TIME TO DELAY NO LONGER

Book by Ruth Agnes Evans

The Marian Antiphon of Francis Bernardone
(Arizona: Tau Publishing, 2017)

TIME TO DELAY NO LONGER

A SEARCH FOR FAITH AND LOVE

Bill and Win Evans

Edited by Ruth Evans

GRACEWING

First published in England in 2022
by
Graceswing
2 Southern Avenue
Leominster
Herefordshire HR6 0QF
United Kingdom
www.gracewing.co.uk

ISBN 978 085244 927 1

Typeset by Gracewing

Cover design by Bernardita Peña Hurtado

Front cover image: Heinrich Hofmann (1824–1911), *Jesus and the rich young man*.

Back cover image: Bill and Win on their wedding day, 25 July 1959, courtesy of Win Evans.

To Father Nicholas Kern
and in memory of Father John Caden
In Gratitude

Jesus answered, 'It is you who say that I am a king. I was born for this, I came into the world for this, to bear witness to the truth; and all who are on the side of truth listen to my voice.' 'Truth?' said Pilate. 'What is that?' (Jn 18:37–38).

CONTENTS

ACKNOWLEDGEMENTS

I WOULD LIKE TO sincerely thank everyone who has assisted me in the difficult task of helping me complete my father's book. Above all, I want to thank my mother who has been tirelessly committed to the book, both by helping Dad with typing and organization while he was still writing and then by writing substantial parts of it herself following his death. In this way she has managed to preserve his theologically based memories and their story. She has also helped me immeasurably by searching for most of the footnote material we needed in Dad's library. Not a task for the faint hearted! The footnotes are the work of my mother and myself, together with some kind assistance at times of desperation.

On the subject of footnotes, I am greatly indebted to Brother Zachariah from Newman's Oratory at Birmingham who helped me with the footnotes from Cardinal Newman and to Father Henry Shea SJ from Campion Hall who helped me with the footnotes from Father Karl Rahner SJ. Father Rob Esdaile had kindly taken me to visit Newman's Oratory on 18 November 2019 and this event proved to be a source of helpful inspiration in the completion of Dad's book. The visit reminded me of my father's debt, and therefore my own, to the recently canonized Cardinal[1] and put me in touch with the Oratory as a resource. I also wish to thank Father Nick Kern who, with the assistance of Michael O'Connor, enabled me to locate a footnote from Hilaire Belloc's letters to G. K. Chesterton. I would also like to express my appreciation of my sister Mary's support when she scoured a book on Newman for me in search of one of the many unlocated footnotes at a moment of discouragement.

Most of the scriptural quotations are taken from the New Jerusalem Bible. Dad actually used the older translation for his work and on the occasions where I thought it necessary to express

Dad's thought and language using the older translation I have indicated this in the notes.

I want to thank my sister Mary, with my brother-in-law Dominic, for their constant encouragement and sound advice on this task. I also want to thank my sisters Sarah and Cathy for their support on this project. Their computer skills were invaluable in its early stages as Dad had no computer skills at all and Mum's were far from confident. As Dad finished his chapters, they were always there patiently to advise my mother about how to type and save the chapters onto her laptop, when she was a beginner. Without their help in rescuing the first chapters, it is unlikely I would have had enough printed material to take up the task later.

Dominic's mother Linda has been a constant source of steadfast support and committed faith in our lives and I wish to thank her for her interest in this project. My gratitude goes out to my mother's cousin Edward Goldwyn and his wife Charmian for their interest in this book and for allowing Edward's correspondence with Dad in 2016 to be included. I am grateful to my nephew Jacob for his much valued and patient help with the formatting.

I would like to express my thanks to Elizabeth Lock and Father Paul Nicholson SJ from *The Way* Journal at Campion Hall, Oxford, for allowing me to use my article 'My Father and the Historical Authority of Jesus' which captures some of my memories of Dad and his pursuit of faith, shared by my mother.[2]

My gratitude is due also to the parish of St Mary of Furness in Barrow-in-Furness, the parish which supported Dad and helped him sustain his practice of the faith during many years of his life, including the last difficult years. I owe gratitude to the late Father Antony Quinn, Father Michael Murphy, the late Canon Frank Cookson, Canon John Watson, Father Andrew Allman and Father Manny Gribben and Deacon Nick Donnelly, among many others. By their enthusiasm and dedication in challenging times they kept St Mary's, now Our Lady of Furness, a vibrant parish, where Dad could practise his faith and contribute to the life of the parish as a respected voice in discussion groups and as a

Eucharist Minister. Our family is also indebted to the late Sister Pierre RSHM for running her Prayer Group which Dad loved to attend and which he never failed to find a source of inspiration and consolation, even when he was ill. We also wish to acknowledge our family friendship with Terry Heaney and his late wife Julia, together with the kind support of our family friends Gerald and Barbara Clinging.

Sister Irene Joseph OSC was a tireless source of support and friendship to Dad when he and Mum visited our Poor Clare Convent at Woodchester, now closed. Dad was also very fond of the late Sister Marie Thérèse OSC, my novice mistress at Woodchester, who was a convert to the Catholic faith like himself. They shared many happy conversations. I am certain he would want them to receive an affectionate acknowledgement.

I am sure that Dad would wish his two dearly loved sons-in-law, Dominic and Derek, who supported him in his old age, to be acknowledged. Also his much loved grandsons Samuel, John, Joshua and Jacob. They all enriched his life through their affection and friendship. And I want to express gratitude for our dear friends Anne and David Faulkner, Rosalind and Tom Simon and Hannah Poland who often treated Dad, looked after him, cooked for him and made him laugh. They brightened his life and his final years.

May I add an expression of my own gratitude to all the kind friends who helped me through the difficult years following my father's death. Some of your names are already mentioned above and, sadly, you are too many for me to mention all of you by name. I wish to acknowledge the late Sister Elizabeth Rees OCV who assisted me towards my present form of religious life, together with Sister Rachel Harrington SND, Sisters Francisca Rumsey, Irene Joseph Lynch, Clare Ruvarashe Chigwedere and Leo Faulkner OSC. I wish to also thank Bishop Mark Davies, Father Peter Dutton and Father Nick Kern for their kind and much appreciated help in this matter. Deacon Tony Ford, with his wife Mary, and our Deacon Chris Wells, with his wife Teresa, have been a continuing source of inspiration and an example of dedication in our parish life.

I would like to gratefully acknowledge my friends Sister Gabrielle Holden OCV, the late Brother Bernard Paul Wassall OSB, Lucy Otton, Bill Dillon, Marie Mulvey-Roberts, Velia and Martin Soames, Carole Browne, Maureen Bysouth, Anne Sturman, Madelyn Dixon, Theresa and John Tabone and Corrinne Newlove. Father Paul Standish and Sister Phyllis Hughes of the Sisters of Evron have supported me with their spirituality and encouragement. I wish to affectionately recall the friendship I shared with the late Angela Code together with her husband, the late John Code. Angela and I spent a happy year together in the novitiate at Woodchester between 1989 and 1990, and in 2018 I had the privilege and joy of renewing this companionship.

I wish also to express my deeply felt gratitude for the friendship I have received within the movement to abolish the death penalty in the USA. In particular, I wish to thank Margot Ravenscroft, Randall Coyne and Anthony Amsterdam.

Finally, I would like to thank Dad himself, for his love and for leaving us with the priceless legacy of his faith.

Ruth Evans,
Eve of the Feast of the Epiphany, 5 January 2022

Notes

[1] John Henry Newman was canonized by Pope Francis on 13 October 2019.

[2] The article included here is based on the piece first published in *The Way*, Vol 57, No 2, April 2018.

PREFACE

OUR FATHER WAS a man who loved this world and he had many interests and passions. But his story ultimately, as he understood it, was a story about the truth, truth searched for and discovered. By 'the truth' he did not simply mean the discovery of personal meaning and consolation in his life, though it certainly included this meaning. He meant the objective and abrasive truth which commands our allegiance, which pertains to everyone and to everything. It was a faith which survived what he suffered. In an age of increasing scepticism he remained true to his discovery that the Gospel of Jesus and identity of Jesus, as interpreted by the Church, could withstand the most rigorous intellectual enquiry. The excitement of this discovery never left him and it animated his approach to life. He was born outside the Catholic Church, so that his intellectual and human discovery of Catholicism was his own profound journey, fuelled by his need for the truth and energized by his intellectual vigour.

Dad retained his mental sharpness up till the last moments of his life. In the New Year of 2017, he spent weeks in hospital. At first Dad was placed in a room with two other local men. Characteristically, Dad bonded with them and they admired his extensive knowledge of Barrow rugby. Dad had a photographic memory and could recall in great detail dramatic moves within matches that he had seen sixty or seventy years ago, as if he was talking about yesterday. His companions were also impressed by Dad because Dad would sometimes talk about needing to get home to finish a book that he was writing. Occasionally, however, they would look at Dad with sadness in their eyes. As he grew weaker, Dad would ask the Mother of God to help him.

Dad was then given a single room which looked out on to a peaceful view of the outskirts of Barrow-in-Furness, the town where he grew up and had lived most of his life. The private room helped him to keep to his prayer devotions and his rosary which he continued to assiduously practice. The dark road and trees that I could see in the night led down towards Furness Abbey, an ancient Cistercian Monastery, despoiled under Henry Eighth when he ransacked the Catholic Church. In my early years at Woodchester Poor Clare Convent I had read and re-read *The Man on a Donkey*[1] by Hilda Prescott and was haunted by her account of the Pilgrimage of Grace, led in protest at the despoiling of the Church by Robert Aske.

The majestic ruins of Furness Abbey retained an atmosphere of prayer and, as I stood near my father's bed, it seemed to me as if that soundless atmosphere reflected back into our lives. As children we would play in the grounds during family picnics. For a short time I enjoyed my father's company during my evening visits. Then I caught a sore throat and I could not visit him anymore.

As he lay there in hospital waiting for me to come and barely able to eat, my father told me I returned into his mind as I had been at four years old when I was in hospital after my tonsils were removed. He would come straight to visit me in the late afternoon after a day teaching and take over the responsibility from my mother, Win, of sitting with me, occupying me and keeping me happy. Bill, or Billy as I called him in my childish songs, was a tall, slim man with fair hair. I found his strong story-telling voice reassuring. He would sit by my bed and every night he read me a story about a tortoise which I loved. I felt calm and safe while he was there. As he got up to go at the end of visiting hours, I would become distressed. Now I had to face this strange world and its problematic negotiations all on my own. I had developed an aversion to the vegetable soup that we were given with an awful predictability each evening and would beg Dad to tell them that I did not like it: 'Tell them I don't like the soup!' I would wail. Bill tried his best to help me by searching for the matron and, despite matron's no nonsense approach to my difficulties, his efforts could not have been entirely ineffective as once or twice I got away with avoiding my supper.

The actual day of the operation Bill and Win had not been allowed to visit but Bill's father, Jack Evans, came and sat beside me, though I was too sedated to respond. Later Jack said what a good little girl I had been but the truth was that I could not even remember him coming. However, I liked the story of Grandad's quiet visit as I lay suspended in a world of dreams and his account of my good behaviour. Jack probably got in to see me because he was known to the nurses through his tireless devotion to a patient who could not be cured. My grandfather would faithfully assist her parents and nurses with her care. Jack was not a demonstrative grandfather but I knew from this story that he cared for me.

Our home as I grew up was full of Catholic books, so much so that for periods in our childhood we took them for the granted, like the wallpaper. But from time to time I would gaze at the haunting titles and feel curious about what lay within. *This Tremendous Lover*[2] and *The Man born to be King*[3] are just two of these intriguing titles. These were Dad's books. Sometimes I would delve into one of them, seeking to penetrate their mystery. At times the lofty language was too much for me but I knew these books were an important part of our family's story. Sometimes I would come across a beautiful passage about Jesus and this would captivate and haunt me. Who was this mysterious man who had lived so long ago and suffered for our sake?

In many ways, Bill Evans was a man of his time, participating in the political and cultural questions of his day. But in this he stood out, in his conviction that if life is to have a meaning then there must be an objective meaning. And he had searched for it. Bill loved the play by Robert Bolt, *A Man for all Seasons*[4] about Sir Thomas More. Truth was important to my father, as it had been for More. Searching for the truth was to them no arid intellectual exercise. Nor were the answers that it delivered always easy. I admired my father's search for its intellectual integrity, its passionate dedication and for its complete openness to the objective grounds for belief derived from Scripture and Church tradition. Ultimately this would bear fruit only in love. It was love of God that gave the quest its meaning, the God who had entrusted so much to us. Even His only Son.

Dad was sensitive to and respectful of the fact that many people intuit their faith in a less intellectual way than himself. For example, he had a devotion to St Bernadette of Lourdes who, disadvantaged by poverty, hunger and deprivation, would fail at her catechism class. Dad was fascinated that God had affirmed the Church's recent solemnly defined doctrine of The Immaculate Conception[5] using this unprivileged girl.[6] For him, this spoke of the inner unity of the Church. Bernadette was devoted to her rosary, as was Dad. Dad used to say the rosary gave her what she needed.

My sister Mary recalls the way that Dad would recite the Nicene Creed at Sunday Mass, not in an automatic manner, but articulating each word and emphasizing each word, 'one, holy, Catholic and apostolic Church', as if it was something precious; something that he had pursued, wrestled with, uncovered and to which he had surrendered. Dad assumed that Jesus is intelligible and that the task of interpreting Him, and our own relationship with Him, is too far-reaching for any of us to achieve unaided. Jesus possessed His own authority, from God and as God, through which He has left us with the resources that we need to achieve this interpretation. I think my father's search was discerning in the centrality it thus gave to the perspective of Jesus as Lord and Teacher. He is the One who has gazed compassionately at the need of our minds and hearts, prone as they are to every error and imbalance. Jesus intended to leave us with a teaching authority for our relationship with God.

For Dad the telling of his story about his search for truth was important. In the last years of his life he was committed to writing his own book, part autobiography, part apologetic which he never finished. And so, very sadly, we cannot present the book he would have written in its entirety, which would have been a work of theology with some autobiographical passages. We can, however, present the heart of this book and interpret its intention. Mum and I have decided, consequently, to weave the early chapters of

Dad's book into a narrative about their courtship, conversion and early married life with the help of her written memories. We have used Dad's own work and completed his intention using our own stories. This has created a book with more dimensions and narratives than the one Dad originally intended and so we will indicate the shifts in time frame and narrative perspective as they occur. We believe that the intermingling of family anecdote and the memory of former times with Dad's story about his intellectual enquiry will cohere. Here then is our tribute to Bill and his Catholicism. We offer here, relying on Win's memories and Bill's legacy, what we can of his thoughts, his writings and his story.

As Bill and Win's second daughter, I will begin the book. I plan to set the scene by looking at my parents as young people, within their family backgrounds and within the complex, troubled world which had brought them to the brink of their adult journey. A love letter always feels like a good place to start. Love letters usually brim over with hope and promise. Certainly the one almost complete letter that has survived out of the many eloquent letters my mother received from my father does.

Let's go back in time to the mid-1950s with Bill as a young man sitting down to write to Win all about his plans and his insights.

Ruth Evans
Feast of St Bernadette Soubirous, 16 April 2021

Notes

1   H. F. M. Prescott, *The Man on a Donkey*, (London, Harper Collins, 1993).

2   M. E. Boylan, *This Tremendous Lover* (Cork: The Mercier Press Ltd, 1959).

3   D. L. Sayers, *The Man Born to Be King: A Play-Cycle on the Life of Our Lord and Saviour Jesus Christ* (San Francisco: Ignatius Press, 1943).

4   R. Bolt, *A Man for all Seasons* (London: Heinemann Educational Books Ltd, 1965).

5   The solemn definition took place in 1854.

6   Bernadette reported that on 25 March 1858 the beautiful woman who appeared to her during her apparitions had said to her: 'Que soy era Immaculada Concepciou.' That is: 'I am the Immaculate Conception.'

Part I

The Story

1 BILL'S EASTER LETTER 1956

I T WAS THE Easter holiday of 1956 and Bill Evans had a five week holiday at home from Durham University to get through before he would again have time with Winifred Klein, whom he had been seeing there almost every day for the last few months. To make things worse, his friends, Terry and Ian, were not yet home from university so that Bill had extra time on his hands during which to suffer. Visiting his two sisters, Margaret and Jean, and spending time with his small niece Susan, Margaret and Tom's daughter, had brought some distraction and enjoyment. And he had enjoyed teasing his mother, Lilian, about an air rifle he had just bought in Newcastle. As he contemplated what seemed like the interminable days ahead, Bill sat down to write to Winifred. It was to be one of his many long and eloquent love letters.

Travelling home to Barrow-in-Furness, he had been buoyed up by learning of the success of his local rugby team. Since he had not known Win all that long and she knew nothing about rugby and could be a little sensitive, he felt a need to reassure her that he was only joking about the fact that even this good news could not wholly console him at their separation. The fact that he planned to tease her showed that he was feeling hopeful about their love and his life in general. Already he and Win shared a delightful world full of ideas and hopes and secrets. The intrigue of accommodating her sensibilities, often unpredictable, and different to his, added to the charm of their encounter. But there could be upsets if he got things wrong.

As he planned his letter, he was aware of a few recent mishaps, including one at the end of term, from which he hoped Win had now recovered. Strictly speaking, he had been the one at fault. College rules for young women were firm in those days and Win was expected to be back at St Mary's College promptly by eleven p.m. at night at the very latest. She was by no means a rule breaker, on the contrary, but, even if she had been, it would have been foolish to risk being reported to the Principal of the College. Once again, unfortunately, on the last Friday night of term, Bill's pleasure at her company had overrun the time deadline with which she so earnestly wished to comply.

Also, Win had been taken aback during a trip to Newcastle the last weekend before the end of term when Bill decided he wanted to buy an air-rifle. Bill had explained it would console him during her absence but she had not been impressed. Bill planned to do target practice with his friends in his back yard during the holiday. To Win, Bill's sudden impulse was bewildering but in fact there was a history to the incident. Bill's father had bought his son an air-rifle one Christmas, promising they would practise together. Responsibly, his father made the condition that Bill never used it unsupervised. Jack Evans was always generous at Christmas but this was a particularly generous gift. Bill was about twelve at the time and overjoyed to receive the gun. The fact that his father showed interest in him on this occasion made the offer all the more important. However, Bill broke his father's rule out of his keen impatience to try out the gift. His father then punished him by permanently taking away the gun.

Knowing Bill was short of funds and seeing the gun as a total waste of money, Win had been shocked by Bill's recent purchase. Bill was generous on dates and had bought her a beautiful skirt and blouse for Christmas. However, he did not organize his money well and was usually running out by the end of term so Win would help him out. This was only necessary temporarily as Bill would then salvage his situation by working through the holidays at Barrow shipyard. Bill was not the greatest practical asset but he did his best and his fellow workers would hugely enjoy discussing sport, politics and religion with him.

The day in Newcastle had got off to a promising start as the young couple wandered around some book shops, hand in hand.

Things started to deteriorate as Bill led Win into a gun shop and asked to see one air rifle after another and then to her utter shock decided to purchase one. But she controlled her disapproval. For lunch they went on into a simple café. Respectful of Bill's financial situation, Win chose the cheapest item on the menu. Meanwhile Bill, who was hungry, went for the best choice which was egg, bacon, sausage and toast. Win had a secret desire to join him but resisted the temptation. She had been brought up in a Spartan way and was trained not to give in to spontaneous cravings, for example, to buy an ice cream. (Her parents, particularly her mother, considered this extravagant behaviour, even at the end of an arduous family climb in Wales.) When he had finished his meal, as he was still hungry, Bill said impulsively to the waitress, 'I'll have the same again.' At this point Win was horrified. Her mother regarded cafes as a total waste of money. The treat they were enjoying that day had scarcely ever come Win's way, leaving her with some feelings of conflict when she saw Bill throwing caution to the winds. Bill was oblivious to her feelings; in fact, he would have been perfectly happy for her to join him at the top of the menu, which would have exhausted their joint funds. Although he had grown up in a poor family, for him this made the odd moment of extravagance all the more exciting. To Win, Bill's behaviour seemed the height of self-indulgence and she stormed out of the cafe. Abandoning his second order, Bill ran after Win who was crossing a busy road in a rather distraught state. She did not notice a car coming her way and for a terrible moment he thought she was about to be run over. Frantically, he called out her name, 'Win!' Unhurt, she then re-joined him but Bill had found their reunion somewhat cool. The day in Newcastle, which he had planned would bring the term to an affectionate end, had been a disaster.

Like many a writer, Bill hoped through his fluid pen to restore the damage. His letter would depict the group of women who looked after him and watched over him — his mother, his sisters, his landlady. They were a caring, supportive group, however on the issue of the gun all of them were against him, some more seriously than others, an issue he was taking up in the letter.[1] He knew Win would not take his side and hoped to make her laugh. More seriously, Bill was aware of deep unanswered questions about Christianity, faith and the future as he wrote.

One of his secrets with Win was the decision that, during the course of their holiday, they would each attend a church service and then share their experience. The reason for this pact was that both of them had received enough Christian education in their school years to be convinced that they wanted to pursue the truth and promise that they believed to be found in Jesus. But neither of them was convinced that they knew the church where they wanted to worship or which represented the fullness of the truth that they pursued. Bill, in particular, was preoccupied by this question. Where could he find a place where you could access the promises of Christianity? These promises were awe-inspiring and wonderful, assuring indeed the fullness of life.

Bill had been influenced by his Methodist upbringing and was haunted by the unforgettable figure of Jesus. The Methodism, with which he had grown up, good and well intentioned as it was, seemed to rely heavily on the talent of individual speakers to whip up enthusiasm in the audience. A gifted speaker would win his audience's admiration. This was an intermittent, unreliable sense of awe and enthusiasm, depending upon individual talent. It seemed an unsatisfactory basis for the Christian experience. Bill was sceptical about how intellectually sound and considered the thinking behind some of the Methodist preaching he had heard really was, although it was interesting, moving and instructive. He had heard preachers, in the flush of their enthusiasm, use Christianity to arrive at conclusions which he considered intellectually unfounded, for example, they would claim that all that was good in the history of humankind was a consequence of Christianity. Bill found this kind of apparent disregard for the intelligence of the listener and the evidence of history annoying. He felt something had to be missing from the Christianity he had experienced so far, an issue he wanted to explore with Win through this letter. His uncertainty and frustration had been confirmed by the Methodist church service he had just attended in order to fulfil his pact with Win.

How Win met Bill

From her ramshackle home in Wimbledon Win, or Winnie as her family called her, was eagerly waiting for Bill's letters which arrived on a daily basis. She would get up early and run down the stairs to seize them. Her boyfriend was a tall, slender young man with a streak of gold in his hair which caught the sun. He was extremely generous and could be very funny. Bill was a graduate training to be a teacher and, two terms ago, he had been captivated by Win at a dance for freshers at Durham during her first week. She was just nineteen, while he was twenty-two. She was small with dark curly hair and deep brown eyes and oblivious to her own charm. She was inexperienced and had been rather shyly present at this dance which had given her a first opportunity to wear a fetching new turquoise dress her mother had bought for her and which suited her. Her mother, with a matchmaking instinct, hoped her daughter would meet a promising, responsible young man with a glowing future. It was the only item of glamorous clothing Win had ever owned. Win wanted to be able to tell her mother she had worn it. As a result, she decided to take up the offer of her girl-friends to go with them to a freshers' ball rather than accept the offer of other friends who were going to a musical evening.

Win was not at all used to attracting attention. Wearing her dress at a ball seemed an exciting event, particularly as young men were then coming up to her to ask her for a dance. Bill was her second partner. He had arrived at the dance rather late following his usual Saturday night pint with friends. As she took in his tall figure and handsome face, she felt glad that the first young man had not absorbed her for the whole evening. Once Bill appeared, they discovered they were both English students and began an animated conversation about English Literature. They danced, a little inexpertly, all evening. Rather than returning to her girlfriends' company, Win accepted Bill's offer to walk her home, braving their raised eyebrows. As they walked about a mile back towards her college, she and Bill continued to talk animatedly with one another. The country walk was atmospheric and passed quickly in the dark; soon they came to a bridge which crossed over a river. Bill reached out to hold her hand, which Win modestly withdrew. As they climbed the steep hill to St Mary's College, Bill asked Win if he could see her again the next night. Win agreed, feeling relieved he had not interpreted her reserve as a repulse. Back alone in her room that night, the young woman felt elated.

And then in the morning... misfortune struck. Win learned that an unavoidable engagement for the new students clashed with the next evening. It was an introductory welcoming event to meet the college staff, particularly the moral tutors, and go over college rules, followed by refreshments. At first she did not know how to contact Bill because he was not in college accommodation. She feared that if he did not hear from her he would think she had stood him up. Then it occurred to her to use his pigeon hole at the college. In her anxiety for him to know she was not delivering a rebuff she earnestly wrote a personal note explaining the situation. Eager for him to arrange another date, she added the potent line, 'I miss you Billy.' She thrust the note into the little square box hoping fortune was on her side and he would discover it in time. As luck would have it, Bill did find the note and opened it with eager anticipation. Win's final line struck him as a wonderful disclosure. He needed no more encouragement.

In the weeks that followed, they walked along the streets of Durham hand in hand. Win was completely immersed in the constant stream of conversation between them about literature, the theatre and their previous lives. Bill was her first boyfriend and she was unselfconscious, free from any preoccupation with her appearance. This was to the point that, much to his displeasure, she had worn her heavy fresher's gown and thick college scarf, which bundled her up, as he saw it, for their first date. She was following college rules on the gown to the letter and was proud of her attire. It had not even occurred to her to make an effort to look more shapely and glamorous on this occasion. 'What's that?' Bill asked, with a note of disappointment, referring to her outfit. Earnestly, Win explained that wearing the gown was the college rule. Bill retorted, 'No one takes that rule seriously!' Confirming her lack of experience in his eyes, Win then told him she would like an orange squash. She had lived close to her mother, governed by her mother's values. Win had never been in a pub before.

Kismet and John

Win's mother, Kismet, who had bought the fateful dress that had influenced her daughter's decision and which had made her beauty stand out on the night in question, was a Jewish atheist. Born in September 1912, she had never identified with the Jewish faith. Her family were poor and her parents occasionally visited the synagogue, but only rarely, in order not to upset the extended family. The sense of Jewish identity in the house where Kismet grew up was strong, but it was a racial identity rather than a religious one. Intelligent, energetic and frustrated, Kismet had desperately regretted her own loss of formal education and was glad to be free of what she felt to be the limitations of the East End working class community where she was born. 'Kismet' was the title of a popular musical and Kismet hated the name because at school the boys used to run after her calling out, 'Kiss me!' As an adult, she preferred to be called Florence.

Kismet and her sisters were all gifted at the piano, a gift they inherited from their father Albert, whose large group of siblings had enjoyed playing musical instruments together at home. Albert would supplement the family income by improvising piano music to accompany silent films at the local cinema. Talented as he was, he had never had piano lessons and consequently had never learned how to read music. Kismet and her sister Gloria played a duet at a prestigious competition at the Albert Hall when they were eleven and ten respectively and won, to the delight of the teacher who had entered them. She was a refugee and had attended the event. But Albert and his wife Fanny[2] were both working in their tobacco shop which was open from dawn to late at night. Subsequently, the girls were not able to receive enough instruction on the piano to fulfil their talent. At age fourteen, Kismet's longings for literature, music and education had ended up behind a boring tobacco kiosk to support her parents' minor business. Eager for more adventure and challenge, she had studied Russian language and literature under a gifted refugee Jewish professor. He was an old man and survived in a garret on a pittance by giving lessons. His life was hard but he was grateful for the safety offered by this country. On one occasion Kismet travelled alone to Russia on a merchant ship. This enterprise was almost unheard of for a young woman at that time but Kismet wanted to find out more about her family's background heritage.[3] In her adult years Kismet would painstakingly make her way through a Russian version of Dostoyevsky and Tolstoy's novels with the help of a Russian dictionary. Her favourite composer was the wonderful Russian composer Mussorgsky.

Kismet identified with her father. Her mother's family, which had been aristocratic, had escaped persecution in a Spanish ghetto in Turkey. According to family legend, they had been expelled from Spain in the fifteenth century as a result of Catholic persecution.[4] Kismet's father's father had escaped persecution from the Christian Cossacks in a farming village of Odessa, near the port city of Odessa, part of the Ukraine, on the northwestern shore of the Black Sea. The region was under Russia at that time, a country which Kismet's grandfather had continued to love despite his cruel experiences.[5] He had disembarked in Britain towards the end of the nineteenth century and the Welsh surname 'Lewis' was given to him, which was officially added to his Russian surname, Lebedinsky. It was apparently a common practice to give Jewish refugees Welsh surnames upon arrival.[6]

(It might be interesting to speculate on what this says about the social status of the Welsh, and of Jewish refugees, in British society!) Lebedinsky Lewis' application to be naturalized as a British citizen, along with his wife and large family,[7] was granted by the Home Department in 1894.[8] Following twelve years residence in Britain, Lebedinsky's application was supported by a number of British born 'respectable persons'[9] who must have been sympathetic neighbours. As they reached manhood, in a heroic effort to give them some security in this country, Lebedinsky set up his five sons in tobacconist's shops.

Kismet had a 'delightfully musical speaking voice' which had almost musical intonations and 'which never changed as she aged.'[10] As a young woman she had waist length, golden hair which her husband sometimes mentioned to his grandchildren. Her appearance was thought of as 'strikingly beautiful.'[11]

Kismet was passionately protective of her people in an emotional way. She was preoccupied by the knowledge that she had survived the holocaust because she was in Britain and was haunted by images of the camps. The anguish and fear of Kismet's war years had been heightened by rumours on the radio of the fate of Jews in Europe. Kismet knew that if Britain lost the war, she and, maybe her children, would be dealt with as Jews. In this event she had no hope for herself. She thought that her best option would be suicide. Since her husband was not Jewish, she thought that perhaps the children would be spared but she did not know. Listening to Churchill's defiant speeches on the radio had helped her to keep up her courage.

Kismet could remember being taunted as a child by other children on her way to the Jewish school as a Christ killer. She could tolerate Christianity in the sense that access to the best local schools meant the Church of England's form of Christianity had to be accepted as part of her children's curriculum. Kismet cherished Britain as a place of refuge for Jews and she accepted Christianity in the sense that it was part of the culture of the country she loved. In this sense, from a great distance, she could acknowledge it, because she had such gratitude to British society. She hoped her children would see Christianity, as she did, as a necessary fact of life which could be avoided most of the time. She could admit that the story of Christ was powerful so there was a faint resonance inside her with the story. She also felt some sympathy with the position of the agnostic or enquirer so that she would not have been unduly concerned by Bill's present undecided state of mind. She thought a position of enquiry on intellectual matters natural and intelligent. She was of course an enquirer beyond the perimeters of her youth herself, although she had a tendency to let emotion obscure her judgement and had difficulty separating the two. In this matter, perhaps, her lack of formal education had not helped. If pushed, she would have admitted that she regarded the Church of England as relatively acceptable compared to the Catholic Church, although she liked neither. She associated the Catholic Church with the history of anti-Semitism which preceded the holocaust. On these matters it was better not to argue with her as her feelings were too strong for her to join in a meaningful debate.

Her husband John was older than herself, an academic teacher of English to international students who had discovered his passion for opera after his formal education was over. Some of his students were Jewish refugees. Discussions on *The Merchant of Venice* would grow heated in his classes as passionate sympathies on tensions evoked by the play were excited. Jews and European Christians would debate the play and Grandpa had to control the discussion, a task which required some diplomatic skill. This illustrates his gift for bringing literature to life. The characters in literature and opera were real to him and excited his deep emotions.

John Klein was touched by the Gospel story and had written a play in his twenties about the trial of Jesus called *Pontius Pilate*.[12] John had grown up in Manchester and he had been alienated from the practice of formal religion in his youth through a conversation with a priest who took an unduly intolerant view of his situation. John's harsh father had been a lapsed Catholic and a poor role model. As a result John never made his First Communion and had hardly ever attended Mass. His mother had a gentle nature and he remembered her affectionately. His parents had wealthy European origins but had lost most of their money by the First World War.

John's father hoped he would be a successful business man and controlled his son's education with this end in view, a career for which he was completely unsuited. As an adult John gave what he could of his time to writing plays and, later on, passionate reviews of his favourite operas. It was here that his deeply sensitive nature found a literary expression. The family was reclusive in its habits but provided a rich cultural environment for the children. Born in October 1899, John had two children by his first marriage, Anne and Rickie. He was left as a heart broken widower in his early thirties and never fully recovered from a sense of tragedy. A few years later in 1935, John met Kismet at the British library where she went seeking to further her education which had been cut short brutally at the age of fourteen.[13] She craved the chances John gave her to be in touch with a culturally richer world. Not long after this they married and together they had three children: Winifred, who was born in October 1936, Joan born in April 1938, and Lawrence born in November 1941.

Kismet was passionate about her children's education in a way that did not always consider their emotional needs or the demands of a particular situation. For example, she sent Win and Joan off to school one morning after a night of severe bombing in the Wimbledon area, assuming too readily they would be safe. The little girls arrived only to find the school deserted and the basement flooded as a result of a nearby hit. A worried caretaker ordered them to get home quickly. Holding hands, they began to run. Halfway home the warning siren sounded and they ran the rest of the way crying.

Kismet was a strong character and particularly protective of her first daughter Win whom she knew to be shy and vulnerable.

Lilian and Jack

If Win depended on her mother for protection and approval, so Bill depended on his mother Lilian. Lilian called her son Billy, her golden boy. At the time of the war, Bill was a young boy and largely protected from danger. Indeed, his evacuation years had been carefree and happy. He had been evacuated with his mother, Lilian, and two sisters, Margaret and Jean, to Milnthorpe while his father Jack continued to work at Barrow shipyard as a crane driver. Barrow-in-Furness' prominent place in the war effort, building ships and armaments, attracted frequent bombing raids which Bill's father encountered with characteristically cool courage. The town was thought to be too dangerous for children. Bill recalled hearing the bombs whizzing down as he sat in an air raid shelter in Barrow not long before their evacuation. Bill had been too small to experience any fear but his sister Margaret was old enough to be terrified.

Lilian had lost her own mother at a young age. Unhappy and unwanted in the care of her new step-mother, she had gone into service as soon as possible to escape, at the age of fourteen. This meant hours of toil, leaving her always tired. And she was always hungry even though the food was good for the time, which meant Lilian spent all her meagre pocket money on food. She was delivered from this exhausting existence a few years later when she moved into rented accommodation with her older sister, Peg, and secured a job in a pawn shop. The two sisters got on well and eventually Lilian obtained a position she liked better as an usherette at the Gaiety Cinema. This meant she could watch the films, introducing her to a romantic popular culture that she loved. Lilian was thought to be a beautiful though no photographs were taken to preserve the memory of this beauty. She was tall with a good complexion and a sweetness of expression.

Jack would have been a brilliant maths student in today's world but his educational opportunities had been curtailed by the poverty of his widowed mother whom he had supported devotedly throughout his youth. He could have gone to the Grammar school on the strength of a scholarship which would have covered most of the expense but his mother could not afford the uniform. Jack worked hard to earn money while still at school, delivering newspapers and provisions on his bike, not only before school started but at the end of the school day. He was good with animals.

It was at *The Gaiety* that Lilian met Jack Evans and they fell in love. Soon after his marriage to Lilian, Jack proved adept at caring for his first baby daughter, Margaret, meaning Lilian could return to evening work at the cinema. In some ways Lilian felt Jack was more competent and less anxious with the baby than she was. However, the young couple, both strong characters in different ways, found it difficult to establish marital harmony in the face of poverty. Lilian had inherited a legacy of anxiety to the point of suffering periods of illness. Even during her fairly harmonious life with Peg at times she felt close to breakdown. Jack's academic gifts, together with his gift for nursing, had been all frustrated, and he had a short fuse. One of the teachers at the primary school his children attended used to say at Parents' Evening to Lilian, 'They are all clever, but none as clever as their father.' In his old age Ruth remembers that Jack enjoyed reading books from Barrow library. On one occasion she recalls that he was reading Frank Slaughter's *The Crown and the Cross: Life of Christ*[14] and he said to her, as one gripped by a novel thought, 'I've never read anything so interesting.' About the same time, perhaps suffering from low spirits, he asked his granddaughter Ruth to paint a small yellow daffodil on their living room wall to brighten it. However, Ruth feared her artistic skills were not good enough.

Jack must have had real potential in maths and science subjects and it is interesting to speculate what he might have achieved with better opportunities. He was, however, less imaginative than his wife, his two daughters and his son.

By the time Bill was born, the couple had grown apart meaning Jack never made the same connection with Bill that he had with his daughters, Margaret and Jean. Lilian adored Bill and was in her own way passionately protective of him, anxious to compensate for the lack of his father's interest. This drove the couple apart even further. She always tried to give Bill the best food that she was able to provide and to make sure his clothes and bed linen were well-laundered and well-aired. Bill in turn deeply loved his mother and as he grew up willingly did her errands, collecting the weekend provisions from the butcher and greengrocer in town.

Lilian was happy to seize the chance to escape war-ravaged Barrow and be evacuated to Milnthorpe with her three children. At Milnthorpe, the family's wellbeing was secured by a local farming community which received them warmly and gave them opportunities to add to their rations. Lilian provided some income by working in a small hotel cleaning and changing linen while Jack contributed out of his earnings. The village teacher noted that the eight year old boy had potential and was kind. He also wrote that Bill was helpful, he would stay behind to help clear up, 'His work is very satisfactory and he is very interested in all his schoolwork. Always willing to help with anything about school. Has a very kind disposition.'[15] And then in 1942, 'Billy is an excellent reader.'[16] His commanding and expressive speaking voice was to become one of Bill's assets.[17] Born in May 1933, the boy now flourished. He made friends with the village boys and roamed the fields with them freely, picking up their rural knowledge, collecting nuts, and making bows and arrows with which to act out Robin Hood and his Merry Men. His mother promptly destroyed the bows and arrows, along with the homemade catapults he brought home. The only thing little Bill Evans had to worry about was his one shortcoming on the school curriculum, his hopelessness in the knitting class. The rural village plan was for boys to learn knitting, as well as girls. But although Bill could knit plain, he could not master the pearl rows without dropping his stitches. The teacher would hold up his handiwork at the beginning of the knitting class and ask, 'Whose is this?' Sometimes Lilian came to his aid and made an excuse for him so that he could avoid the ordeal.

The chestnuts and blackberries Bill collected contributed to the family diet. During the war every resource was valuable and he acquired knowledge about berries and hedge flowers which would come in useful as an adult when he would encourage Win to start making homemade wine. All three children made friends and did exceptionally well at school and were more contented living with their mother than they had ever been before. The two girls were taken by a bus to the grammar school in Kendal. An unmarried aunt and uncle visited regularly with gifts for the children but Jack rarely came. Jack and Lilian's marriage was now in deep trouble and eventually Lilian's anxiety about this brought their country haven to a close, years before the war was over. Returning to Barrow, the three children experienced a great loss of security and happiness.

Bill's Letter

It was only when the war was over that Bill became aware of the scale of the tragedy in Europe and this left him with a lasting love and compassion for the Jewish race. At some point as he grew up, Bill began to see filmed evidence from the concentration camps in post-war footage at his local cinema and was appalled. These tragic images stayed indelibly on his mind and profoundly influenced his understanding of the world. His horror and grief remained with him all his life, so much so that he could never bear to watch cinematic attempts to portray the holocaust. When *Schindler's List*[18] eventually came out he would be unable to watch it, despite the film's great historical and artistic merit. To him, Win's Jewish origins added to her appeal and enhanced his growing identification with her and his desire to make her happy. Bill respected and loved the Jewish people and valued their immense contribution to European literature, music, art, drama and culture. He also, increasingly, would value their religious understanding of the world and their religion as a faith from God which he understood to affirm the Gospels. Later on he would be glad that his children were part of this great people.[19] To Bill, it sounded as if Win came from an ideal family setting, cultured, studious, stimulating, family gatherings constantly enriched by a flow of animated discussion about productions at the London theatre. This kind of academic critique was an area where he himself was talented and he was looking forward to being included. The young man also had some confidence in the insights from his own working class background. If they had not granted him the truth, they had, he believed, given him a basis for seeking it.

By the time Bill wrote his letter, he had developed a few strategies for winning Win round again when he knew he had been at fault. In late 1955 and early 1956, he and Win had spent time getting to know each other—going to films, to pubs, and dances. Bill was a few years older and had had many girlfriends, only a few of them were students. Bill would quickly realize that Win was the girl he loved and now, by Easter, he felt committed to her. On that awkward first date, however, he had hesitated, because, in her simplicity, she was not behaving with the sophistication and poise of other girls he had met. It seemed naïve to him to ask for an orange squash in a pub on a romantic occasion. As his mind struggled with the adjustment, he wondered if he had made a mistake. Concerned not to hurt Win, he arranged another meeting at the end of the evening but without much conviction. He could see she was a sweet girl but he felt he had probably been mistaken to encourage her and that he would have to bring the relationship gently to a close next time. That night, uncertain in his mind, he fell into a troubled sleep. In the course of the night, however, unknown to his conscious mind, something mysterious happened within him. When he woke up, he was desperate to see Win again.

Occasionally, as I have already mentioned, he would make her cross and anxious by not being sufficiently diligent about the college rules, in particular, for failing to get her back at night just before 11 p.m. Sometimes he would like the idea of buying chips for them both on their way back, and, although Win enjoyed sharing the chips with him, it could bring her rather too close to the deadline if there was a delay in the shop. Win was frightened of upsetting the college gate keeper who was a retired jailer and threatened to report to the Principal anyone who was late. One such incident had occurred at the end of term. Bill had tried to avert trouble by putting his watch back and then pretending that their tardiness was due to the watch being five minutes slow. He had even shaken it in mock concern and contrition. But Mr Robinson had not been convinced. Bill could not help but see the funny side.[20] As he began his letter, Bill was torn between hoping Win was not still displeased with him and amusement at the memory of her troubled face. His immediate task was to ensure he was forgiven. Using exercise paper, he began to write to her swiftly in his firm strong hand.

Tuesday

Dear Win,

How are you? I hope you are settled down again to home life and are getting down to the business of work. I am not perfectly settled myself though I feel much better than I did when I first arrived home. On Saturday the thought of five weeks away from you seemed well-nigh intolerable and I could willingly have slept 'out this great gap this time...'[21] It certainly is a novel experience for me to leave Durham with a sinking feeling and to enter Barrow with the desire to be on the way back. In previous years my feelings have been just the opposite. Even the thought that Barrow had drawn at Wigan (which is no inconsiderable feat) which I discovered on buying a paper in Penrith didn't help matters very much. (I trust you know me well enough by now not to take that last remark too seriously—but you know Win I never can be too sure with you, can I?)

I am still a little unhappy about last term but I suppose I will get over it fairly soon. At least it was an experience which I should never have to repeat, thank heaven. It has however taught me one or two important things which should prove valuable later on-such as that teaching is by no means as easy as I once thought and that to be done well it requires a tremendous amount of patience and hard work. Despite some of the more unfortunate aspects of last term I still feel reasonably confident that I want to teach and that I can do it fairly well. The important question now is whether the Education Department will be kind enough to give me a diploma. I still have nightmares involving that weird unblendable (there's no such word I'm sure) mixture of myself, 3c, Mr Hewitt and *Julius Caesar. Julius Caesar* and 3c might have something in common somewhere but if they have, they need a more effective intermediary than myself. It is some consolation however to know that there are other forms than 3c—though on the other hand it's a rather desperate thought to think that I might be faced with the prospect of a secondary school where even the best forms might be considerably worse than 3c.[22] So you will realize that, though the thought of a future in the teaching profession is on the whole a pleasant one, its pleasantness is tempered not a little by some rather serious doubts.

I hope you have got over our rather unfortunate experience of last Friday night. We seem to be in the habit of ending the term on a not altogether pleasant note-remember last Christmas term—or is it best forgotten?[23] I hope you are not like Giles Winterbourne[24] and remember and judge an evening (or a term) by its unfortunate ending. (If this had been an essay by one of the boys at Bishop Auckland School[25] I would have underlined the last 'unfortunate' and put an 'R' (Repetition in the margin.) We will as you say have to make a big effort to improve ourselves on this serious question of time. No doubt your watch will be a big help. It still worries me a little to think that you might misjudge my apparent amusement at your concern at such times, but really Win I'm sure that if you could see yourself, your serious worried look when you're a bit worried about getting past Mr Robinson in time you would agree that it was amusing in a pathetic sort of way. Please don't think it a sign of my indifference to your predicament.

Last Saturday morning found me in a position similar to that of the previous term—a lot of things to do and not much time to do them in. This time however I managed to catch the train. Fortunately the station is much closer to Mrs Bell's than to Miss Tindale's. Mrs Bell was clearly relieved to see the departure of the gun. She has no wish to see it again—so if I decide to do some shooting in Durham I'll have to smuggle it up and hide it in St Mary's College. You wouldn't mind would you? Just think of the stir we could cause in the rooms opposite to yours if people saw us shooting out of your window. Apart from her unconcealed relief however Mrs Bell was very pleasant when I left her and said she would be very happy to have me for another term. As you know, she has been an excellent landlady and I think I am very lucky to have such a good place to go back to. I don't think she will mind in the least you coming round once or twice a week if we wish to work together. You appear to have made quite an impression on her Win judging by the number of times she refers to you (always as 'your young lady') and the emphasis with which she expressed her confidence in the fact that I was going to miss you a lot.

Poor gun, I'm afraid it seems doomed to being unwanted. As you can well imagine it didn't meet with an altogether welcoming reception at home. When I arrived home there was only my mother to greet me as father had gone to Wigan to see the match. When I told her that the big parcel I was carrying contained an air gun she didn't believe me at first. She was so confident that I was pulling her leg that she smiled in a way which said 'Don't be so silly I know you've got more sense than to buy an air gun.' When I insisted however her face changed to an expression of mild alarm and her next comment was, 'Well you can sell it.' (This or words to the same effect has been her remark ever since whenever the gun was mentioned.) When the weapon was eventually taken from the box and assembled she became really anxious—a little panicky in fact. 'Is it loaded?' she said in a very alarmed tone. I don't know why it is but some women, my mother and Mrs Bell in particular, seem to have the notion that guns go off on their own and have a natural and quite independent tendency to kill everybody in view. My mother seems to believe that in touching 'the wretched thing' as she calls it, she is undertaking a grave risk. Mrs Bell on the other hand wouldn't clean my room until the gun had been taken to pieces. I'm sure she believed it could load itself and go off on its own.

My father appeared just as I was putting the final touches to the assembling of the gun. 'What on earth's that?' was the characteristic comment. 'Has he carted that thing all the way from Durham?' he asked my mother in a tone with disgust mingled with incredulity. (He invariably directs his criticisms of me at my poor mother as if she was herself in some way to blame.) However on examining it he admitted it was a beautiful piece of work though he said it was too dangerous to use on the premises. On Sunday morning in fact he forbade me to use it outside, but since then he has cooled down a little and has even talked of getting a target rigged up in the house.[26] So the chances are that we'll be doing a little shooting together before very long. I have done a little myself over at my sisters[27] and was very pleased with it. It is very powerful, easy to handle and very accurate. I found I could set a match head on fire at ten yards. Terry and Ian[28] and I should get fun out of it during the vac.

On Sunday morning I went over to pay my respects to the rest of the family who all seemed to be well and in good spirits. My sisters were very amused when I told them about the gun and my parents' reaction to it. (I showed them the picture of the party incidentally and you will be no doubt flattered to hear that they thought you looked very nice.) Some of the comments on some of the other 'characters' (their words not mine) were not I'm afraid to say quite so flattering. 'Peculiar' was the word they used. I think they must have been looking at our psychology friend with the beard. They didn't specify. Susan[29] was in fine form—she gets bonnier every time I come home. Her present craze is drawing-she will draw for hours on end and is very pleased when you praise her work. She is remarkably good too although I say it myself. I will have to show you some of her masterpieces.

In the afternoon I took her over to see her grandparents as is my custom on Sunday afternoons. There is rather an amusing tale to be told about this particular occasion. Last Thursday was my father's birthday and as Susan didn't see him on that day it was decided that her mother would buy a small present for Susan to take over on the Sunday. The present in question was a pair of socks. On entering then Susan proudly goes up to her grandfather with the socks and promptly gives them to him without saying a word. My mother and father wishing her to perform her duty properly asked her what they were for, trying to get her to say 'For your birthday.' Susan however remained dumb and continued to be silent when the question was repeated. Finally after being questioned several times the poor child with great exasperation and contempt burst out with 'To put on your feet you silly thing.'

Incidentally Susan too was not altogether happy at the sight of the air rifle. When she saw it she ran away in terror to her mother. No doubt after seeing one or two cowboy serials on television she had formed a fairly clear idea of the essential function of such things. She was quite worried when her father and I went outside with it and insisted at once that he came back.

On Sunday evening (true to our agreement) I went to church. Did you? In fairness to you I must confess that it was rather a special occasion as the service was conducted by a former minister of the church who was a very popular preacher during his stay in Barrow and who I had known personally quite well. It was in fact the man I have mentioned to you before—the one who was formerly a quite famous comedian on the stage. It was in fact the man I suggested as a possibility when you told me of your going to church last Christmas. He is incidentally a resident minister in some part of London at present. If you remember it was he who I saw on two occasions in Durham last term. He was born somewhere in Durham County and was once the minister at a church in Spenemore. He is a sensible and interesting preacher and he has quite a powerful emotional appeal. The church incidentally was literally packed out which gives you some idea of his popularity. Usually it is barely half full. I enjoyed the service though I found Mr Sloan's sermon less exciting than I might have done five or six years ago when I used to hang spellbound on every word. (At that time I would probably have been a natural member of Dicu.[30]) His sermonizing technique is interesting, and, as far as my experience of Methodist ministers goes, quite original. It is not perhaps basically sound. What he does is to take a significant situation (usually from the New Testament) and dramatize it verbally for his congregation by describing exactly how it came about (i.e. what led up to it) what the various feelings and motives of the protagonists were and what its ultimate significance was. Using this as his basis he then proceeds to relate the situation to the eternal human predicament.

One of the best examples and one I may have mentioned to you before, was his sermon on Mary's meeting Christ on the first Easter Sunday. Here after a brief introduction to and explanation of the situation he concentrated his attention on the one word 'Mary' which was to her the revelation of Jesus' identity.[31] He then proceeded to analyse, interestingly if a little presumptuously, exactly what was taking place in Mary's mind in that great moment. She realized three things he declared with supreme confidence. The 'three things' (round which, by relating them to our own position he built his sermon) were that (a) nothing mattered i.e. she no longer had anything to fear (b) everything mattered i.e. everything in life assumed a significance in terms of the divinity here revealed and (c) she mattered i.e. she was important in that she was one of the loved ones of God. All these things are no doubt true of human life if we accept Christianity but you will see what I meant now when I said his technique was a little doubtful—to attribute such a full and complicated realization to Mary at that time is to say the least a little imaginative. You may say that this is not important provided that his points are sound when related to ourselves but it has a distinctly irritating effect on the listener—it's like having a good argument founded on a faulty premise or rather one in which the premise has been 'cooked' (used in Wimbledon?) by working backwards. The subsequent result is that you begin to wonder how (in what order) and why (with what real purpose) the sermon was conceived— and I'm afraid you are left with just a faint suspicion of the arty crafty, of the man being a little too excited by the dramatic and imaginative possibilities of the sermon and being led by these into a rather extravagant embroidery of the certain facts, and a rather facile readiness to see relationships and significances which are not clearly there.

You can't help feeling in fact that the sermon's conception and realization have not proceeded from an entirely pure and sincere desire to tell the truth—which would have established automatically its own rigorous veracity—that they are in fact partly the product (perhaps unconsciously) of a desire to shine rhetorically. You would appreciate this feeling better had you been with me—it's one I have very often when I listen to various people preaching. To love the dramatic too much is I'm sure a very unhealthy thing—in the long run it can result in you never being able to see things as they are.

The sermon on Sunday was perhaps an even better example. He took the case of Peter's denying Christ and eventually concentrated on 'Jesus looked at Peter and Peter remembered it.'[32] Again Peter remembered three (very conveniently for the purpose of the sermon) significant things—(a) he remembered his fault i.e. his former pride revealed in his boastful promise that he would stay by Christ till the end—leading of course to a discussion of the sin of pride (b) he remembered his frailty—that in being human he was a sinner and (c) he remembered his future—sinful and weak though he was he had nevertheless through the grace of God a glorious future of devotion awaiting him in which he would establish the new church. Again one felt there was a slight straining of the historical imagination in order to impregnate the phrase with a profundity of significance applicable to the world in general.

Another thing which irritates me about him in particular and Christian preachers in general is the supreme confidence born usually of ignorance with which they see the movements of history and human behaviour as a particularly clear expression of pro-Christian or anti-Christian tendencies. All that is good in history or man they attribute to belief in Christianity and all that is bad to rejection of it. They will pervert, ignore or over-emphasize to make this the case. The arrogance of their assertions is at times quite alarming. In the face of the bulk of historical, psychological and philosophical controversy their unqualified certainty is to say the least a little disconcerting. I used to like to think that their confidence was the product of a firm and illuminating faith which resolved the complexity of things into a clear and imperturbable simplicity, but the more experience I have of them the more inclined I am to suspect that it is the result either of an underlying feeling of uncertainty or more often of a complacently self-satisfied closure of the mind—a refusal to examine anything that threatens and an almost greedy readiness to seize what seems to confirm.

Moreover the emotion infused into so many sermons (particularly those of Mr Sloan) is becoming more and more vulgar and embarrassing for me. Particularly is this the case (as it was last Sunday) when you feel the preacher is partly motivated by a desire to indulge his love of the dramatic and the rhetorical. It seems at times as though these preachers, failing to derive any deep spiritual or intellectual satisfaction from their faith, endeavour to compensate for their dissatisfaction in striving for a vicarious thrill which they obtain by straining to the utmost the emotive possibilities of language and sentimental notions. The effect of their efforts on the congregation (an effect which they take to be a spiritual uplifting) is simply to titillate their emotions and generally make them feel very pleased with themselves and the world in general. You can tell this by what is said after the service and by the expression on people's faces during it—they gaze admiringly up at the preacher as if in some sort of pleasing daydream. No Win I'm afraid that judging by what I've seen of it I haven't a great deal of faith in the Methodist church—What's the answer? You tell me.

To return to more mundane subjects—I knew that Ian wasn't home when he hadn't been round over the weekend so I went round to the house on Monday and learned that he is coming home on Friday of this week. Terry will also be coming on Friday so until then I am more or less on my own. Ian apparently has been doing rather well in his interviews for various education departments. He has been accepted at Sheffield, Leeds and Liverpool. He must have made quite an impression at the last two as it is rather difficult to get accepted at another university as most of the places are kept for their own students. I think however that he will stay in Sheffield as he has quite a lot of friends there. Incidentally, he may come through to Durham for a day next Summer term after his finals are over so you may have the opportunity of meeting him. Have you by the way mentioned anything about the possible holiday at Stratford at home? Let me know if you have come to any decisions as to whether you still intend going, whether you have fixed a time yet, whether Joan would object to my going etc—so that I can get to work on Ian straight away—I will write to my aunt sometime this holiday to see what the position is there. There should be no difficulty about getting fixed up for a fortnight.[33]

I have been once to the pictures since I have been home. I went on my own on Monday to see *Genevieve*[34] which I hadn't seen before and *Doctor in the House*[35] which I had. I'm afraid I was a bit disappointed with both of them. I think your enjoyment of such films depends largely on the mood you are in and I can't have been in the right mood. *Genevieve* had its moments of course but it lacked (for me) variety of incident—I got fed up by the constant stoppings and explosive startings and was glad when the race (and the film) was over. You have seen it haven't you? I'm sure I would have enjoyed it had I seen it with you in Durham and had been able to have a whispered discussion on all that was happening. It doesn't seem the same going to the pictures without you.

By the way how did you enjoy the opera on Saturday night?—You must tell me all...[36]

The end of the letter has not survived. Although Bill may not have fully realized it at the time, the questions implicit in its pages were to be the prologue for the intellectual and spiritual journey that encompassed his life. But now let's allow Bill to speak for himself, as he writes down the key events of his life from the perspective of old age, his voice alternating with that of his wife.

Notes

[1]   In fact, towards the end of the Easter holiday Bill took his mother's advice and sold the gun.

[2]   Albert Lewis and Fanny Behar were married at the synagogue in Singers Hill, Birmingham on 18 January 1909. Both were aged twenty-one. See family documents.

[3]   Beginning in the 1880s, anti-Semitic pogroms swept across different regions of the Russian empire for several decades. More than two million Jews escaped Russia between 1880 and 1920. Many of them fled to the United States and what is today the State of Israel.

[4]   Account by K. Turner. See family documents.

[5]   Letter from K. F. Klein to R. C. C. Evans at the Poor Clare Convent of Woodchester, 1 April 1989. See family documents.

[6]   Account by L. Klein. See family documents.

[7]   In all there were ten children. K. Turner. See family documents.

[8]   The Certificate of British Naturalization was granted to Lebedinsky Lewis on 25 April 1894. See family documents.

[9]   From a report of the result of inquiries concerning the Application for a Certificate of British Naturalization by Lebedinsky Lewis, issued on 11 April 1894. See family documents.

[10]   K. Turner. See family documents.

[11]   *Ibid.*

[12]   J. W. Klein, *Pontius Pilate: Biblical Drama in Five Acts* (29 Ludgate Hill: A. H. Stockwell, 1923).

[13]   Account by L. Klein. See family documents.

[14]   F. G. Slaughter, *The Crown and the Cross* (Norwich: Jarrolds, 1972).

[15]   G. A. Tallet, Milnthorpe school report, 12 December 1941. See family documents.

[16]   F. Casson, Milnthorpe school report, 3 July 1942. *Ibid.*

[17]   When Bill reached the sixth form Lilian was overcome with pride when she heard him reciting the poem, 'The Highway Man', at a school public speaking event.

[18]   *Schindlers List* is a 1993 epic film directed by Steven Spielberg.

[19]   On one occasion Bill would tell Ruth that it was a privilege to belong to a hated people.

[20]   A few years later he would have his small daughters giggling helplessly as he mimicked a particularly stern and fear-provoking school teacher.

[21]   W. Shakespeare, *Antony and Cleopatra*, Act 1, Scene 5, line 5.

[22]   Bill's teaching practice was at Bishop Auckland Grammar school where, as a trainee, he had been given the least academic class. In fact Bill soon learned to win the interest of children of all abilities.

[23]   Bill had invited Win to the Castle Christmas Ball. This was considered a prestigious event and it lasted until the early hours of the morning. Once again Win went to the occasion wearing her turquoise dress. After a few dances and some refreshments, Bill invited Win into a friend's room for a glass of wine. It was a sweet fruit wine and Bill assured Win that it was like drinking lemonade. However, Win had never drunk wine before. She had several glasses on the strength of his assertion. A little later, to her alarm and mortification, she was suddenly overcome with nausea and was repeatedly sick. Bill was very concerned and contrite, saying that the wine had never had that effect on him! Obviously, this was not the kind of evening he had anticipated.

[24]   Giles Winterborne is an honest young suitor to Grace Melbury in Thomas Hardy's novel *The Woodlanders*. Her boarding school education has, in

her family's view, placed her above him in society but, armed with a strong affection, he still hopes to win her. The incident to which Bill refers is a fateful evening between the two young people which, despite the young man's best efforts to further his cause, goes disastrously wrong at a pivotal moment. After the occasion Giles is left anxious, with good reason, as to how Grace will evaluate him. See T. Hardy, *The Woodlanders* (London and Basingstoke: Macmillan London Ltd, 1974), pp. 105–110.

[25] Bishop Auckland Grammar School for boys.

[26] 'In the house' must mean in the back yard that belonged to the house.

[27] His two sisters, Margaret and Jean, and their husbands, Tom and Eddie, were temporarily sharing a house together until Jean and her husband Eddie had saved enough to take out a deposit for their own home.

[28] Terry and Ian were close friends of Bill from his schooldays at Barrow Grammar school.

[29] Susan would not yet have been at school.

[30] This was an extreme evangelical movement.

[31] Jn 20:16.

[32] Lk 22:61.

[33] In fact this plan never materialised, as next term Win impulsively and idealistically signed to help Austrian refugees rebuild their homes and when Bill heard about her plan he also signed. So then, the first part of the 1956 summer holiday, was spent with Bill working in the Barrow shipyard and Win serving in a Lyons cafe to earn money for the fare to Austria. They had signed themselves up for several weeks including a week's final holiday which the young couple needed to finance themselves.

[34] *Genevieve* is a 1953 British comedy film produced and directed by Henry Cornelius.

[35] *Doctor in the House* is a 1954 British comedy film directed by Ralph Thomas.

[36] Letter from William Evans to Winifred Klein, Easter holiday 1956. See family documents.

2 EARLY INFLUENCES

Bill 1933–1951

WHO CAN SAY when a conversion begins? Scripture says that: 'before the world was made, God chose us, chose us in Christ' (Ep 1:4). It speaks of 'the kingdom' that 'is close at hand,' (Mt 4:17) of the 'light that gives light to everyone' (Jn 1:9). It proclaims the God whose reality is evident in the things He has made, (Rm 1:20) and who, in the fullness of time, has revealed Himself definitively to the world, through word and sign, in the person of His Son, (Heb 1:2).

One thing I do know is that, in my own case, a Catholic was in the action from the beginning. I have it on the best authority that, early in the morning, when the midwife arrived to deliver me, Mrs Tranter, our next door neighbour and an Irish Catholic, got out of bed and said the Rosary for my mother and me. No doubt the main part of her prayer was for a safe delivery, but, knowing these Irish Catholics as we do, I don't think we can exclude the possibility that she slipped in something else, the fruit of which was to be born twenty-nine years later when I was received into the Catholic Church.[1]

The story of a conversion is often, to some extent, the story of a person's life, because you move towards the Faith through many influences, you embrace it as the answer to the deepest questions, and you persist in it through its capacity to answer those questions. 'The Catholic Church is the natural home of the human spirit,' wrote Hilaire Belloc. 'The odd perspective picture of life which looks like a meaningless puzzle at first, seen from that *one* standpoint takes a complete order and meaning, like the skull in the picture of *The Ambassadors*.'[2] Well, obviously I cannot deal here with the whole 'meaningless puzzle' and with the 'complete order' which the Faith offers, but I will try to indicate those aspects of my own experience and reflection where, hopefully, I have felt the truth of Belloc's words.

My home background in Barrow-in-Furness was not very religious. My father never went to church and seemed sceptical towards all forms of religion. My mother went to church only occasionally, but she lived by good values and said her prayers regularly. Of the two, my mother exerted the stronger moral influence on my two sisters and myself. We were brought up knowing the difference between right and wrong, as they say, but without any specific religious guidance.

It was not a happy marriage. My parents often quarrelled: some of the quarrels were violent and the three of us grew up frequently frightened and generally insecure. I think this background of fear and insecurity had some bearing on my subsequent attitude to marriage, and on my conversion.

But if we were not given religious instruction at home, we were all sent to the Methodist Sunday School and to Church from an early age and, in my own case, this was an important influence. According to Scripture, faith comes from hearing what is preached.[3] At that time, in the forties, a Catholic child would have the experience at home, from his parents, and in the catechesis received at school, particularly in the preparation for the reception of the Sacraments. A Protestant child had it above all in the Sunday School. The French Protestant minister, Jean Rilliet, describes this experience far better than I could myself, so I'll let him speak for me:

As a young child, the Protestant listens with wonder to the beautiful stories of Jesus ... Having reached his sixth year, he joins Sunday school where ... ordinary lay people ... mingle prayer and the singing of hymns with the narrative of the miracles and the parables ... The birth of Christ through Mary, His ministry of mercy, the hatred of the Pharisees, the abandonment by His disciples, the denial by Peter, the crucifixion, the Resurrection are engraved little by little on their hearts, and, with these, Faith enters for life ... From then on, should a crisis of conscience occur, the adolescent at war with his passions will return to the Name which he was taught to place above all other names ...; he opens the Gospel and reads it with a fervent desire to find truth! He finds it by finding Him who said, 'I am the Truth ...'[4]

Such, broadly speaking, was my own early formation in faith, and such, broadly speaking, was the nature of my return to it as I hope to show later.

In addition to Sunday School, of course, I attended day school: first the local primary school, and then the Barrow Grammar School. There also I was given religious instruction, non-doctrinal, Bible-based, but helpful in building up a knowledge of the Scriptures, with that great Figure at their centre.

Tot Sloan

In my late teens I met someone who was to prove an important influence for me. He was the Reverend Norman Sloan, our minister at the local Methodist Church. He was a little man, known affectionately to all as Tot Sloan. He had come to the ministry late, having been a comedian on the stage for many years. He knew the world, and used to shock certain parishioners from time to time by talking about Christ's compassion for prostitutes and sexual outcasts (Mt 21:31). Now, as far as I know, there were no prostitutes among the congregation of Greengate Methodist Church, but the idea stuck and was remembered later: Christ came 'to call not the upright but sinners to repentance' (Lk 5:32). It was the first of many pennies which were to drop for me in the years ahead.

Above all, he taught me that unbelief is not necessarily clever, a conviction that has never left me from that time onwards, even through the years when I was not a committed Christian. He was an eloquent, emotional and dramatic preacher who brought the Scriptures alive for me intellectually, imaginatively and emotionally. He made me realise that the divinity of Christ was credible, that the Gospels were deeply illuminating and challenging, that Jesus had to be taken seriously. Not then, perhaps, nor later, at university, on Saturday night, but sometime, when it was more convenient, Jesus would have to be taken seriously.

As far as I can remember there was no systematic doctrine at the heart of his preaching, nothing like the doctrinal clarity of the old Catholic Penny Catechism, or of the new *Compendium of the Catechism of the Catholic Church.*[5] The essence of his message seemed to be that Jesus stands at the door and knocks (Rev 3:20), and that we enter into a relationship with Him in response to the preaching of the Gospel and, at home, in prayer, by opening that door and letting Him into our hearts. If we do this, He will transform our lives. That may be an over-simplification, but that is how I remember it. I can't remember any coherent doctrine of sin, faith, grace, repentance, the Sacraments and certainly no clear theology of the Church.

And yet he appeared to hold a high doctrine of the Eucharist. For Methodists, Holy Communion used to be administered only once a month, after the Sunday Evening Service. It was never at the centre of worship as it is for Catholics; the central thing was the sermon. Nevertheless, for Tot, Communion was very important. He used to quote the passage from St John's Gospel:

> In all truth I tell you,
> if you do not eat the flesh of the Son of Man
> and drink his blood,
> you have no life in you (Jn 6:53).

I don't think he ever communicated to me any precise idea of what those words meant, certainly nothing approaching the realism of Catholic doctrine, but the words stuck and with them the realisation that Communion was important. It was another penny to be recalled later.

When I was eighteen, after a short period of instruction from Tot, I was received into full membership of the Methodist Church. This was formally done in a service, which, as far as I can remember, did involve a profession of faith, probably the Apostles Creed. Anyway I went through the service and made my commitment and this meant I could take Holy Communion. I felt at the time that I was taking the commitment seriously, and I continued to attend Church and receive Communion up to the time of leaving Barrow for Durham University.[6]

Win 1936–1955

My own early influences were very different to Bill's. Whereas he was born into a working class family in a small tidy terraced house in the ship-building town of Barrow-in-Furness, I was brought up by a middle-class family in a large, rather ramshackle, semi-detached house in Wimbledon, a prosperous suburb of London.

Bill, from a young age, was taken by his uncle to watch his beloved Barrow rugby team and his hero, Billy Horne, on Saturday afternoons. He remembered the sense of passionate shared antic-ipation, as eager crowds flocked to Craven Park, excitedly discuss-ing the team selection, whereas for me the highlight of Saturday evenings was being taken to the theatre and opera by my parents. We would sometimes go up to Sadler's Wells or Convent Garden at the crack of dawn with my mother to queue for seats in the gallery and when we came home she would play on the piano the most beautiful arias, so that we wouldn't miss them.

Influenced by his mother Lilian, Bill inherited a love of the cinema and local popular music. For example, his mother loved 'Danny Boy'[7] and 'Jeanie with the Light Brown Hair',[8] a song after which she named her own daughter Jean. From his mother's songs, he derived moral values which tended to hold a high ideal of romantic love. Later on, his love of music would expand to include the operatic passion of my family and gifted song writers such as Bob Dylan and Leonard Cohen. I, in my turn, responded to the music of Bill and his family. I particularly liked Paul Robeson singing 'Shenandoah'[9] and folk music. My mother also liked folk music and sometimes played and sang her favourite songs to us on the piano.

At home Bill's reading was confined entirely to comics until he was introduced to classical literature when, at the age of eleven, he did so well in the eleven plus that he was put in the express stream of the Barrow Grammar School, whereas we were encouraged to read Scott, Dickens, George Elliot and the Brontes at an age when we could barely understand their content or vocabulary. Comics were frowned on by my father to such an extent, that, when my mother surreptitiously bought some in a desperate attempt to encourage my younger brother to read, they had to be hidden out of sight before my father came home.

Bill was sent several times on Sundays to his local Methodist Chapel with his two sisters, encouraged by his mother, who could then enjoy a little peace and quiet in their cramped living room, whereas my parents would have felt threatened by their children attending any church service.

Yet, when we met at Durham University, none of these differences counted for anything. We felt the excitement of dancing at the freshers' ball, of talking animatedly about plays and novels and expressed a hope maybe at some time to find a church, which would inspire and deepen a mutual sense we shared that Christianity was true and should be addressed at some time in our lives.

My Birth in Wales

I was born in Bangor Hospital on 9 October 1936, a few weeks premature and weighing 5 pounds. At the time, my parents were renting a small, primitive cottage in North Wales on the side of a mountain with a stream running beside it. They had moved to Wales, after their marriage, as my mother was already pregnant with me, but couldn't face her parents' disapproval. My father was hoping to make a living as a successful playwright and so they were living very cheaply off the modest inheritance my father had received on the death of his parents.

My birth must have come at a most inconvenient time for my parents, although they never said so, as my father was having to return frequently to London to oversee the rehearsals and then the production of his play, *Charlotte Corday*,[10] which was performed at the 'Q' Theatre from Monday, October 26 until Saturday, October 31 with Beatrix Lehmann, a leading British actress, in the title role.[11]

When my mother and I were discharged from hospital, it was clear that the cottage was totally unsuitable for a new born baby, so I am told my parents walked up and down the streets of Bangor, looking for a sympathetic couple who would take in my mother and myself in return for a small remittance while my father was away in London. Such a couple were found in the minister of the local chapel and his wife, who were very welcoming and kind to my mother and myself.

When the time came for the return to the cottage, my parents warmly thanked the minister and his wife, but were taken aback when the minister asked if in return he might ask a favour of them, to baptise the baby. Touched by the faith of that gentle pastor, they felt unable to say no, although it went totally against their beliefs, as my mother was a Jewish atheist and my father agnostic. I have since wondered if my baptism bestowed a grace, which found fruition later in my life. I have always been touched by the words of Isaiah:

> I have called you by your name. You are mine (Is 43:1).

My parents' apprehension about the suitability of the cottage proved to be well founded as soon after our return there, I caught pneumonia and nearly died. After I recovered, my parents left the cottage, and, as my father's play had not been the hoped for success and most of his inheritance had to be spent buying a house in Wimbledon, my father had to return to teaching English in a school for foreign students in London.

He was able to buy the lease of the house because properties in the suburbs of London were going very cheaply at this time. People were beginning to fear a second world war was imminent and that London would be a prime target for bomb attacks. It would have taken only a relatively small sum of extra money for my father to buy the freehold but he was so impractical that he missed this chance.

This house, from which later I would hold my reception when I married Bill, was spacious and had a Victorian charm with large elegant rooms opening on to a generous garden where I had hours of childhood freedom with my brothers and sisters. Accustomed as we were to my parents' Spartan regime, we were oblivious to the dilapidated condition and furnishings of the house and accepted the intense cold in winter.

I look back on my childhood as basically secure and happy, although my father could at times become depressed and bitter, as he suffered from chronic insomnia, ill health and also felt he had failed to fulfil his ambitions as a playwright. In addition, his first wife had died tragically from a heart attack in her twenties, leaving my father with a four-year-old son, Rickie, and a two-year-old daughter, Anne, who had then to be looked after for several years by a maiden aunt, who lived in a villa in Italy and could afford a nanny and tutor for the young children. After the birth of my younger sister, Joan, when I was a year and a half, Anne and Rickie came to live with us. With war looming, my father feared that they would be trapped indefinitely in Italy unless he acted swiftly. Then when I was five, Lawrence was born. I felt we were a close, although rather reclusive family and I was very fond of all my brothers and sisters, with each of whom I had a different, but enriching relationship. Rickie was the first to leave home and I remember how excited Joan, Lawrence and I were, when he returned from West Africa, where he was working as an engineer supervising the installation of water pipes to local communities, and brought with him exotic presents. He had film star looks and I felt proud when he attended a school open day and my friends were all hoping to be introduced to him. Then, there was Anne, who was so kind, caring and patient, that she felt like a second mother. She would take us up to the Common most days in the Easter and Summer holidays, where we would spend hours fishing for tadpoles and newts and listening fascinated to the stories of the films Anne had seen with her friend and the latest instalment about 'Slug Minor', a naughty little boy who Anne invented, chiefly to entertain our little brother. Slug Minor was always getting himself into trouble. Lawrence was full of mischief and fun, independent and adventurous, yet he showed a touching concern for his sisters, as, when I had an interview for a place at Durham University, he worried that I might arrive late, because of all the changes of train I had to make. Joan was the nearest in age to me and we felt close, as we shared a bedroom, knew each other's friends, walked to school and the swimming club together and understood each other's anxieties, fears and hopes for the future. When Ruth was born a year and a half after Mary, just the same age gap as between Joan and me, I thought it would be good for them and that has certainly proved to be the case.

Although my parents were against all forms of organised religion, I felt we lived by good values, partly imbibed from the books we read, such as Hardy's *Tess of the D'Urbervilles*, Charlotte Bronte's *Jane Eyre*, George Elliot's *Middlemarch* and the plays and operas we were taken to. When we were still very young, Joan and I went to see *Madame Butterfly*[12] at Covent Garden and were moved to tears by the figure of the loyal, trusting little Madame Butterfly waiting hopefully through the long night for the return of the faithless, heartless Pinkerton. I remember my father would read to us Oscar Wilde's 'The Happy Prince', 'The Nightingale and The Rose', 'The Ballad of Reading Jail' and Byron's 'The Prisoner of Chillon', which we would find unbearably sad.

On Sunday afternoons, if the weather was fine, we would go for an excursion, as Dad named our Sunday walks, in the Box Hill, Leatherhead, Epsom Common and Richmond Park areas. Occasionally, we would climb Leith Hill and on the way back we would visit the grave of Audrey, my father's first wife and enter the country church at Cold Harbour. Here my father would kneel down and become lost in thought or prayer and so perhaps he did have his own private faith. This made an impression on me and I think I also sometimes prayed, particularly in a crisis.

I went to Wimbledon High School, a Church of England School, with my two sisters. Here, I was indebted to the Religious Studies lessons, which made a powerful impression and brought the Gospels alive for me. I remember being particularly moved by the arrest, trials and crucifixion of Our Lord and haunted by the sublime magnanimity of the prayer of forgiveness for His cruel tormentors:

> Father, forgive them; they do not know what they are doing (Lk 23:34).

I was also deeply moved by the good thief's reproach to the other criminal, as he acknowledged his own guilt and, alone among the mocking crowd, recognised Jesus' innocence and kingship and begged to be remembered:

> Have you no fear of God at all?... You got the same sentence as he did, but in our case we deserved it: we are paying for what we did. But this man has done nothing wrong. Then he said, 'Jesus, remember me when you come into your kingdom.'

And the wonderfully comforting response:

> In truth I tell you, today you will be with me in paradise (Lk 23:40–3).

I felt pained by Jesus' lonely cry of despair,

> My God, my God, why have you forsaken me? (Mk 15:34)

I remember on one particular Good Friday, going into a room on my own and praying, saying I was sorry Our Lord had to suffer so much, even betrayal and desertion by His own disciples, and wishing I had been there to comfort and support Him.

I had a black, long-haired cat, Bella, whom I loved dearly. I would brush her fur tenderly, sometimes buy her fish heads from the market with the penny we were given to buy a bun at break at school or pass her a little of my meal, where she sat in readiness under the table. She was very much a one-person cat, often waiting at the bottom of the road for when I returned from school and coming up to my bedroom to sleep at the end of my bed, which annoyed my mother. My father wasn't fond of animals and would push her brusquely off the chairs and she in response would hiss at him.

Once when I was about ten, I entered my bedroom to find Bella had climbed into a half opened drawer, probably for warmth, and somehow managed to get her head stuck in the gap at the back. In my panic to release her, I at first pushed the drawer the wrong way, which tightened the grip on her neck, before realising my mistake and managing to free her. When I put Bella in her basket, she looked limp and lifeless and I thought I had killed my cat. I remembered Jesus' words on prayer:

So I say to you: Ask and it will be given to you (Lk 11:9).

and similar words on the effectiveness of prayer and so all night prayed that my cat would not die. Miraculously, or so it seemed to me, Bella slowly recovered. Nevertheless, I don't remember praying regularly and I am sure there were long stretches of time when I never prayed at all. But it was at the times I felt most vulnerable, most alone and in need of help that I would then turn to prayer.

When I was about fourteen, my friends at school invited me to join the local church youth group, which they attended. They made it sound very exciting, talking about the debates, table tennis and outings they shared with boys from King's College and other local schools. Rather apprehensively, I asked my parents' permission to be met with a hostile silence from my mother and a firmly negative response from my father, who replied decisively that it was out of the question, as we would be bombarded by the vicar calling round to find out why he didn't see us at church on a Sunday. If I am honest, my interest in the youth group was mainly to join in with my friends and be part of their animated discussions rather than feel an outsider, but, nevertheless, I remember thinking to myself that one day when I was independent, I would be free to make my own decisions and might like to join a church. So, when several years later, in 1955, I gained a place at Durham University, I felt excited but also a little apprehensive at the prospect of my new independence and wondered whether, among other things, I would find a place to worship in such an inspiring city dominated by the imposing cathedral.

Notes

[1]   Bill was born on 19 May 1933.

[2]   This comes from a letter from Hilaire Belloc to Gilbert K. Chesterton on 1 August 1922. To clarify Belloc's point, the skull in the picture appears bizarre and meaningless from one angle but is completely coherent from another. See M. Ward, *Gilbert Keith Chesterton* (London: Penguin Books, 1958), p. 305.

[3]   '[T]he word of faith, the faith which we preach,' (Rm 10:8).

[4]   L. Cristiani and J. Rilliet, *Catholics and Protestants: Separated Brothers* (London: Sands and Co Ltd, 1960), pp. 52–53.

[5]   *Compendium of the Catechism of the Catholic Church* (London: Catholic Truth Society: Publishers to the Holy See, 2006).

[6]   This was October 1951.

[7]   'Danny Boy' is a ballad by the English songwriter Frederick Weatherly in 1913 and set to the traditional melody of 'Londonderry Air'.

[8]   'Jeanie with the Light Brown Hair' is a parlour song by Stephen Foster who lived from 1826–1864.

[9]   'Oh Shenandoah' is a traditional American folk song from the early nineteenth century.

[10]   J. W. Klein, *Charlotte Corday* (Great Britain: C. W. Daniel Company, 1927).

[11]   Beatrix Alice Lehmann (1 July 1903 – 31 July 1979) was a British actress, theatre director, writer and novelist.

[12]   *Madama Butterfly* is an opera by the Italian composer Giacomo Puccini that premiered at La Scala opera house in Milan on 17 February 1904. The work is one of the most frequently performed of all operas.

3 UNIVERSITY INFLUENCES

Bill 1951–1954

I SAY THAT I took the commitment seriously, but it couldn't have been too seriously, because I hadn't been at university for more than a few weeks before I had stopped going to church on Sunday. Attendance at Sunday service was not considered obligatory for Methodists and I didn't feel I was doing anything wrong in not going. Anyway, away from home, I soon lapsed from my Methodism, and never took it up consistently again.

Notional and Real Assent

In his book, *The Grammar of Assent*, Cardinal Newman, a major influence, writes of the difference between notional and real assent in matters of religion. We give notional assent to beliefs he maintains, when we accept them as true, but only in the mind, without actively committing ourselves to them and to their implications. Real assent, on the other hand, involves the element of self-commitment; it means that we not only believe, but really take on the Faith. It becomes the moral and spiritual compass which shapes our lives. Newman gives as an example the belief that slavery is evil.[1] Many people, no doubt, would acknowledge the truth of that notion, but it took a Wilberforce to take on the real implications of it and to do something about it. Now the kind of belief I held during the time of Tot Sloan's influence, and in some sense continued to hold, was more what Newman calls notional belief. I regarded Christianity as wonderful in many ways, and probably true, but I wasn't ready yet to embrace its demands, in particular its moral imperatives and constraints.

Hilaire Belloc describes this tension, which belief creates for the young, in this book *The Path to Rome*:

> Of its nature it struggles with us. And we, we, when our youth is full on us, invariably reject it and set out in the sunlight content with natural things. Then for a long time we are like men who follow down the cleft of a mountain and the peaks are hidden from us and forgotten. It takes years to reach the dry plain, and then we look back and see our home.[2]

Anyway, I certainly drifted into 'the sunlight'. Many of my friends were unbelievers, and that helped the drift.

At Durham I studied English Literature, and here the influence of Christianity was inescapable. 'The Faith is Europe. And Europe is the Faith' wrote Hilaire Belloc.[3] That is clearly an exaggeration, but one with a good deal of truth in it as anyone who saw Kenneth Clark's wonderful TV series: *Civilization*[4] will realise. It is significant that after making that series that Clark was received into the Catholic Church. Surely no narrative has irrigated the culture of Europe: its philosophy, literature, art, music and architecture more thoroughly than the Judaeo-Christian narrative, particularly as articulated in the Catholic tradition. Certainly it was impossible to study English Literature without recognising the enormous influence of Christianity on its development. So many of the major writers were Christians.

As well as English, I studied Modern History as a subsidiary subject. One of my tutors was a man called Ellis, a brilliant man, who wouldn't accept any opinion from you unless it was supported by hard evidence. I received a bit of a shock one day when I heard that he had been converted to Christianity. His ground had apparently been the Resurrection of Christ, which he had come to believe was a historical fact.

Impressive though these testimonies were, of the writers I was studying, of rationalists like Ellis and of certain good Christian minds I encountered at Durham, they made little difference to the way I lived. Like many of my contemporaries I enjoyed myself and was not a model of good behaviour and had little sense of sin. As far as I can remember I never prayed, not even at times of personal crisis, of which there were a number.

And yet, if pressed, I wouldn't have called myself an unbeliever. Time and again, with friends, in the pub, I would find myself taking the Christian side in argument. I wasn't at that time or any other really impressed by the arguments of unbelievers. Chesterton in his great book, *Orthodoxy*, claimed that before his own conversion to Christianity he had never read the Christian apologists; the atheists and agnostics with their shallow and conflicting testimonies conspired to make him a believer.[5] And that was how I felt myself and have continued to feel ever since. It would require an extraordinary act of faith and of arrogance for me to conclude that all the biblical and historical testimonies were grounded in relentless mendacity or delusion. The miracles of unbelief have always struck me as more improbable and astonishing than the miracles of faith. Of this more later.

But, if I remained notionally a Christian, I was in no way Catholic, notionally or otherwise; all my life up to this point I had been suspicious of Catholicism. I had been brought up as a Protestant and had inherited many of the prejudices which Protestants then held against the Catholic Religion. I thought of Catholics as superstitious, idolatrous, priest-ridden, not very respectable. They confessed their sins and then did what they liked. They distorted and ignored the Scriptures in the beliefs they held. They worshipped the Virgin Mary, putting her before Christ. They had persecuted Protestants, and would do so again given half a chance. There had been bad popes and periods of appalling corruption in the history of their Church, and yet Catholics still believed in the teaching authority of the Church, in particular, in the authority of the pope. Catholics were not allowed to think for themselves, and held strange moral beliefs on questions like birth control and divorce. And yet, in spite of all this, they had the arrogance to believe that their religion was the only true one.

At University I did, however, have one Catholic friend, Terry Heaney, whom I had known at school. We used to argue about religion from time to time. Most of our arguments were about moral issues such as contraception and divorce. I used to think that Terry's positions were too rigid. But there was one point he made which impressed me. It was when we were discussing the difference between Catholic and Protestant congregations that Terry would say, 'What about Tommy Minnican?' Tommy was a neighbour of Terry's, a non-Catholic, who used to get drunk occasionally, and had to throw his cap in before his wife would let him into the house. Terry's point was that the Church should have something to say to Tommy and not just to pious and respectable people. It was an echo of Tot Sloan's point about Christ's compassion for sexual outcasts, and it stuck. Not only were there no prostitutes among the Methodist congregations I was used to, there were no Tommy Minnicans either. It was another penny.

While at Durham I did, from time to time, hear distinguished Christian preachers, mostly Anglicans. The only Catholic preacher I heard was Father Holland, who was later to become the Bishop of Salford. He spoke on the last things. I remember being impressed by the intellectual rigour and clarity of his talk, but feeling it was a bit dry and over rigid in some of its positions, on the finality of judgement for instance. One point he made, however, did stay with me and was taken up later. Speaking of the profound coherence of Catholic doctrine, he quoted the philosopher, Hegel, to the effect that Catholic theology was an indissoluble whole. If you could accept the premise of God's existence, everything else followed with irresistible logic. It was another penny, which others, notably Newman, would develop for me in the years ahead.

Moreover, from my study of English Literature, I was becoming increasingly aware of the many important Catholic writers, both in the past and the present. Among the poets, for instance, there were Chaucer, Campion, Traherne, Pope, Dryden, Hopkins,

Francis Thompson and others. There was the flock of writers, who had joined the Church in the twentieth century, notably G. K. Chesterton, Evelyn Waugh and Graham Greene. Clearly a Church, which could attract and hold such men, must have something to say for itself.

Win 1955–1958

At the beginning of October 1955, as I travelled to St. Mary's College, Durham University, to study English Literature, I felt a mixture of excitement and trepidation at the prospect of starting a new, challenging, independent part of my life. I hoped to find the lectures inspiring, to make interesting friends and possibly make a serious religious commitment, as I knew Durham was steeped in Christianity and the impressive Cathedral dominated Palace Green, where the English lectures took place.

Unsurprisingly, the early weeks were a mixture of highs and lows. When things were going well, I enjoyed my new-found freedom, but when there were setbacks, I felt home-sick, unsure and missed the safety and security of home.

The first setback came very shortly after my arrival at St Mary's College. We were told that when we attended lectures, it was compulsory to wear an undergraduate gown and so it would be advisable to purchase one from the second hand stall and also some of the second hand set books, which were now on sale. I went to the Bursar's Office to collect my State Scholarship grant, only to be told that there had been a delay in these particular grants arriving. I left the Bursar's Office almost in tears, as I had no money at all. In a panic, I rushed to the station to see if they would give me money in exchange for my return ticket, only to be met by a firm negative response. I didn't feel any of the students I had met I knew well enough to ask to borrow money from them, and, as my parents had no phone, I couldn't contact them quickly enough either. After several hours of anguish, I returned to the Bursar's Office and tearfully explained my situation. She was kindly reassuring and lent me £5.00 until my grant arrived. At a later date, when I told Bill about my panic, he said with characteristic generosity he would have been only too happy to lend me the money.

On the other hand, one of the early highs was meeting Bill. On the Saturday of Freshers' Week, we were given the choice of attending the freshers' dance or a musical evening. I was undecided at first, as two of my new acquaintances had opted for the musical evening, which seemed the safer option and two for the dance, which felt the more exciting. My mother had bought me an attractive turquoise dress in the Elys sale. This decided me in favour of the dance. With hindsight, it was a momentous decision, as it was here that I met Bill. Had I not gone, it is unlikely our paths would have crossed, as Bill had already graduated and was in his Dip Ed year and so was not attending lectures on Palace Green. Without Bill's influence, I think I can certainly say I would never have become a Catholic.

My first impression of Bill, when he asked me for a dance, was that he was tall, slim, with a streak of golden hair, good looking, intelligent, sincere and spoke eloquently about literature. We discussed the plays I had seen in the London theatre and which Bill had studied at Durham and the course I was about to start and Bill had completed. We danced most of the evening and the time seemed to pass in a flash. At the end Bill asked if he could walk me back to St Mary's and we continued to discuss plays and books. We made an arrangement to meet again the next evening. I remember that night I felt elated. Bill was my first and only boyfriend.

But the next morning disaster struck again! We were told that on Sunday evening all first year St Mary's students were invited to attend a formal college meal followed by meeting the Principal, their tutors and moral tutor. My dilemma was how to let Bill know, so that he didn't think I had stood him up. After several anxious hours, I decided to write to explain the situation, place the letter in the cubby-hole for post for Castle students and hope that he checked it.

Fortunately, Bill did receive my letter and we arranged another meeting. As time went on, as well as discussing plays and books, Bill spoke of his Methodist experience and I of the impression the religious studies lessons had made on me and we felt at some later stage in our lives we would like to explore our religious faith together and perhaps find a church, which would inspire us. In my mind, this would certainly be a Protestant church, as from my school and my mother I had inherited many prejudices against the Catholic Church. In History lessons, we learnt of bad popes, corrupt priests, the cruel Inquisition, the scandal of indulgences, idolatrous worship of Mary and the saints and from my mother the belief that the Catholic Church had been responsible for much of the persecution of her race, the Jewish people.

However, for the time being, I was preoccupied with my course, the demands it made on my time, new friendships and experiences, and, above all, the developing relationship with Bill. Bill also was taking his Dip Ed year seriously and it proved to be demanding with lessons to prepare together with the prospect of an inspector coming in at any time to assess Bill's progress.

Nevertheless, we found time to see plenty of each other, going to college dances, walks and rowing on the river, attending university talks and debates, going to the cinema and at times through to Newcastle to see plays or unusual films. Bill was full of fun and enthusiasm for life, generous and loving. He would be amused, as he saw it, by my taking the rules and regulations too seriously, such as, when I arrived for our second date proudly wearing my college gown (bulky and unglamorous and a rule largely ignored by the students) or worrying about arriving back at St Mary's College no later than 11 p.m., where an impatient Mr Robinson would be waiting to check that all the students, who had signed out, had returned on time so that he could lock up. On at least one occasion, when we were a few minutes late, Bill put his watch back to claim innocence!

During my second term I received a shock when Bill arrived with a frying pan, plus eggs, bacon and sausage! The other girls would use the small kitchen to make a hot drink and at the most perhaps toast a tea cake or boil an egg. Bill and I were in the habit of spending a couple of hours together in the late afternoon from about 4.30 to about 6.30 p.m., the slot of time between the end of his teaching practice and the bell at St Mary's, to be followed by our supper, which required all young men promptly to leave the college premises for the night. When I expressed misgivings about the meal, Bill persuasively talked me round, arguing that it would enable him to spend more time with me and make a quick start on his lesson preparation after leaving. I was embarrassed about the cooking of the fry up, which made me rather conspicuous in the corridor but I saw the sense in Bill's argument and gave in. However, I had never wanted to look different and I used to dread someone coming into the kitchen and seeing me!

During the Christmas and Easter holidays we wrote to each other every day. We hadn't forgotten our commitment to look into the possibility of joining a church together and arranged on a few occasions that we would go to a church service on a Sunday, Bill in Barrow and myself in Wimbledon or Raynes Park, and discuss with each other our experience. Bill went to the Methodist Church, which he had attended before university, but about which he now had quite serious reservations. I tried one or two Protestant churches, and found the services to some extent uplifting, but not sufficiently so to feel that this was the church I wanted to join. Whether I told my parents where I was going or not, I can't remember, but if I did, they made no objection.

At the end of my first year at Durham, I signed to work voluntarily in a rural work camp in Austria, helping desperately poor refugees rebuild their homes which struck me as more in keeping with Jesus' idealistic teaching than the more traditional style of holiday.[6] When I told Bill, without a moment's hesitation, he also decided to go, although it would not have been his natural choice for a holiday. It was a hard three weeks, but also at times rewarding and uplifting. We were assigned to different sites and on one occasion Bill and I were helping to dig the foundations of a house. It was exhausting work in the blazing sun, but I remember Bill saying that when he saw how diligently the young widow and her two sons, who looked only about eight and ten, persevered, he couldn't but give it his best. In the evenings, Bill would recover with a large beer while I asked for an apple juice! He would say:

Ein großes Bier und ein Apfelsaft, bitte. Danke schön!

On one occasion, we were sent to a site where the houses were at a more advanced stage and I was consigned to stand on, as I remember it, a narrow wooden platform high up and unload bricks from the pulley. Each time I reached for the bricks, and looked down, I felt dizzy, as though I might fall. When I confided my fear to Bill at the break, without a moment's hesitation, he said, 'Well then, you're not going up there again!' and, to my great relief, went straight to the supervisor, who changed my work to one at ground level. I never for one moment doubted Bill's concern for me or that he would come to my rescue.

After this arduous holiday, Terry, a close friend of 'Lord Bill', as he jokingly nicknamed him, would ask, 'What has she got lined up for you next year?' In fact, my mother had torn up the next application form when it arrived a few months later because I had come back with a skin infection on my face and hands. Although Bill and I did not know about this at the time, she and Bill would have been in agreement.

As I started my second year at Durham, Bill began to apply for teaching jobs in the area to be near to me. He was accepted to teach English in a Secondary Modern School at Seaham Harbour starting in January. He found his early years teaching demanding and stressful. He planned his lessons very conscientiously and had to find a way to interest boys of widely different ability.[7] He also set a lot of homework, which he carefully marked.

I too was working very hard, putting a lot of time, possibly too much, into reading widely and writing essays, but we would meet at weekends, usually in Durham and continue to go to the cinema, the theatre, university talks, play tennis, row on the river and country walks. We also now visited each other in holidays in Barrow and Wimbledon. I was welcomed warmly by Bill's parents, sisters and friends in Barrow and felt at home and somehow special. Despite my anxiety that Bill's friends would perceive me as very southern and middle-class, Bill told me I had received 'The thumbs up' from them and in fact one of them had said to him about me, 'She breaks the mould.'

Bill was accepted by both my parents, especially my mother, who was impressed by the eloquence, enthusiasm and intelligence with which he analysed the plays we saw and also his obvious devotion to me. My younger brother, Lawrence, later told me that he found Bill's presence a breath of fresh air, as, at the time, when his far from satisfactory school reports arrived and my father, in particular, but also my mother, would look very grim, Bill lightened the atmosphere by bursting into laughter. He also said that he would listen admiringly to Bill's analysis of books and plays. Lawrence and Bill went on to form a life-long friendship and enjoyment of each other's company.

Bill and I decided to marry after I finished my degree at Durham and, although we hadn't relinquished our desire to find a church in which we would worship together, it had been put on hold, partly as the demands of teaching and finals were so time-consuming and also I felt it would be easier once we were married and living together in the same place, free of family constraints.

Notes

1   J. H. Newman, St, *An Essay in Aid of a Grammar of Assent* (London: Longmans, Green, and Co, 1903), p. 36.

2   H. Belloc, *The Path to Rome* (London, Edinburgh and New York: Thomas Nelson and Sons Ltd, 1902), p. 142.

3   H. Belloc, *Europe and the Faith* (London: Constable and Company Limited, 1920), p. 331.

4   *Civilisation*—in full, *Civilisation: A Personal View by Kenneth Clark*—is a television documentary series written and presented by the art historian Kenneth Clark. It was first shown on BBC2 in 1969.

5   'Almost thou persuadest me to be a Christian.' See G. K. Chesterton, *Orthodoxy* (London: Bradford and Dickens, 1957), p. 137. See also Ac 26:28.

6   It was the summer of 1956.

7   Initially, Bill taught boys at Seaham Harbour but while he was there girls were included in the school.

4 MARRIAGE AND CONVERSION TO CHRIST

Bill 1955–1959

AT THE BEGINNING of my last year at Durham I met Win, the girl I was to marry four years later. This relationship was to be a very important one both for my life generally and for my conversion. Win herself had been baptised and had gone to an Anglican High School where the Christian Religion was taught in a non-doctrinal way. When she came to university her attitude to Christianity was agnostic but sympathetic. She came hoping she might find faith there. In this she was to be disappointed, at least for the duration of her course at Durham. I didn't feel ready for religion yet, certainly not for the commitments it involved, and my negative attitude had its effect on her.

After I had finished my university course, I obtained a teaching post near Durham so that we could continue our relationship while Win was still at university. A year after Win graduated, in the summer of 1959, we were married at a registry office near Win's home in Wimbledon.

After the marriage, we set up house in a small rented flat in Sunderland, moving a little later into a larger flat, when our first daughter was born, and eventually, two years before our return to Barrow, into a house. I have a very special affection for those homes[1] because they recall for me a period of extreme happiness in which I found fulfilment in work and in love and in which, more importantly, Win and I found the faith.

Shortly after we were married, we decided that we would do what we had sometimes talked of doing—we would really look hard at the Christian religion and make up our minds about it. I think our motive was in part to give our marriage the best possible base for its future. Belloc says it is the experience of evil, encountered daily, which causes the return. This I am sure is true. But it can be equally true of our experience of good. There is a terror which underpins all extreme happiness, a sense that it will be fleeting, short-lived, which makes us seek some more lasting, more secure basis which is deeper than itself. I was particularly aware of this as the child of an unhappy marriage, and because even in my relationship with Win there were times, inevitably, of tension and difficulty. Anyway, for these reasons and others we decided, as a joint venture, to look at Christianity together.[2]

The Nature of Conversion

Conversion is rarely purely intellectual. Newman makes that very clear as I hope to show later. Ideally it involves the whole person: mind, heart, imagination, conscience, will. I think we are ready for conversion when our self-sufficiency has been shaken in some way, when we feel the need for something more than what has hitherto seemed enough, when, to quote Belloc again, 'the sunlight' is no longer sufficient. Conversion takes place in the moral heart of ourselves, when, not only do we see the truth of the Gospel, but we are prepared to let it reshape us. It is a radical reorientation of the self, a kind of death. My daughter, Ruth, put it rather well, I thought, when she said: 'The mind comes alive only when something else has been awakened.' In Win's and my own case, hopefully, that awakening had occurred.

For Win and me, the inquiry did not begin with the philosophical arguments for the existence of God, based on reason reflecting on the natural world. Fascinating though these are, for us, the case for God and everything which pertains to Him rested ultimately on Revelation, more specifically on the claims of the Judaeo-Christian Revelation. For Win and me, the vital question was: can we trust the Bible, in particular, can we trust the New Testament, for it is there that the most astonishing and challenging claim is made: that the God, who has revealed Himself to humankind in the things He has made (Rm 1:20), and who has spoken to Israel through her prophets and her scriptures, has Himself become incarnate in Christ and, through Him, has delivered His definitive Revelation to the world. So, together, we began to re-read the New Testament and all the works of Christian apologetics we could lay our hands on.

How does an inquirer come to faith in Jesus as God's messenger? For it is as His messenger that we first apprehend Him: the acceptance of His Divinity, in the full Nicene sense, comes later, as it did for His followers. I think we each do this in different ways, guided and prompted by the action of the Holy Spirit within us. As I said earlier, faith comes from hearing by those who seek with truly open minds and hearts. Jesus Himself says: 'Ask, and it will be given to you; search, and you will find; knock, and the door will be opened to you' (Lk 11:9). The action of the Holy Spirit is as important here as the work of our own minds, because according to Scripture: '[N]obody is able to say, 'Jesus is Lord' except in the Holy Spirit' (1 Co 12:3). It is God's Spirit, the Spirit of Truth, who, acting within us, confirms in our minds and our hearts the Word of the Gospel and prompts our commitment to it.

Win and I came to that first act of faith in Christ very quickly, in a few months. I think we were able to do this because we were both familiar with the Scriptures through our upbringing. The difference was that now we were willing to reflect on them more deeply and commit ourselves unreservedly to their demands. As I have indicated, our predispositions are always a necessary factor in conversion. It will never be embraced by an arrogant scepticism, only by those who seek it with open mind and heart. That is why faith is not just a cognitive, but a moral act, a fundamental, existential reorientation of our whole selves.

Win 1958–1959

At this point I feel I need to further clarify how this book has developed out of Bill's original intention for his book. Bill had intended to complete a work of theology, an account of his spiritual journey towards Catholicism and his unshakeable belief in its truth up to the end of his life, despite the problems that have beset the Church in recent times. Sadly, he died before finishing the book and, as explained by our daughter Ruth, in the Preface, we are trying to rescue what he left and, where possible, comple-ment his theological insights with my memories of my early influences, our meeting in Durham, our wedding and early married life, my own conversion and the birth of our first two daughters, Mary and Ruth, up to the time when Bill was received into the Catholic Church in September 1962. Within three weeks of Ruth's birth, Bill was received into the Catholic Church and so this seems a natural point at which to end the story. We are sustaining Bill's storyline and theological perspective as far as possible and supplementing them with my memories which attempt to capture the atmosphere of our life in the late 1950s and early 1960s. And for me it has been helpful at an early stage of grief and loss to recall these happy times.

I graduated from Durham University in June, 1958, but Bill and I decided to delay our marriage by one year. This was mainly because Bill had found his early years of teaching demanding and stressful and wanted to feel fully prepared for marriage. He decided to try to drink little or no alcohol in the months ahead and I was touched by the sacrifice he was making. I was also content to spend a last year with my parents. I obtained a job in Harrods Query Office, where I answered phone calls and letters of complaint and Bill and I saved some money towards our wedding and honeymoon. Harrods was one of the most prestig-ious London stores where wealthy women would come to buy elegant and exclusive outfits for special occasions, among their other purchases. However, as I was not well off or interested in fashion, this aspect of the store did not intrigue me. On the contrary, dealing with the complaints of these women about their outfits and trying to ascertain which ones were genuine was a great worry and source of stress for me. I often felt I would have been happier working for *The Reader's Digest*[3] but unfortunately they offered me an interview for a post after I had already been accepted at Harrods.

The Query Office was a completely new experience for me. It was quite a large office staffed by some middle-aged women, who had worked there for many years and a few young women, who like me were filling in a gap year. We were given each morning a thick bundle of letters and told how vital it was carefully to distinguish between those who had a genuine cause for complaint and those who were trying to avoid paying their bills, as we must not lose loyal customers but neither must we let fraudsters get away with non-payment. This involved rushing around to check when the item in question left the appropriate department, when it was packed, when posted, whether the customer was up to date with previous payments or had a history of bad debt and so on. Accurate dates were of the greatest importance, because some people claimed an outfit bought for a special occasion had arrived too late and so was being returned.

I tackled the job with my usual conscientiousness, often working through my lunch hour and found the job stressful. I was, however, met with good humour and kindliness by the staff, whom I related to warmly and who probably thought I took it all far too seriously! When I left, I was given a lovely card signed by everyone in the office and a gift of Prestige kitchen utensils, some of which I still have and use to this day. Two mature ladies, who had been particularly helpful to me, came to our wedding and reception. For this work, I was paid somewhere between £7–£8 a week, which increased to about £10 a week in the lead up to Christmas when we worked overtime. Bill, at the time, as a graduate English teacher, was earning £12 a week. When I gave my notice in, I was offered a promotion, but I can't say I was sorry to leave, although I had been touched by the generous well wishes of the people I worked with.

When Bill first started teaching, he had been staying in lodgings, where he had a room, his meals provided and his washing done. However, as time went on, this did not prove entirely satisfactory. The landlady complained that Bill was using a lot of electricity, as he stayed in in the evenings preparing lessons, marking books and reading, whereas her other lodgers went to the pub every night and he gave her more clothes to wash than she was used to. There was also an atmosphere of bickering between the wife, her husband and teenage daughter, which Bill found unsettling. Bill tended to be good naturedly tolerant. However, when a cousin visited for the day and remarked that he was surprised Bill was staying in such an atmosphere, Bill decided to look for an independent flat.

This Bill found in Toward Road. It comprised one middle sized room with a double bed, two chairs and a gas fire, which had a meter, a small adjoining room with a cooker, table and two chairs but no running water. However, there was a bathroom on the floor below, where washing up could be done in the basin and which was shared with the other four lodgers.

The landlady was a kindly widow, who had been left with one son. She had recently bought a small mongrel puppy, which she joked was growingly alarmingly big, but was proving to be a very good house dog. She told Bill the price of the flat was £2 a week and, when at a later date, Bill told her we were planning to marry, she said that was no problem. I could come and live there too. There was a pleasant, free and easy atmosphere in the house and Bill felt much happier than he had been in his previous lodgings. As he was not used to looking after himself, Bill often ate out and at this time discovered Chinese food, which he thought was wonderful. At other times, he cooked himself a fry up. Not the healthiest of diets! He sent his washing to the laundry, which they collected each week and returned, beautifully ironed.

We decided to marry in a registry office, as, despite believing in the truth of Christianity, neither of us belonged to a church and so it seemed the right and honest decision and also a decision with which both sets of parents felt comfortable.

A few weeks before our wedding, my mother encouraged me to hand in my notice at Harrods. As she was working in the Civil

Service, she said it would be a great help to her if I spent the time weeding and planting flowers, mowing the lawn in the large garden, as we planned to have the reception at home and hoped for a sunny day, when the guests could spill out into the garden with their refreshments. Also, she wanted to get a kitten, but, as she worked, she didn't have time to housetrain it, which I would then have time to do and I was happy to agree.

My much-loved cat, Bella, had recently been put to sleep at the age of about seventeen while I was still at university. She was half Persian and had long fur, but once I left home for university no-one brushed her fur and so she developed sores on her skin under the matted fur. I was sad to hear of her death, but didn't grieve for her the way I would have done had she died when I was a girl. My mother always liked to have a cat in the house, partly because she was an animal lover, but mainly to keep the mice down.

My mother knew someone who was looking for a home for a little black and white kitten which we duly collected. It was the last one of the litter, small, delicate and timid, but also gentle and responsive and proved very easy to train, as she spent most of the three weeks outside in the garden with me.

One day I went up to London, looking for a dress for my wedding day, but I have never been too sure what suited me and became more and more confused, as I went in and out of shops. I tried on dresses, affirmed by strong minded saleswomen, but, unconvinced by any of them, I eventually returned home empty handed. So I put myself in the hands of my sister, Joan, who was an actress and very good at fashion. She took me to a small, but exclusive dress shop in Wimbledon, where I chose a simple, but stylish navy blue dress, which everyone said suited me and which Bill thought was lovely.

My mother threw herself into the preparations for the reception with enthusiasm. Our large house was rather rundown and shabby, but she decorated and bought a new carpet for the main living room. She helped me with weeding and planting flowers during the evenings, so that the garden looked beautiful, full of colour and perfume. My mother ordered a buffet meal from Lyons, choosing the most expensive option and it proved to be very good and unusually imaginative for the time.

The day before our wedding, Bill's sister Margaret and her little daughter, Susan, came to stay and in the evening they, together with my parents, Joan, Terry, Bill and I went to the Royal Court Theatre to see Arnold Wesker's play *Roots*.[4] Although Susan was only about seven, she was excited by the new experience and watched the play intently, making quaint little comments on it. When we returned home, I felt proud of Bill, as he animatedly joined in the discussion of the play with his usual eloquence, intelligence and enthusiasm. He looked handsome, slim and tall; his skin tanned and his fair hair accentuated by the sun.

The next day we were joined at the registry office by close family members and also by some friends. Although we were in a registry office, I felt I said the marriage vows with utter sincerity and full commitment, and I am sure Bill did the same. Looking back on our life together, despite inevitable difficulties, which we did not foresee at the time, and human failings, I think we both did our best to honour those vows:

> To have and to hold from this day forward,
> for better, for worse,
> for richer, for poorer
> in sickness and in health,
> to love and to cherish,
> till death us do part.[5]

When we returned home, the sun was shining brightly and everyone was in good spirits. My father and Bill had decided they would be more relaxed and enjoy the day better if they didn't have to make a speech, but my Jewish grandfather, who loved to hold forth, spoke with kindliness and goodwill towards everyone. The excellent buffet was appreciated by all and the guests spilled out into the garden with their drinks and food, as we had hoped. I remember feeling joyful and hopeful.

About five in the afternoon, Bill and I departed for Stratford-upon-Avon, where we stayed in a small guesthouse for a week. The glorious weather continued and we went for walks by the river in the beautiful countryside. We also queued for tickets for Shakespeare's plays, which we enjoyed and afterwards discussed animatedly the actors' performances. I remember it as a very happy week.

When we returned to Sunderland, somewhat to my relief, the teaching jobs in the area had been already filled. For the first time in many years of hard study, I had time on my hands and so this felt the right time to read about Christianity, deepen my belief and find a church, where we could worship together. I felt this would help and strengthen our marriage, as the deeply unhappy atmosphere in which Bill had grown up, had left him prone to stress and anxiety. Also, in marriage there are inevitably adjustments to make, as two very different people seek to live in loving harmony. Bill also shared my feeling and we both felt open and ready to explore Christian faith and commitment together, free from family constraints.

Notes

1   Bill's high opinion of these flats as lodgings was based on romantic and spiritual memories rather than practical concerns!
2   This passage is an expanded version of the equivalent passage in Bill's book. It actually comes from an earlier piece of writing on his conversion, given as a talk to the Methodist Men's Fellowship in the mid-1970s.
3   *The Reader's Digest* is an American family magazine, published ten times a year and covering topics of general interest. Formerly based in New York, it is now headquartered in Midtown Manhattan. The magazine was founded in 1922.
4   *Roots* is the second play by Arnold Wesker in *The Wesker Trilogy*. The wedding party saw it on 24 July 1959.
5   From *The Book of Common Prayer*.

5 OUR SEARCH: WHICH CHURCH?

Bill 1959

THE NEXT QUESTION for both of us was: which Church? We had no intention of being freelance Christians. We realised that Christian commitment meant membership of the Church and regular worship. Interestingly, I felt no inclination to return to the Church to which I owed so much for my Christian formation, the Methodist Church. Win herself had never been attached to any particular denomination and, fondly though I remembered it, I knew by then that Methodism was only one of many Christian options. So we decided we would bide our time and survey the possibilities. But events were to take a hand here, prompting us to move more quickly than we had intended. One evening, quite by chance I remember, Win and I tuned into a radio programme. It was a debate on the existence of God between the agnostic, Bertrand Russell, and the Jesuit, Father F. C. Copleston.[1] It was a brilliant debate between two experts in their own fields. The result appeared inconclusive, but we both felt that Copleston had more than held his own. What stayed with me more than the arguments themselves were two ideas. When they wanted someone to argue with Russell they went for a Catholic. Why was that? Also, more significantly, any religion which could claim the assent of a mind like Copleston's had to be reckoned with. It was another penny.

On the staff of the school at which I taught was a man called John Harrison. He was one of the dominant personalities in the staff-room, an excellent raconteur, and very popular. He was also a Catholic convert, though he rarely spoke about religion. One lunch-time, shortly after hearing the radio debate, I asked John why he had become a Catholic. He told me that his chief influence had been Cardinal Newman, in particular Newman's *Apologia Pro Vita Sua*,[2] in which he gave the account of his conversion. Many pennies were about to drop.

The following Saturday I happened to be in a bookshop in Sunderland when I saw Newman's book on display. I bought it for three shillings and sixpence, the cheapest and most important purchase of my whole life, and began to read it straight away. What impressed me first about it was its style. It was clearly the work of a brilliant mind but also of a poetic sensibility. Its effect was both to stimulate and re-orientate my own mind and inflame my imagination. It left me haunted by powerful ideas and images, above all by the image of the Catholic Church as the true bride of Christ, which was the historical successor of the Apostolic Church and which taught with the authority of Christ. From then on my search for the Church took a specifically Catholic direction, though Win was not to follow me in this immediately. In fact, when I told Win I might become a Catholic she burst into tears.

Sensing my interest in Catholicism, John Harrison brought me another book: *This Tremendous Lover*[3] by the Irish Cistercian writer, Father Eugene Boylan. This book impressed me in many ways, above all in demonstrating the beauty, depth and integrity of Catholic doctrine. It hung together in a profound organic unity, its central concepts reverberating through all its parts. This echoed and developed what, according to Father Holland, Hegel had said about the irresistible inner cohesion of Catholicism. It was an idea which would be developed for me later by Newman and others.

A newspaper advertisement provided another providential push. It was from the Catholic Enquiry Centre, an offer of a free course of booklets on the Catholic Faith, or, if you were prepared to pay for it, you could have the whole course in a single volume. I opted for the latter and was promptly sent the book. This was not the best work of Catholic apologetics I was to read but it was useful. Above all, it was helpful in bringing to my attention many biblical texts, which I had scarcely been aware of as Protestant, texts which were clearly tolerant of a Catholic interpretation. For me it was a shower of pennies.

There were the texts relating to the Church, to the authority given to Her by Christ, in particular, to the authority given to Peter:

> All authority in Heaven and on earth has been given to me. Go, therefore, make disciples of all nations: baptise them in the name of the Father and of the Son and of the Holy Spirit, and teach them to observe all the commands I gave you. And look, I am with you always; yes, to the end of time (Mt 28:19–20).

The threefold all: all nations, all commands, always, is highly significant. There is only one Church to which they can reasonably be applied.

> So now I say to you: You are Peter and on this rock I will build my Church. And the gates of the underworld can never hold out against it. I will give you the keys of the kingdom of heaven: whatever you bind on earth shall be considered bound in heaven: whatever you loose on earth shall be considered loosed in heaven (Mt 16:18–9).[4]

And

> Simon, Simon! Look, Satan has got his wish to sift you all like wheat; but I have prayed for you, Simon, that your faith may not fail, and once you have recovered, you in your turn must strengthen your brothers (Lk 22:31–2).

Also

> Jesus said to him [Peter], 'Feed my lambs ... Look after my sheep ... Feed my sheep' (Jn 21:15–7).

With regard to these Petrine texts, two things struck me as immediately apparent. Firstly, that powers are being conferred which are foundational necessities, essential to the well-being of the Church, and, secondly, that these are powers, which we normally associate with Christ Himself, (the Rock and the

Shepherd.) If Christ had not intended to found the Papacy here, it is strange that He should have left us with what seems such a powerful invitation to embrace it.

Equally challenging, were the texts relating to the Sacraments:

> In all truth I tell you, no one can enter the kingdom of God without being born through water and the Spirit; (Jn 3:5).

> In all truth I tell you, if you do not eat the flesh of the Son of man and drink his blood, you have no life in you … For my flesh is real food and my blood is real drink (Jn 6:53).

> 'As the Father sent me, so am I sending you.' After saying this he breathed on them and said: 'Receive the Holy Spirit. If you forgive anyone's sins, they are forgiven; if you retain anyone's sins, they are retained' (Jn 20:22–3).

> Any one of you who is ill, should send for the elders of the church, and they must anoint the sick person with oil in the name of the Lord and pray over him. The prayer of faith will save the sick person and the Lord will raise him up again; and if he has committed any sins he will be forgiven. So confess your sins to one another, and pray for one another to be cured; the heartfelt prayer of someone upright works very powerfully (Jm 5:14–6).

These texts represented a totally unfamiliar ground to me. Apart from Tot Sloane's insistence that Holy Communion was important, as a Methodist I had received very little in the way of sacramental doctrine. The whole emphasis was on having a personal relationship to Jesus. I knew nothing of baptismal regeneration, despite the frequent references to it in the New Testament. Confession was never mentioned; the idea that priests had the power to forgive sins would have struck me as unfounded and absurd, as would the doctrine of the Real Presence of Christ in Communion. Again, of the Sacrament of the Sick I knew nothing. Yet here were all these doctrines, clearly present, at least embryonically, in the New Testament.

There were texts relating to Mary, in particular, one from John's Gospel:

> Near the cross of Jesus stood his mother and his mother's sister, Mary the wife of Clopas, and Mary of Magdala. Seeing his mother and the disciple whom he loved standing near her, Jesus said to his mother, 'Woman, this is your son.' Then to the disciple he said, 'This is your mother.' And from that hour the disciple took her into his home' (Jn 19:25–7).

I came to see this text as an illustration of the difference between Protestant and Catholic interpretation of Scripture. Many Protestants would see it as merely meaning that Jesus wanted Mary and John to look after each other when He was no longer with them. The text is open to that interpretation, but if you look at it carefully it suggests more: that Jesus wants Mary and John to receive one another in a new relationship of mother and son. This is the interpretation given to it in Catholic tradition and, seeing it as a part of a constellation of texts in both testaments relating to the maternity of Mary, the Church here sees Christ declaring that Mary is now the new 'mother of all those who live' (Gn 3:20), prefigured by Eve, exercising a motherhood, not of the flesh, but of grace for all humankind. Far from indicating an infidelity to Scripture, the Catholic interpretation illustrates a deep reverence for the sacred text. It rarely merely means only one thing, but when read with an open ear it is often an ever more, particularly when texts are read in the context of Scripture as a whole.

So, singly and collectively, all these texts made a strong and lasting impression on me. It was like having lived in a forest all my life and, for the first time, beginning to see the trees. From then on, as I read more and reflected more, the conviction deepened that, far from being disrespectful to Scripture, the Catholic Church was the one most fully faithful to it.

Win 1959

When we returned to Sunderland, we decided that now was the time to do what we had so often spoken about and search for a church to which we felt we could commit ourselves. We both believed in Christianity and felt that this would be a way of strengthening our faith and our marriage.

Our quest was also to be given a certain sense of urgency by the fact that Bill had suffered throughout his childhood the traumatic experience of overhearing violent quarrels between his father and beloved mother, due to his father's infidelity, during which Bill was terrified. This had left him prone to anxiety and at times depression. We, therefore, were not as secure and confident of our future, as we would otherwise have been and unsure where to turn for help. I think it is sometimes in our times of vulnerability and need that our hearts are more open to God or so it has been in my experience.

Bill initially was attracted to the Catholic Church before me. His interest was awakened after we had heard by chance a debate on the radio on the existence of God between the agnostic, Bertrand Russell, (whom my parents greatly admired) and the Jesuit priest, Father Copleston, in which they both made a strong case for their own positions. Bill was impressed that it was to a Catholic Jesuit priest that the media turned in order to match Bertrand Russell point by point and it led to Bill's asking John Harrison, a popular member on the staff at Seaham Harbour, why he had become a Catholic. He told Bill that his chief influence had been the writings of Cardinal Newman, in particular, his *Apologia Pro Vita Sua*,[5] which Bill proceeded to buy the following weekend and began to read with increasing enthusiasm.

Meanwhile, I was becoming alarmed by Bill's growing interest in Catholicism and when, in fact, he said he was considering the Catholic Church, I burst into tears. All my prejudices from my Church of England School and, more importantly, the fact that my mother viewed the Catholic Church as responsible for the persecution of her race came flooding into my mind and I feared that the search, which I had thought would strengthen our marriage, could, in fact, come to divide us.

I had always felt particularly close to my mother and had never wanted to cause her any distress. Nor had I found this particularly difficult until this point. But now I realized I might have to make a painful choice. So I thought to myself, 'Oh no. Any church but that one.'

Bill was not to be dissuaded but he was, to some extent, reassuring saying he had also shared many of my prejudices. However, in intellectual honesty, we had to consider the claims of the largest Christian Church, even if it was to reject it. He gently suggested that we read together with open minds the Gospels to judge whether, in fact, they supported Catholic beliefs, as well as reading books, which put the case both for and against the Catholic Church and also a book on the Catholic Faith, which he had sent for from the Catholic Enquiry Centre.

I knew I believed in Christianity and had been deeply moved by the teachings and life of Our Lord, but I was only familiar with selected passages from the Gospels, mainly the miracles, the parables, the Sermon on the Mount and Our Lord's Passion and death on the cross. I don't think I had ever given any thought to doctrine and would have felt quite content to join a church with an inspiring preacher and a friendly, supportive congregation. But now I was forced to consider which church was closest to the teachings of Jesus and slowly, almost imperceptibly, over the ensuing months, I found my prejudices slipping away, as we examined Jesus' words in the Gospels to see whether or not they really supported Catholic beliefs.

I remember being impressed by Jesus' final words to His disciples, before His Ascension, when He was giving them instructions for establishing the early Church:

> And look, I am with you always; yes, to the end of time (Mt 28:20).

Surely the Church had not been deserted by Christ and gone disastrously wrong for sixteen centuries only to be corrected by Henry VIII, whose motives for breaking away from Rome were far from disinterested and edifying! Henry would, in fact, have been perfectly content to remain loyal to the Catholic Church had Cardinal Wolsey been able to persuade the Pope to grant him the divorce he so desperately desired from his wife, Catherine of Aragon, so that he could marry Anne Boleyn and, as he hoped, produce a male heir.

As I considered this, some of the other prejudices from the history teaching of my school years started to be challenged. That some of the popes and priests had been corrupt and betrayed their calling, no longer seemed such a powerful argument against the Church and in favour of the Reformation. When I considered the frailty of human nature, I knew there will always be people who betray their beliefs and are unworthy of their vocation in every church, just as there will also be shining examples of great courage and sanctity. After all, one of the twelve disciples, Judas, who had followed Jesus for three years, heard His teaching and been His friend, had betrayed his master to His enemies for thirty pieces of silver, Peter had vehemently denied three times he knew Jesus and all the disciples had fled when Jesus was arrested in the Garden of Gethsemane. Surely, I now began to think reform could have come from within the church with no need for schism.

I had also wondered how Catholics could possibly believe in the infallibility of the Pope, why, in fact, they even thought it necessary to have a Pope, when it had seemed glaringly obvious to me that, at certain times in the past, some of the popes had been very fallible, corrupt men. However, as we studied Catholic doctrine, I came to realise that the infallibility of the Pope did not apply to the character or lifestyle of the Pope, but only to the extremely rare occasions 'When, as supreme pastor and teacher of all the faithful—who confirms his brethren in the faith—he proclaims by a definitive act a doctrine pertaining to faith and morals'⁶ and this must be in consultation with the other bishops. Most Popes had never exercised this charism.

Then, again, my attention was drawn to the great Petrine text:

> You are Peter and on this rock I will build my Church. And the gates of the under-world can never hold out against it (Mt 16:18).

It was eminently clear that Simon Peter was far from rocklike. Though often well intentioned, he was always getting it wrong. In fact, almost immediately after these words, when Peter tried to dissuade Our Lord from His destiny of going to Jerusalem where He would be 'put to death' (Mt 16:21), Jesus said to him:

> Get behind me, Satan! You are an obstacle in my path, because you are thinking not as God thinks but as human beings do (Mt 16:23).

Texts such as these, I had never been aware of before and they made me realise there was biblical support for the position of the Pope, that Peter, despite his human failings, had been chosen by Jesus to be the first pope and that therefore the doctrine of infallibility was not disproved by the failings of an individual pope.

We were occasionally taken to a church service from school. I, of course, would not receive Communion, but some of my friends did. If I had thought about it at this time, I think I would have regarded Communion solely as an act of remembrance of the Last Supper. After all, we are told in Luke's Gospel:

> Then he took bread, and when he had given thanks, he broke it and gave it to them, saying, 'This is my body given for you; do this in remembrance of me (Lk 22:19).

But now I had to consider whether there was convincing evidence in the Gospels:

> In the celebration of the Eucharist, when the presiding priest repeats the words of Christ, by the power of the Holy Spirit the bread and wine are consecrated, cease to be

bread and wine and become the Body and Blood of Christ
really present to us.[7]

As I read John's Gospel, I started to realise that the words of Jesus
did support the Catholic belief in the Real Presence. Soon after
the Feeding of the Five Thousand, Jesus taught this doctrine 'At
Capernaum in the synagogue' (Jn 6:59).

> Anyone who does eat my flesh and drink my blood
> has eternal life,
> And I shall raise that person up on the last day.
> For my flesh is real food
> and my blood is real drink.
> Whoever eats my flesh and drinks my blood
> lives in me
> and I live in that person (Jn 6:54–6).

We are told that 'After this, many of his disciples went away and
accompanied him no more' (Jn 6:66). Surely if Jesus had not meant
these words to be taken literally, He would have called them back
to tell them they had misunderstood His meaning, but instead
He said to His twelve disciples,

> What about you, do you want to go away too? (Jn 6:67)

Peter answered with his wonderful profession of faith:

> Lord, to whom shall we go? You have the message of
> eternal life, and we believe; we have come to know that
> you are the Holy One of God (Jn 6:68–9).

Passages such as this, I had been unaware of ever having heard
before, but now I felt I could not disregard them.

Another Catholic belief that had struck me as far-fetched and
without a Scriptural basis was the extent of the devotion to the
Virgin Mary. Catholics prayed to her almost, or so it seemed to
me, more than to Our Lord. Here, too, I was soon to modify my
opinion as I learnt more about the Catholic doctrine on Our Lady.
When Catholics prayed to Our Lady, it was to ask her to intercede
for them to Our Lord and they were encouraged in this by the

way Our Lady interceded at the Marriage Feast of Cana for the young bridal couple, whose celebration was in danger of being ruined when they ran out of wine. We are told Mary said to Jesus:

They have no wine (Jn 2:3).

And to the servants:

Do whatever he tells you (Jn 2:5).

So now I began to appreciate that Our Lady points the way to her Son, not detracts from Him. This also suggested to me that it was not only in the gravest of matters that Our Lady would intercede for us, but also about our more mundane concerns, something that appealed to me, especially in times of difficulty.

Then, again, I had always interpreted Our Lord's words from the cross to His mother:

Woman, this is your son (Jn 19:26).

And to His disciple John, only literally:

This is your mother (Jn 19:27).

Jesus was making sure that Mary was cared for by His beloved disciple in an age when it would be difficult for a woman to live on her own with no surviving husband or son to protect her. But now I realised that the words could also be understood to mean that Christ was bestowing His mother to all of us, as our heavenly mother, a wonderfully magnanimous gesture when He had been betrayed, tortured and crucified by us.

As I considered these and other Catholic beliefs and teachings and saw that they were supported by passages in the Gospels, passages I had either been unaware of, never thought about or interpreted differently, I was no longer so confident of the basis of my prejudices and, in fact, found myself gradually attracted to the Catholic faith to the extent that when Bill suggested we should attend Mass one Sunday evening in December, about five months after our marriage, I felt prepared to give it a cautious try.

Notes

[1] The Copleston–Russell debate was a dispute concerning the existence of God between Frederick Copleston and Bertrand Russell first broadcast in 1948 by the BBC Radio. The debate focuses on the metaphysical and moral arguments for the existence of God.

[2] John Henry Newman, *Apologia Pro Vita Sua* (London and Glasgow: Fontana, 1959).

[3] Boylan, *This Tremendous Lover.*

[4] We have retained this key passage in its older translation from the Jerusalem Bible, knowing it was this translation that Bill used and loved.

[5] Newman, *Apologia Pro Vita Sua.*

[6] *Catechism of the Catholic Church,* 3:891.

[7] H. McCabe OP, *The Teaching of the Catholic Church: A New Catechism of Christian Doctrine* (London: Catholic Truth Society, Publishers to the Holy See, 1985), p. 17.

6 FIRST MASS

Bill December 1959

B Y THIS TIME, Win was beginning to come with me and, shortly before Christmas, 1959, we decided we would go to Mass together. We chose to go to the evening Mass at St Mary's, the church in the centre of Sunderland, thinking that there would be very few people there. We were in for a shock. The church held about six hundred people and it was jam-packed. Not only was it jam-packed, but it was full of the sort of people I'd never seen in Protestant churches. It was like the crowd at Roker Park, the local football ground. I don't know if there were any prostitutes there, but there were plenty of Tommy Minnicans. The church was full of them. But there were respectable looking people there also, and, judging by the awesome silence and the intensity of the devotion, plenty of devout people too.

Thomas Merton had a similar experience when he went to Mass for the first time in New York in the late nineteen thirties. He describes it in his autobiography, *The Seven Story Mountain*:

> The thing that impressed me most was that the place was full, absolutely full. It was full, not only of old ladies and broken-down gentlemen with one foot in the grave, but of men and women and children, young and old-especially young: people of all classes and all ranks, on a solid foundation of working men and women and their families.[1]

The image of that congregation and the experience of that first Mass have stayed with me and have been helpful in reflecting on the state of the Church since the Second Vatican Council. Above all, they established for me a unique and important feature of the Catholic Church: it is the Church for everybody, for every kind of person without distinctions of any kind. I already knew that it could attract and hold intellectuals. Now, it was apparent, it could attract ordinary working class people in great numbers. Even as a Protestant, I had gathered there had been great Catholic saints. Now I began to realise that the Catholic Church was, pre-eminently, the Church of sinners. Sadly, some of this comprehensiveness has been lost in certain parts of our country in the post-Conciliar decades, when working class congregations have declined in numbers. But it is still apparent in many parts of the world and even in our own country, in Westminster Cathedral, for instance, where the multi-racial, socially inclusive character of the Church is evident at all Masses, Sunday and daily, and in the endless stream of people who pour into the Church, all day and every day, to pray and to receive the Sacrament of Reconciliation.[2]

The Mass was celebrated in Latin. Some people followed it, using English translations, some people prayed the Rosary and some simply followed the Mass and prayed. But I felt throughout, particularly at the consecration and immediately afterwards, that there was a reverence, a depth and intensity of inward prayer there which I had never experienced before. The faith and devotion near the altar were almost tangible; you could cut it with a knife. The booklet from the Catholic Enquiry Centre had already introduced me to the idea of the Mass as a sacrifice. Here I had my first experience of it as a reality. Scott Hahn in his wonderful book, *The Lamb's Supper*, describes this experience very eloquently. At his first Mass he knew he was in the presence of Jesus, in His eternal act of sacrificing Himself for us.

> I remained on the sidelines until I heard the priest pronounce the words of consecration: 'This is my body...This is the cup of my blood.' The experience was intensified just a moment later, when I heard the congregation recite: 'Lamb of God ... Lamb of God ... Lamb of God', and the priest respond, '*This* is the Lamb of God' ... as he raised the host.

> In less than a minute, the phrase 'Lamb of God' had rung out four times. From long years of studying the Bible, I immediately knew where I was. I was in the Book of Revelation, where Jesus is called the Lamb no less than

twenty-eight times in twenty-two chapters. I was at the
marriage feast that John describes at the end of that very
last book of the Bible. I was before the throne of heaven,
where Jesus is hailed forever as the Lamb.[3]

Again, sadly, one does not always experience the Mass today in its
blinding truth. Karl Rahner lamented the fact that, after great
upheavals, which the Council undoubtedly was, there is inevitably
loss as well as gain.[4] Devotion springs from doctrine firmly grasped,
and internalised, but in the determination to make the Bible more
accessible to the faithful, there has, perhaps, been less in the way
of clear doctrinal instruction from the pulpit, resulting in a loss of
devotional fervour. But this fervour can still be found in the
Church: in traditional Catholic countries such as Poland, in
churches close to the Marian shrines as in Lourdes, and also in our
own country, where congregations really know what the Mass is.

The sermon we heard that night was brief and practical, very
unlike the ones I was used to, which could last up to three-
quarters of an hour. It was given by an elderly Irish priest, a man
of deep and simple faith, whom I came to love. The subject was
Christmas, and the message: that we should consider giving
Christ a present by coming to the Sacraments. It confirmed what
I had gathered from the Catholic Enquiry Centre about the
centrality of the Sacraments in the life of a Catholic.

This sermon and ones we heard at subsequent Masses illustrates the point I was trying to make about the relationship
between doctrine and devotion. Catholic preaching at that time
did not always have the eloquence, the emotional impact, I was
familiar with as a Methodist. But the more I heard, the more I
came to realise that here was a Church, which knew what it
believed and taught. Hilaire Belloc, in a letter he wrote to
Chesterton after hearing of his friend's reception into the Church,
described the Faith as something 'Corporate, organised, a personality, teaching. A thing, not a theory.'[5] And this was what
became more and more apparent to myself: that the Church had
a rich corpus of doctrine which she had preserved faithfully down

the centuries and which she delivered to a people who received it with deep faith. Thomas Merton had been similarly impressed by the first Catholic sermon he heard:

> [The sermon] was not long: but to me it was very interesting to hear this young man quietly telling the people in language that was plain, yet tinged with scholastic terminology, about a point in Catholic Doctrine. How clear and solid the doctrine was: for behind these words you felt the full force not only of Scripture but of centuries of a unified and continuous and consistent tradition. And above all it was a vital tradition: there was nothing studied or antique about it. These words, this terminology, this doctrine, and these convictions fell from the lips of a young priest as something that were most intimately part of his own life. What was more, I sensed that the people were familiar with it all and that it was... part of their life also.[6]

According to Scripture, true faith comes from hearing those who have been mandated to preach (Rm 10:17); it comes from an implanting of God's Word (Jm 1:21), and it is sustained through an inhabitation of that Word (Jn 14:23). Over a period of time, Win and I heard the whole range of Catholic doctrine expounded by priests who had been instructed to do this systematically by their bishops. This preaching reinforced and developed the catechesis the faithful had received at school, so a clear 'hearing' and 'implanting' were affected, resulting in a fruitful 'inhabitation' of the truths of the Faith. This became increasingly evident to us in the fervent sacramental and devotional life of the faithful.

Win December 1959

I had come a long way by December, 1959, when I agreed to go to the evening Mass with Bill at St Mary's Church. I was interested in giving it a cautious try. I had, after all, on a few occasions visited other churches. This time, I particularly hoped to remain inconspicuous, because I didn't feel ready yet for anyone approaching or in any way pressurising us.

I was, of course, aware of the distress this would cause my mother with whom I had always had a very close relationship. Until now I had not found it difficult to comply with her wishes.

Fr Caden, a young curate whom we were soon to meet, describes Mass attendance at St Mary's in Sunderland around this time like this:

> There would be a lot of people in the church, and St Mary's was a huge square church, with a very large choir gallery. It was possible to pack a thousand people into that church—something we did regularly every Sunday night in the 1950s, once we had started a Sunday evening Mass![7]

So I had no need to worry about our being singled out. In fact, the large church was so full that there were no seats at all available at the back. Several good-looking young curates were patrolling the aisles and ushering late comers to the front, close to the altar, where there were still a few empty places. To my alarm and contrary to my intentions, we were given places at the very front. It was a completely new experience. Here the people around us prayed with an intensity and earnestness I had never before sensed. I think I felt that, maybe, here was a place we could turn to for help. Amazed, humbled and unnoticed, I felt able to relax and absorb the experience.

I was also surprised by the nature of the congregation. Everyone seemed to be there, rich and poor, middle class and working class, old and young, families with surprisingly well-behaved children. The Mass was celebrated in Latin, but booklets with the English translation were available. As I had studied Latin at O and A Level, this so far from being a hindrance for me, was an attraction. It lent the Mass a sense of sacredness and mystery, which I hadn't experienced in other church services. As '*Credo in unum Deum, Patrem omnipotentem, Creatorem caeli et terrae ...*', '*Pater Noster ...*', '*Corpus Christi ...*' and '*Ave Maria ...*' rang out, I had the sense of the power and universality of the Mass, as I thought how the same words would be said in every Catholic

Church in the world. At the moment of Consecration, a deep hush descended on the church. Everyone seemed to be absorbed in prayer. You could have heard a pin drop.

The sermon was given by an elderly Irish priest, Father O'Donovan, whom Bill and I came to respect and love and who was extremely kind and helpful to me. The sermon was brief by the standards of Protestant Churches, but direct, heartfelt, not aiming for heights of eloquence, but to give his parishioners practical advice on how best to live their lives. Above all, he said that the weeks leading up to Christmas should be a time of spiritual preparation and renewal, by receiving the Sacraments of Penance and the Holy Eucharist, spiritual reading and prayer.

As we left, I felt uplifted by the experience in a way I hadn't by other church services, but also troubled. I sensed that we were drawing closer to joining the Church and that this could give our marriage the help and strength we needed, which might otherwise be lacking, because of the lasting effects of Bill's troubled childhood. But I was also aware that it would cause difficulty between my mother and Bill. My mother had always disliked all forms of organized religion,[8] even her own, the Jewish religion, but above all the Catholic Church, which she saw as responsible for the cruel and unforgivable persecution of her race.

Bill and I continued to go to Mass on Sunday, both in Sunderland and during the Christmas holidays in Barrow. Bill's mother had told us that she had had very good Catholic neighbours, in particular Mrs Tranter, who had prayed for her at the time of Bill's birth and who would frequently give small gifts like an egg, apple or home-made cake, saying, 'This is for you, Mrs Evans', as Bill's father was out of work at the time and Bill's mother was rundown, anxious and depressed. She did this despite being very poor herself and having a large family to feed. Nevertheless, Bill's mother told us at a later date that she felt uneasy about us attending Mass.

Notes

[1] T. Merton, *The Seven Story Mountain* (New York: Harcourt, Brace and Company, 2009), p. 207.

[2] Bill drew strength from Westminster Cathedral, with its reminder of the atmosphere of his first Masses in Sunderland, throughout his life.

[3] S. Hahn, *The Lamb's Supper: The Mass As Heaven On Earth* (New York: Doubleday, 1999), pp. 8–9.

[4] This was a recurring theme in several late and often personal reflections by Fr K. Rahner on the decline of previous practices and devotions following the Council. See, for instance, his 'Eucharistic Worship,' in *Theological Investigations*, Vol. 23, trans. J. Donceel and H. M. Riley (New York: Herder & Herder, 1992), pp. 113–116; 'Devotion to the Sacred Heart Today,' in *Theological Investigations*, Vol. 23, pp. 117–128; 'Courage for Devotion to Mary,' in *Theological Investigations*, Vol. 23, pp. 129–139; 'The Status of the Sacrament of Reconciliation,' in *Theological Investigations*, Vol. 23, pp. 205–218.

[5] Letter from Hilaire Belloc to G. K. Chesterton, 1 August 1922. See Ward, *Gilbert Keith Chesterton*, p. 305.

[6] Merton, *The Seven Story Mountain*, p. 209.

[7] J. Caden, *Game, Set and Match* (Durham: The Pentland Press Ltd, 1997), p. 98.

[8] However, she had some sympathy with the Quakers, whom she admired for their relaxed way of gathering, tolerance and lack of formal doctrine. She also had some respect for the Salvation Army. As a girl she and her three sisters would sometimes accompany Annie, their Irish live-in servant, to hear the Salvation Army band on a Sunday afternoon and Kismet saw them give sweet tea and buns to revive people weak with hunger. This memory of faith in action stayed with her.

7 FATHER CADEN AND WIN'S RECEPTION

Bill 1960

A FTER THAT FIRST Mass, Win and I continued to attend
Mass together, both in Sunderland during the school
terms, and in Barrow-in-Furness during the holidays.
While I was at school through the week, Win frequently used to
pop into St Mary's Church, as I did myself at weekends and in
the holidays. The natural, deep piety of the Catholic faithful
continued to impress us. I was particularly impressed whenever
I saw people preparing for Confession. Watching them, noting
the length and obvious seriousness of their preparation and
thanksgiving, I could no longer believe that Catholics did not take
their sins seriously.

Soon after Easter, our first daughter was conceived. This new
responsibility lent a new urgency to our interest, particularly to
Win's. She felt that, if possible, she would like to become a
Catholic before the birth.

I think it was shortly after Easter 1960, that we first spoke to
a Catholic priest. It was while she was in St Mary's, Sunderland,
that Win met Father Caden, who was one of the curates. He had
noticed her browsing through Catholic Truth Society pamphlets
at the back of the Church and came up to speak to her. She told
him that she and I were not Catholics but were interested in the
Faith, so he arranged to come and see us. At the end of a pleasant
evening he asked us both to make a novena of Masses during
which we were to pray for our conversion. We agreed to do this
and Win also agreed to go to him for a course of instruction. I,
myself, did not feel ready for this yet. However, we both began
the novena, which meant getting up at 7 a.m. in the morning for

nine consecutive days, and dutifully saw it through. Win began her instructions and kept me informed about all that went on.

Win's instructions continued through the summer and on into the autumn, this time under an Irish nun called Sister Peter, a woman of considerable intellectual and spiritual stature, who was to prove a great help to us both. Also, throughout the autumn and early winter, we went to a course of public instructions at Corby Hall, a local retreat house, run by the Jesuits. The instructions were competent and thorough and were certainly an additional help.

Just before Christmas, 1960, Win was received into the Church by Father Caden. For myself, there was still a lot to resolve, though I was well on the way and felt no difficulties about Win's decision, nor about having our baby daughter, Mary, baptised into the Faith after her birth in February of the following year. Win's first experience of her new faith was one of great joy and it was a considerable help in seeing her through the ordeal of her first childbirth. The Sacraments, in particular, were a source of strength to her.

Win 1960

After the Christmas holiday in Barrow, we returned to Sunderland, where we continued to go to Mass at St Mary's every Sunday and to be impressed by the prayerfulness of the congregation, but we were happy to remain quietly anonymous at the back of the Church. By this stage, we felt no desire to experiment with other churches.

Bill's teaching was going well. He could hold the attention and inspire a love of literature in pupils of all abilities. His discipline was good, but he also had the common touch, playing cricket with the boys, discussing sport with them and treating them with fairness, sensitivity and kindliness.

Around this time, the head master must have become aware of Bill's interest in Catholicism. Up until now Bill's timetable had also included some R E lessons, which he had enjoyed. The R E syllabus was non-doctrinal, based on stories from the Old Testament as well as the New Testament. Bill had readily brought these stories to life. However, at the start of the new academic year Bill's R E lessons were replaced by Geography, about which he knew very little. Nothing was said, but it suggests a certain atmosphere of suspicion present at the time towards Catholicism.

A few years later, when Bill was applying for the Head of English in the Barrow-in-Furness Technical School, Freda College, now the Head Teacher of Seaham Harbour Grammar School, wrote among many glowing tributes,

> Mr Evans' own deep interest and his sensitive approach to his work, particularly in literature and poetry, have brought an excellent response from his pupils.

She emphasized that Bill's successful approach included the pupils who struggled to keep up in class. Then she continued:

> There is always an atmosphere of industry in the classroom where Mr Evans is teaching and his thorough preparation of lessons and care to fulfil the needs of his pupils helps him to maintain a sound discipline while establishing friendly relations with them.[1]

While here in an extract from the Deputy Head, Francis Masterman is an equally enthusiastic testimonial:

> He manages the pupils in a sensible, kindly way, with a sympathetic understanding of their problems, and, in consequence, he quickly gains their confidence and ready co-operation in the work undertaken, so that throughout he has had a fine influence on the classes in his care.

He added:

> He is popular with staff and boys alike, and his prowess in the cricket field has made him an excellent cricket coach.[2]

In the evenings, after Bill's marking and preparation for the next day's teaching were completed, he continued reading voraciously both the writers who presented the case for the Catholic Church, but also those who argued against it and he said that these thoughts were never far from his mind.

I also continued to read books of Catholic apologetics, but didn't feel the need to read as extensively as Bill. I did, however, feel drawn to St Mary's Church and started to visit it frequently in the week day mornings. I was able to do this at the time, as, when we had returned to Sunderland after our honeymoon the previous August, all the teaching jobs in English Language and Literature had been already filled. I was doing a little coaching in the evenings and a correspondence course on writing books for children, but these left me with plenty of time on my hands.

I was in the habit of walking into town in the morning and going into the market and nearby shops, buying things like fluke freshly caught from the sea, rabbit pieces, chicken livers, eggs, mushroom stalks, plenty of vegetables and stale cheese, which once grated and placed between layers of piping hot vegetables and potatoes melted and tasted fine. These provided very cheap, but nutritious meals, which Bill later often said he remembered as delicious. We were living in the small flat, which Bill had moved to the year before we were married but were trying to live economically in order to save for the deposit on a house. Instead of sending the washing to the laundry, I did it by hand in the bath in the shared bathroom and, as we didn't go out for meals, as Bill had often done before our marriage, we were probably spending no more than when Bill was living on his own, if as much.

It was during one of these weekday morning visits to the Church, when I was browsing through the pamphlets of the Catholic Truth Society, that a young, very good-looking priest came up to me and asked if I was new to the area and a Catholic. I told him that Bill and I had been recently married and were interested in the Catholic faith, whereupon he asked if he could come and visit us, which we arranged for a few evenings later.

The priest was Father John Caden and Bill and I both felt inspired by his infectious enthusiasm and total dedication to his vocation. The evening went very well and Father Caden soon became a friend, visiting us fairly frequently. He was a priest with amazing energy and lots of interests, which enabled him to reach out to many people in all their different situations. He was well read and prayerful, understanding and sympathetic, a man who also loved the theatre and sport, was a talented footballer and tennis player and was there for people in their times of difficulty. Sister Peter, the headmistress of St Mary's Primary School, who later instructed me, said how the children in the playground flocked around him rather like the Pied Piper, begging him to play football with them.

Father Caden suggested that we made a novena of Masses to pray for our conversion, which we did conscientiously, although it meant getting up very early in the morning, which normally Bill would have found difficult, especially when he had a demanding day's teaching ahead of him.

It was about this time that we decided to follow the Catholic Church's teaching on birth control. Looking back, I am in some ways quite surprised that we did this without any qualms, as our original plan had been that I would apply for a teaching job in good time for the autumn term, so that we could save seriously for the deposit on a house and only after that would we think about starting the family, which we knew we both wanted.

The rather run down flat we were living in suited Bill and me fine on our own, as it was cheap, we were free to come and go as we pleased, there was a friendly atmosphere in the house and Bill had added moreover a book case, a television, radio and record player to the bedroom cum living room, but with no running water in the tiny kitchen, the washing up of dishes and clothes had to be done in the bathroom on the floor below, which was shared by four other lodgers plus the landlady and her son. Then, the clothes and bedding had to be wrung out firmly by hand, as I had no access to an outdoor area, so that it wouldn't drip on the carpet and dried in front of the gas fire in the living room. Hardly a flat suitable for a couple with a baby![3]

Nevertheless, when I became pregnant with our first daughter, Mary, in the late spring, I remember feeling a surge of joy and elation. Bill also said he felt happy and it gave him a feeling of responsibility, a desire to make sure that our marriage never caused the suffering that his own parents' violent quarrels had been responsible for in his sisters' and his own life.

The knowledge that I was pregnant made me feel that perhaps this was the time to take a step closer towards commitment to the Catholic faith, so, when Father Caden asked if we felt ready for instruction, I replied that I thought I was, while Bill said he needed more time to read and convince himself intellectually. Father Caden said he would instruct me and that he respected Bill's position. He felt confident that Bill would eventually be received into the Church and that, when that time came, he would like to be the one who received Bill. He also warned Bill that, in seeking for total intellectual certainty, a time might come when he was in danger of sinning against grace; that sometimes one has to make the final leap of faith.

About two and a half years later, soon after the birth of our second daughter, Ruth, when Father Caden was no longer at St Mary's, Bill phoned Father Caden, who said jokingly, 'So, you're giving yourself up at last!' Bill went through to Dipton and was received into the Church by Father Caden, when Ruth was just a few weeks old. Bill said that he remembers that as one of the happiest times in his life.

Bill was pleased that I was starting instructions but told me he felt a little envious that I had reached this position before him and he prayed that he too would receive the gift of faith. He was keen to hear all about my lessons, but, in fact, I had very few, because suddenly around this time Father Caden heard that he was being moved to St Patrick's Church, Dipton. We felt a real sense of loss. He arranged for my instructions to continue in the autumn with Sister Peter, a dedicated, learned and enthusiastic nun.

Recently, I have been reading Father Caden's book, *Game, Set and Match* and it brings back vivid memories of how vibrant the

Church was in our Sunderland days. I hadn't realised the extent to which Father Caden's fourteen hour days were packed full with:

> [T]he daily Masses, whether in the Church or at one of the convents, the routine daily visitation of the homes of parishioners, the twice-weekly calls at the school, the frequent interviews with callers at the door, [including] 'knights of the road', as we called the daily half-dozen tramps and beggars.[4]

This was in addition to his responding to hospital and parishioners' calls, often at night, as his bedroom was the nearest to the phone, also running several societies and clubs, including a successful Youth Club and spending five hours in the confessional every Saturday night. And yet Father Caden writes that he found his departure from Sunderland 'shattering' and that he 'had spent nine wonderful years at St Mary's.'[5] He also refers to these days as 'halcyon days.'[6]

One incident, which Father Caden describes in his book, struck me as typical of the dedication of the priests and the trust, which their parishioners placed in them at St Mary's at this time and which inspired Bill and me. Father Caden describes how 'At one o'clock in the morning, and a very foggy winter morning it was, the doorbell of the presbytery rang loudly several times.' As he 'stumbled to the door', he saw 'a distraught woman in her thirties, with two young children. She had a coat on over her nightdress as did the frightened, shivering children ...' Hysterically and tearfully, she told Father Caden, that her husband was a Catholic, and had come home drunk and very late. He had tried to get 'his rights' as it was sometimes termed at the time. When she refused, he began to hit her and with the children now awake and crying, she had grabbed her coat and their coats, and told him she was going for the priest.

Although Father Caden had no idea how large or violent the man was, he hurriedly dressed and put on his 'flying jacket', in the hope it would make him 'look much bigger and more powerful than [he] really was.' The wife 'looked much calmer and happier and the children's eyes were turned in [his] direction,' as she led Father Caden to the bedroom. He says, '"My heart was beating fast but I knew I could not let the unfortunate woman down at this stage...". I loomed nearer to him and said, "What sort of a man are you to drive out your wife and bairns on a night like this? You ought to be ashamed of yourself."' Then grabbing the 'bedspread and shirt, which he was pulling up over his chest,' Father Caden continued sternly, 'If you ever lay a finger on your wife again, I will give you the hiding of your life.'[7]

This impulsive, brave action might not be considered advisable today or even at the time. Nonetheless, witnessing total commitment and courage like this, Bill and I started to feel we had found in St Mary's the answer to the church, which we would be happy to join.

After Bill's reception into the Catholic Church, we lost touch completely with Father Caden. I think we felt that parishioners should leave a priest free to settle into his new parish and devote his energies there and, although this is probably advisable, as the priest has to move on to his new parishioners' needs and, of course, we had only known Father Caden for a few months and our lives were very busy with two young children, I, nevertheless, felt a certain sadness on reading his book, that we had not written from time to time or found a way to visit him, as some of his other parishioners had done.

However, when he died at the age of eighty-nine and we read the glowing tributes to him in the newspapers, they brought back vividly our warm memories of him. We were pleased that his vocation had remained inspirational until the end of his life. Lizzie Anderson's headline was 'Hundreds attend the service for Fr John Caden.' The journal 6 March 2013 had the headline, 'Tony Blair attends funeral of "A spirited priest"' and the ITV Tyne Tees headline was 'Funeral of one of County Durham's "best loved characters."'

Father Jim O'Keefe said of him,

Father Jack knew no distinction between human life and spiritual life. He was committed to the fullness of life, to people's happiness and well-being and immersed himself in all sorts of things to bring that about.[8]

He was Tony and Cherie Blair's parish priest, baptising their four children and receiving Tony into the Church. He was also his doubles tennis partner. At his funeral, Tony Blair said,

John Caden was a charismatic, lively, warm and great-spirited priest and public servant. He was a constant presence in my life and always there for us with friendship and good advice.[9]

These words reflect the Father Caden we came to know and whose friendship we valued so dearly. He obviously maintained his youthful enthusiasm, his ability to reach out to all and sundry and his dedication to his vocation throughout his life. He was buried in Sedgefield Cemetery next to his mother's grave, at his request, on 5 March 2013.[10]

Notes

[1]   Teaching reference from F. College, 26 February 1964. See family documents.

[2]   Teaching reference from F. Masterman, 26 February 1964. See family documents.

[3]   This was the case even by the standards of 1960 when central heating, washing machines and refrigerators were for many people unattainable luxuries.

[4]   Caden, *Game, Set and Match*, p. 88.

[5]   *Ibid.*, p. 124.

[6]   *Ibid.*, p. 78.

[7]   *Ibid.*, pp. 82–84.

[8]   L. Anderson, 'Hundreds attend service for Father John Caden', *The Northern Echo*, 4 March 2013.

[9]   D. Leatherdale, 'Former Prime Minister Tony Blair leads tribute to popular Sedgefield priest', *The Northern Echo*, 24 February 2013.

[10]   Anderson, 'Hundreds attend service for Father John Caden', *The Northern Echo*.

8 SISTER PETER AND WIN'S RECEPTION

Win 1960

A T THIS POINT in the narrative, I am unable to alternate Bill's account with my memories. This is because, as Bill will explain later, what he hopes to offer 'is an account of ideas developed early and expanded and consolidated over many years.'[1] At this point our writing diverges, as despite my early reservations and very real prejudices against Catholicism, I was able to reach a position of conviction much sooner than Bill.

Happy in my faith and the support it gave me; my focus now shifted more to domestic matters and the care of our young daughters, Mary and Ruth. Bill, too, was very much involved in his young family, but still felt the need to read everything he could lay his hands on about Christianity and his preoccupation with the question, which church was truest to the one Jesus wished to establish. He would say that these questions were never far from his mind. This preoccupation and his passion for theology and the truth, as he saw it, remained with him till the day he died.

We will continue with Bill's own written account later. For now, I will take up the story in the summer of 1960.

During the summer holidays, we went to stay with my parents in Wimbledon, who, and, in particular, my mother, were delighted that I was pregnant. For my mother, the baby would be a first grandchild. She was very concerned that I was eating sufficient nutritious food and resting, as I had been suffering from morning sickness and put on a risk list by the hospital, as my blood pressure was high, which tended to be a problem on my mother's side of the family.

However, as I feared, she viewed with alarm our growing interest in the Catholic Church. I think she blamed this all on Bill, which was true only in so far as initially I wouldn't have considered the Catholic Church without his influence. Sadly her feelings towards Bill cooled.

This wasn't helped by Bill, who, full of his youthful enthusiasm, believed that through argument he could dispel my mother's prejudices, just as his own and mine had been. However, my mother was an emotional rather than a logical thinker and Bill's strong, fervent manner of argument only served to confirm her dislike of the Catholic Church. Bill often said in later years that he deeply regretted his manner of debating and wished he'd been aware at the time of the advice given in the Legion Handbook when talking to someone about the Faith: 'There must be nothing of the controversial, nothing overbearing. Every word must breathe humility, affection, sincerity.'[2]

Later, Bill, reflecting back on this time, would write about it. He begins with his early discussions on Christianity with my mother, before the argument became vehement.

> I was still at that stage, when, though not a committed Christian, I was prepared, for the sake of argument, to take the Christian side. I would argue with Win's father and mother about the credibility of the Gospels—particularly with her mother. At that time Win's mother found the arguments stimulating. She said she had never heard the Christian case put so well. It was only when our interest in Christianity had ceased to be purely academic, when we were thinking of becoming Christians and then Catholics that her opposition became strong and our arguments became bitter. For that I largely blame myself—in the first flush of conversion when, [in the spirit of Chesterton], you are arguing against the world for Catholicism and with yourself against it—one tends to come on a bit strong and such arguments do no good.[3]

We returned to Sunderland in good time for the start of Bill's term and in some ways relieved to be on our own, although I always felt sad saying goodbye to my parents and I know, in particular, my mother did also. The local Boys' and Girls' Secondary Modern Schools in Seaham Harbour had decided to amalgamate and form an O Level Class, which would be made up of the most promising pupils and Bill was to take this class for English Language and Literature. This was a tribute to Bill's success as a teacher. He felt excited by the new challenge and put much effort into the preparation of his lessons, as well as pursuing his extensive reading of Catholic theology.

I continued my instructions, but now with Sister Peter, who was the headmistress of St Mary's Girls' School. Father Caden writes of her in his book:

> Sister Peter was, for me and for most other priests at St Mary's during her teaching days, the epitome of the perfect nun. Cultured, well-read, gentle, humorous yet full of empathy, she was a wonderful support, not only to me, but to all my fellow curates at St Mary's, as well as to her teaching staff.[4]

He also writes of her sense of fun and broad mindedness. Father Coughlin, a fellow curate and great friend of Father Caden, was also befriended and supported by Sister Peter, who, he writes,

> Was never taken aback or in the least fazed by our irreverent joking. Leo was a great mimic and he could have people in convulsions of laughter with his impersonations of Father Dan, myself, and many others.[5]

That also describes the Sister Peter that Bill and I came to know. I would go to the school once a week in the dinner hour during the autumn term. When I arrived, Sister Peter would often be taking one or two children for an extra catechism lesson. She told me that, as they had learning difficulties, they needed more help so that they would be allowed to make their First Communion. At the time, a priest would ask each child questions from the Penny

Catechism to make sure they understood their faith sufficiently well to receive Holy Communion. The class was already at ease with the priests because they would join them in the playground for games and football. And I wouldn't be surprised if Sister Peter didn't ask Father Caden or Father Coughlin to give the vulnerable children the most straightforward of questions!

Sister Peter set me at ease straight away. She was warm and kind with an infectious enthusiasm. I remember her saying that, like a loving parent, Jesus gave us the Sacraments to help us at every stage of our life, starting with Baptism when we became a child of God, receiving Sacramental Grace for the start of our journey. Then, Penance and Holy Communion to help us to make the correct choices, as we reached the age of reason and could distinguish between right and wrong. During the difficult years of adolescence, when we could so easily be led astray, Confirmation was there to strengthen us and when we became adults, the Sacraments of Marriage and Holy Orders gave us help to persevere and remain true to our vows in the difficult times as well as the good. Finally, the Sacrament of the Sick was there to give us the strength to recover in times of sickness, but, if that were not possible, help to face death, confident our sins had been forgiven, with peace of mind and in a state of grace. 'Such gifts,' she would say. 'She [the Church] overwhelms us with her gifts. We cannot cope with them.'

It is often said that Catholic churches were so full at this time, because Catholics attended out of fear of mortal sin rather than from love of God and, although there is some truth in this, I can honestly say Bill and I weren't aware of this emphasis in our own encounters with Father Caden, Father O'Donovan and Sister Peter, who were full of enthusiasm, positivity and humanity.

Sister Peter was very interested in Bill's position, having heard from Father Caden of his extensive reading and she would ask me how he was doing. She used to visit the families of the children she taught on Saturday afternoons, particularly those in need of support, and she said she could include us in these visits, but warned that they would be well spaced out, as she had so many pressing calls to make. When she told me she was visiting in our area, I remember I would look out of the window eagerly to see if she was coming. Bill also looked forward to seeing Sister Peter and she usually came with a book or two for him and eager to discuss what he was reading. She would also ask how I was feeling, and Bill and I felt moved when she said,

There will be a special blessing on this baby.

I think it was about this time that we decided, if the baby were a girl, we would call her Mary.

We attended a course of lectures on the Catholic faith given at Corby Hall by the Jesuits. Bill remembered that it was about this time, although I thought it came earlier in our exploration of which church to join. Be that as it may, I remember a certain reluctance to go, as I thought the Jesuits might be fanatical, pressurising and over-bearing, but, far from this, they struck me as learned, gentle men. The lectures were well attended and the priests systematically explained Catholic doctrines and beliefs, supporting them mainly by quotations from Jesus' words in the Gospels. There was also a question and answer time, when people felt free to challenge their interpretations. I remember Bill and I rereading the Gospels and believing that they reinforced irrefutably the Catholic position.

As Christmas was approaching, I felt ready to be received into the Catholic Church. Sister Peter agreed that this would be the ideal time. Her lessons would end after Christmas, but she asked me to bring the baby to see her in the New Year, which I did in February, soon after Mary's birth. I felt proud and happy, as Mary slept peacefully throughout the visit and Sister Peter said what a beautiful child she was.

So now it just remained for me to phone Father Caden, as he had said he wanted to be the priest, who received Bill and me into the Church. He was pleased by my request, quickly arranged a convenient date and with his usual generosity offered to pick us up and drive us through to his new parish church, St Patrick's in

Dipton, which he told us was very different to St Mary's. This is how he describes it in *Game, Set and Match*:

> After the bustle and noise of the busiest street in Sunder-
> land, St Patrick's had a silence that was almost palpable.
> The parish was situated nearly a thousand feet up in the
> hills of north-west Durham. It was prone to very frequent
> hill fog, and in the winter the snow could linger there from
> November until April or May. There were no hospitals or
> institutions to look after, but the people were a hardy breed
> of mining stock, whose strong faith was typical of north-
> west Durham. I knew that the myriad demands of a
> downtown parish like St Mary's would be sadly missed in
> my new habitat. However, I was sufficiently spiritually
> focused to realise that this was what God wanted for me
> at this stage of my priesthood. Somehow, this quickly gave
> me an indescribable calm that was strengthened by the
> anticipation of getting to know all the people in and
> around those hills and valleys.[6]

The parish priest, Father Duffy, had been left suffering from claustrophobia and anxiety after the trauma of his experiences as an army chaplain and so found it very hard to go out and relate to his parishioners. In addition, he had been without a curate for several months, as his previous curate had suffered a nervous breakdown. Father Caden was obviously desperately needed there and I am sure that both Father Duffy and his parishioners must have welcomed with open arms such an outgoing, enthusiastic curate! I think it also says much about Father Caden's faith and humility that he was able to accept unquestioningly his new appointment and throw himself so wholeheartedly into such a different parish.

In *Game, Set and Match,* he describes his new parish,

> Dipton parish was completely different in its demands
> from St Mary's. Apart from visitation of the homes and
> attending to a much larger number of housebound, there
> was a calm, hardly ever experienced in Sunderland. The

curate in Dipton parish was expected to take on full
responsibility for all the parishioners and for all the sick
and housebound, as well as the bulk of the church services.
This, however, was no great burden, because there were
no other demands to distract one from this routine
work—after St Mary's I found it all quite leisurely. Despite
the prophesies of some of my priest friends that the
'Country' would bore me stiff and the frustration would
drive me mad, I quickly came to terms with it. Indeed, after
a couple of weeks, I was actually enjoying it. For nearly ten
years, I had never been able to fit all my day's work into
the same day. Here, I could not only complete it, but still
have time to 'do my own thing' as well. I was able to join
a tennis club, in fact, two tennis clubs and was able to take
an active part in both the competitive side and the social
side of the clubs.[7]

Father Caden also in time became 'manager, coach, secretary,
trainer, cheerleader and, occasionally, player'[8] of 'The Pats'
football team. All these activities would have quickly endeared
Father Caden to his new parishioners.

When we arrived at St Patrick's, it did indeed feel bleak, quiet
and cold. I don't remember that we saw anyone other than Father
Caden in the presbytery. We went into the church, where I
received the Sacrament of Baptism (conditional in case my
original baptism had been invalid), followed by my First Confession. I had prepared thoroughly beforehand, but still felt nervous.
However, when I heard the words of Absolution, I had a wonderful feeling of relief, of starting afresh and then, when I received
Holy Communion for the first time; I had a sense of the Real
Presence. I felt a flood of joy and peace, that all would be well. I
remember I prayed for a long time.

This was followed by simple refreshments in a rather sparse
room. We were interested in hearing how Father Caden was
settling into his new parish. Although he said he was missing the
busy life at St Mary's and all the friends he had made there, we

had the impression that he had embraced his new life with an unquestioning whole heartedness.

Father Caden reminded Bill of his promise to let him know when he was ready 'to give himself up', as he jokingly put it. He was impressed by the extent of Bill's reading and knowledge of theology, but again warned him that at some point he would have to make that final leap of faith. However, he felt Bill would know when that time had come. So we returned to Sunderland, feeling happy and optimistic about the future and looking forward to the birth of our first child.

Notes

1 See Part Two, Chapter One: The Intellectual Grounds.
2 *The Official Handbook of the Legion of Mary* (Dublin 7: Concilium Legionis Mariae, 1993), p. 313.
3 From Bill's writings.
4 Caden, *Game, Set and Match*, p. 75.
5 *Ibid.*
6 *Ibid.*, p. 124.
7 *Ibid.*, p. 128.
8 *Ibid.*, p. 127.

9 FATHER O'DONOVAN AND THE BIRTH OF MARY

Win 1961

E ARLY IN JANUARY, we returned from visiting our parents during the Christmas holidays and were greeted by our landlady. She was a kindly widow, who supported herself and her son by letting rooms in the two adjoining terraced houses she owned. She gave us the welcome news that an upstairs flat had become vacant and would be much more suitable for us than the one we were at present renting. It consisted of a living room with an open fireplace, two bedrooms, a bathroom and a little cubby-hole, which served as the kitchen and contained a cooker, a few open shelves, but had no running water. What is more, she said, I could hang washing out in the backyard and put the baby in the pram in the small front garden. At that time, it was believed fresh air was so good for a baby, who, well wrapped up, should be put out in all weathers.[1] The rent would be £3 pounds a week, only a pound more than we were paying at present.

We straightaway gratefully accepted. She did apologise for the colour of wallpaper in the living room. The previous tenants had rather strange tastes, she said, and had decorated it mainly in black, but we were free to redecorate ourselves. She also gave me a pot of white paint and a brush and suggested I might want to go over the chipped skirting board and door, which I did. However, neither of us were practical, and, what's more, Bill continued to give much time to his lesson preparation and his reading of Catholic theology, while I was still doing some coaching and preparing for the birth of our first child due early the following month. I can honestly say that the rather dilapidated, dark state of the flat didn't worry either of us and we made no attempt to redecorate!

I started to go to Father O'Donovan, the parish priest, once a week on Saturday evening, to make my confession. After receiving absolution, I would sometimes ask for his advice and he was invariably patient, kind and helpful, although the priests at this time in St Mary's were usually hearing a hundred confessions each during their five-hour Saturday stint.[2]

Bill was worried that our marriage wasn't valid in the eyes of the Catholic Church, as it had taken place in a Registry Office. This had been done in good faith at the time, as we weren't members of any church, but now he asked me to consult Father O'Donovan, which I did. Father O'Donovan seemed uncertain himself, said he would have to look into the matter and could I come back the following Saturday at the same time, when he would give me an answer.

When I returned the next week, Father O'Donovan was kindly reassuring. He said:

> My dear, tell your husband not to worry. The actual moment when the Sacrament of Marriage is conferred is when the couple make the vows to each other and say in turn; 'I do take thee (name) to be my lawful wedded wife/ husband, to have and to hold from this day forward, for better, for worse, for richer, for poorer, in sickness and in health, to love and to cherish, till death us do part.' What I want you both to do is solemnly repeat these vows to each other in case, in the Registry Office, you didn't say them with complete fullness of intention.

This, Bill and I did solemnly, determined that, whatever problems life might throw up against us, we would honour those vows.

I also wondered, with some amusement, if Father O'Donovan thought Bill was trying to wriggle out of the marriage and that, in his kindly way, he was keen to show him there was no way out!

Shortly after we had moved into the new flat, we noticed mice in the kitchen, which made us very uneasy. We worried about how hygienic the surfaces of the shelves were and we were put off eating the food, which was left overnight, as the mice might have been running over it, even though I did my best to make sure it was well covered. I, therefore, went to a stall in the market, which sold traps and rat poison. I didn't feel I could face seeing the mice caught in the traps, so opted for the poison, which I proceeded to put down by the holes in the skirting board. However, I felt troubled when I read about the death it caused. Again, I consulted Father O'Donovan, who again was reassuring, saying: 'Sure, sure, you can't be overrun by vermin!' The poison very effectively solved the problem of the mice.

As I recently read Father Caden's book, *Game, Set and Match*, fond and nostalgic memories of this time came back. Father O'Donovan was obviously very concerned for the moral welfare of his four young curates and didn't want to put any temptation in their way. Father Caden writes:

> Father Dan was not too keen on his curates going out after supper, and he would sometimes be guilty of lengthening the 'supper talk' before he would eventually say Grace. When he did finally rise to say grace after meals, that was the signal for us to leave the dining room. Supper was actually quite a modest meal usually, and if it did not officially end until 8:30 or 8:45 p.m., it did not give us much time to go out and back again—the front door, the only practical entrance to the house, was 'Locked and chained' at 11 p.m.[3]

I was also interested in what Father Caden writes about the house keepers of priests at this time, as few priests now-a-days have them, most being expected to look after themselves and organize the finances of the parish. I thought it might be worthwhile to look at their role in the presbytery, because it does emphasize how much times have changed and how these dedicated women could be a valuable help and support to the parish priest, as indeed Miss Walker must have been to Father O'Donovan, leaving him free to concentrate solely on his pastoral duties. Father Caden writes that,

> In those halcyon days, being a housekeeper to a priest was regarded very much as a special vocation and there were certainly plenty of takers. The remuneration was usually derisory; but then, cooking and domestic work in the 1940s and 1950s was not well paid. It was nearly always done by ladies who were single and unattached. Many priests' housekeepers were happy to have the opportunity of working, because the presbytery gave them a secure home. They realised, too, that they could be 'serving God' by looking after the daily needs of the priests who were 'working for God'... The Old Church rules suggested that housekeepers should be 'of advanced years' and indeed, most of them in my curate days, would have fitted very comfortably into that category! In those days, too, many parish priests could become very dependent on their housekeepers, especially if their housekeepers had other talents as well as cooking and cleaning. Painting, decorating, coping with the doorbell and the telephone, handling money—these were all bonuses. Needless to say, Father Dan had become completely dependent on Miss Walker.[4]

I never remember meeting Miss Walker but Father Caden's gently humorous, but affectionate description of her and her ceaseless, uncomplaining long hours of work for little material reward seem to reflect the atmosphere of dedication, which so impressed us in St Mary's and therefore I felt it was worth giving it some time. He continues,

> Even by 1950 standards, Miss Walker was different. She was a quaint little lady who could have been no more than 4' 11". She must have been pushing sixty but did not look it; her long dark-brown hair was always plaited and taken up in a bun. I can never remember her wearing anything else but black-ankle length dresses, relieved only by the white apron and the white headdress.[5]

He also continues:

> Even in my early days there, she hated to go out shopping
> at all. However, when I arrived on the scene, she was
> confident that, because I was English and came from
> Hartlepool, I would be well equipped to negotiate in the
> covered market or at the fish shop or the bakery, and
> consequently she coaxed me to take on these extra respon-
> sibilities. Aware that she had an almost pathological fear
> and dislike of being 'In the outside world' at all, as she
> called it, I was soon cajoled into reducing her journeys over
> the presbytery threshold virtually to nil. During my nine
> years at St Mary's, I never remember her taking a single
> day off, nor do I remember her ever missing a day's work
> through illness. A day's work for Gert [the curates' name
> for her among themselves] lasted from six o'clock in the
> morning until two o'clock the following morning! She
> slept, or rather, retired to an attic in the higher part of the
> house. No priest had ever seen beyond that attic door.
> Most of her day, however, was spent in a large, rather bleak
> kitchen. She refused to let Father Dan have it more
> comfortably furnished, mainly, I think, because she was
> genuinely a very ascetic person, and would not have money
> spent on her or on her quarters. She did not want any
> domestic help in the house at all. Even her niece, Mary,
> was not allowed to help in the 'waiting on' when there was
> a special lunch, since Mary was not prepared to wear an
> ankle-length dress for the occasion.[6]

Father Caden was left in charge of the presbytery and parish on
Mondays from 9 o'clock in the morning until late in the evening,
as it was the day off for Father O'Donovan and his other curates.
However, Father Caden says Father O'Donovan would frequently
return early about 4 in the afternoon to check everything was in
order and, if Father Caden was out, would greet him on his return
with, 'God, Jack, who is on duty here?' Father Caden realised that
he must always inform Miss Walker, when he was called out to

the hospital, who 'would then tell [Father O'Donovan] with great unction, "Father Caden is out at the Royal Infirmary."'

As Father O'Donovan relaxed over a cup of tea, he would explain the reason for his anxiety, 'You see, Jack, this is a busy place. We need good men here and fit men.' Father Caden refers to him as 'simply [a] pastor of souls.'[7] These recollections fit in with my memories of Father O'Donovan and remind me of the kindly concern for my welfare I always felt when I asked him for advice.

Mary's Birth 1961

On the 8 February, after our evening meal, suddenly, quite unexpectedly, I realised my waters had broken. I had been asked to phone the hospital when this happened, so I told Bill and quickly checked I had packed everything I needed. We both felt anxious but also excited. The time had arrived for the birth of our first child. When I phoned, I was told that an ambulance would be sent shortly. At the hospital gates, we said, 'Goodbye', as, at this time, husbands and relatives weren't allowed to stay. I remember saying to Bill how strange, but also wonderful it was that the next time we met, there would be three of us. Then, Bill walked back to the flat, praying for me, while I was taken to a ward, where there were several women in various stages of labour.

As I remember it, the curtains were drawn round the beds and, at fairly frequent intervals, a midwife would come to examine us. The woman in the bed next to me was crying out for her mother and some of the other women were groaning. I think they would have appreciated the support of a loved one and must have found it a lonely, terrifying experience, but actually I didn't mind being on my own. I think this was because I felt it would only distress Bill too much. He did say, at a later date, when it was becoming fashionable for husbands or partners to stay, that he felt he might have been more of a liability than a help and in danger of fainting! I prayed and I remember thinking, if I can keep praying through this, then it will help me to pray when I face death. As the contractions became more frequent and intense, I tried to continue praying. I also felt relieved to join in the groaning, knowing that there was no one there, who loved me and would be in anguish. When the midwife decided the birth was imminent, I was wheeled into a room where there was also a doctor and nurse. I remember that their voices seemed to come from very far away, as I felt locked within myself in a cycle of pain with brief moments of relief, when I felt so exhausted I longed to sleep, but then the next contraction relentlessly started to gather force. Yet, strangely, once the baby, a sweet little girl with dark brown hair and a clear, lovely complexion, was placed in my arms, I felt such a flood of joy and exhilaration, that I didn't feel tired at all. She weighed 6 pounds 2 ounces. I thought she was the most beautiful baby in the world and longed for Bill to see her. I also felt like writing straight away to my mother and Bill's mother to tell them about their new little granddaughter. It was 9 February, the very date that had been predicted.

Bill arrived promptly at 7 p.m. for the visiting hour. He had had a sleepless night worrying about and praying for me. Early the next morning he had phoned the hospital and was delighted to hear that the baby had been safely born, was a little girl and that we were both well. When he saw Mary, who was sleeping peacefully in the cot beside my bed, he said, 'She is absolutely adorable.' He said he had hoped the baby would be a girl. We both felt proud and happy.

I think the specialist in charge of maternity in the hospital was in advance of the times. He had a firm belief that breastfeeding was best for mother and child. We had the babies in cots beside our beds. I was told, because Mary was a small baby, I should feed her every three hours, but that I didn't have to stick to it too rigidly. This suited Mary perfectly, who soon got into a peaceful routine, and, to be honest, I don't remember much crying on the ward from any of the babies nor can I remember ever seeing a bottle, though some of the women did say they had asked their mothers to buy bottles and milk powder, so that when they left they would be free to leave their babies from time to time.

However, the day of my return home everything went disastrously wrong. First, I was told to change Mary onto four hourly feeds, which would make life easier for me at home, but this totally unsettled her routine. Then, after lunch, I was told to expect the ambulance, which was to take me home, at any time, so I didn't know if there was time for a feed or not, but, in fact, the ambulance didn't come for a couple of hours. By the time I reached home, nothing would stop Mary crying.

To make matters worse, the carrycot and pram ordered for Mary as a gift from my mother and grandmother had not arrived. Showing that he could think practically in an emergency, Bill suggested we made a little bed for her out of a drawer which, lined with a soft cot blanket, turned out to be the perfect solution. (Incidentally, Bill's mother would go on to use this story to illustrate his practical aptitude in a crisis.)

Bill's mother, who had come to help, suggested that she should give Mary a long bath to tire her out, wrap her tightly in a shawl to make her feel safe, then I should feed her again and put her in her cot and leave her for five to ten minutes to settle to sleep, but even this sensible advice was to no avail. By this time, Bill was looking anxious, I was in tears and even Bill's mother, who did say she had had days like this, looked worried. With hindsight, I think longer gaps between feeds followed by a succession of short panicky feeds had given Mary either painful wind or stomach cramp. I started to wish I was back in the hospital, where everything had gone so serenely. However, eventually that night Mary did settle to sleep and by the next day she was back in her peaceful routine on three hourly feeds. Bill's mother couldn't believe what an easy baby she was and said she had never had one like that and I felt happy and proud. Bill felt nervous of handling Mary, because she looked so small and fragile that he was afraid he might drop her, but he loved to watch her having her bath in the evening and was delighted when she started to smile at him at five weeks old.

After I had been back home a week or two, I went to confession to Father O'Donovan as usual on Saturday evening. I also explained to him that we would like to arrange for Mary to be baptised, but didn't know what to do about godparents, as we didn't know any Catholics in Sunderland. In his usual kindly, fatherly manner, he told me not to worry, all we had to do was bring the baby to church the following afternoon at a certain time and he would see to everything else.

When we arrived at the church, there was another couple already there, also with a baby girl, and a middle-aged woman, who I thought could have been the grandmother. She told me that Father O'Donovan had asked her to be Mary's godmother as well and that she was very happy to accept the privilege. The baptism service went very well and at no point can I remember either baby crying. After it, Mary's godmother placed a half crown in my hands, which was quite a lot of money in those days and asked me to buy something for the baby. With hindsight, it seems perhaps a pity that we didn't suggest keeping in touch. When we returned home, Lilian and I celebrated with a cup of tea and a cake while Bill had a few glasses of his homemade wine, which his mother viewed with suspicion.

Looking back, it was such a different atmosphere to that which we often see today in our church at baptisms, when the pews can be almost full, often with many young people, sometimes dressed in all their finery, more as if they are going for a night out than to church, but whom we may never see again.

Towards the end of that year, with profound shock and sorrow, we would become aware of the terrible tragedy that had afflicted new parents like ourselves across the country. Around December 1961, it was becoming known that some women, who had been prescribed the drug Thalidomide for nausea in pregnancy, had given birth to babies with damaged limbs and other serious health problems. Now I had suffered from sickness in the early weeks of my pregnancy with Mary and had gone to see my doctor, Dr Runge, who had prescribed a pill to counter this. When the news broke, I went and asked her if she had given me Thalidomide. She replied that she had never prescribed it, as she had always had reservations about new, strong drugs. I had always found her a very caring, supportive doctor with whom I felt a special bond, partly as neither of us belonged to Sunderland, but now I felt even more gratitude to her. Wise decisions such as hers will have spared some of her patients and their babies such terrible suffering. I prayed for these parents and their children.

Notes

[1]   These were more trusting times.
[2]   Caden, *Game, Set and Match,* p. 89.
[3]   *Ibid.,* p. 70.
[4]   *Ibid.,* pp. 70–71.
[5]   *Ibid.,* p. 71.
[6]   *Ibid.,* p. 72.
[7]   *Ibid.,* p. 73.

10 BILL'S RECEPTION AND THE BIRTH OF RUTH

Win 1962

First House

LIFE CONTINUED SERENELY. Mary was a happy, contented baby and was putting weight on nicely. We enjoyed all the little milestones like her first smiles, words and steps, and, when we visited Wimbledon and Barrow in the summer holidays, my mother and also Bill's mother loved her dearly. I have photos of our first visit to Wimbledon when Mary was six months old and she is always smiling, smiling in my arms, also in the arms of my father and sister and laughing as my mother bathed her.

In Sunderland, we felt well supported by the Church. We still received visits from Sister Peter and also, now that Father Caden was in Dipton, from his friend and fellow curate, Father Coughlin. I remember his calling one morning and how tenderly he looked at Mary. I also felt relieved that his visit hadn't come any earlier, as I had just finished feeding her!

In the mornings, when I pushed Mary in the pram into town for my daily shop, I also would call into St Mary's to say a prayer. There were always other people, mostly women, in church and one elderly woman would say: 'Here comes the little flower,' as Mary beamed at her. I had the impression that Mary's smile lit up her day.

Bill and I had been quite content in our flat up till now, but in the autumn of 1961 Bill's mother came armed with Bill's sister, Margaret, her husband, Tom, and their two children. They took me aside and said that they really thought it was time we looked for a house. Bill's mother said she couldn't sleep, thinking that soon Mary would be crawling on that dirty, worn out carpet, which looked as if it had been down a hundred years! What's more, she said, she hadn't been able to sleep on the rickety old sofa bed in the second bedroom with the windows rattling every time it was windy, when she had come to help at the time of Mary's birth. They said that Bill had always had his head in the clouds and that I was the one with the time and common sense to start things moving!

I did have a word with Bill and we agreed that Tom would drive us all round Sunderland to see whether any of the houses for sale were within our means. This we did and, surprisingly, we saw one, which looked in good condition and seemed very reasonable. Bill's mother and sister thought we should go ahead and put in an offer straight away. However, fortunately Bill made enquiries about it at school and he was told we should avoid the house with a barge pole, as there was an abattoir at the back of it and houses in that area were plummeting in value.

Nevertheless, we did look at the flat in a more critical way and started to save in earnest. We had already begun making home-made wine, which had become an enjoyable hobby. We had bought some books with recipes and winemaking equipment and it was fun walking along the lanes collecting elderflower or blackberries, rose hips and elderberries, according to the season. Bill could identify the hedgerows and knew which berries to pick from his evacuation days in Milnthorpe. We stepped up the wine making, mainly because it would be a good way of saving more money. Bill had always enjoyed relaxing with a pint in the pub at weekends, but now he took pride in producing his own wine, which he would drink in the evening at weekends and, if friends called round, they were invited to join in. So beside our fireplace, there were always large, glass gallon containers with the air locks popping away, as the wine fermented. Bill took great pride in his wines and enjoyed them all, but many of them tasted too bitter and strong for me. Occasionally, a friend was taken by surprise by the strength of the alcohol, with unfortunate consequences! I remember my favourites were the blackberry and rose hip, which were sweeter and lighter, but Bill and some of his friends liked the maize, which they thought resembled whisky.

On one occasion, when we were travelling to Barrow for Christmas by train, Bill suggested we took some of our bottles of wine with us. In the cold flat they had stopped fermenting, but I will never forget the startled expression on the face of the woman sitting behind us, when corks started flying into the air! The underfloor heating had started the wine fermenting again.

In the afternoons, instead of taking Mary to the lovely parks, I now started to trudge up and down the streets in Sunderland, pushing the pram, looking at the houses for sale, and, just before Christmas, I saw a small semi-detached house, which looked in reasonably good condition and seemed possibly within our price range. The search for a house had now become more vital, as I was expecting our second baby, Ruth. The couple who owned the house had two boys and said that, as the house was high up on a hill, the air was very healthy and that their two sons had ailed for nothing. They also said they would be leaving some of their furniture. Bill, who was now doing very well at his teaching and had had a pay rise, agreed that it sounded ideal if we had enough for the deposit, so I went to see a solicitor. Unfortunately, he said we were £100 short, which was a lot of money in those days. When I looked really disappointed, he said maybe he could give us a loan. I thought at the time he was being very kind, but only later realised the high rate of interest he was charging.

We did, however, go ahead with the purchase of the house in Stannington Grove and, on the day of Mary's first birthday, 9 February 1962, we moved. Bill went to school as usual and I hired a small van to take care of our possessions, which consisted mainly of a bed-settee, a cot and pram, a television, two book cases, a wireless, record player, some books, records and many large glass bottles of wine. The removal men kept pointing to Mrs Henderson's furniture in the flat and I kept telling them that no, that wasn't ours, but that there were more bottles of fermenting wine in the spare bedroom. They looked rather bemused, but, good-naturedly, allowed Mary and me to travel in the van to our new home, just over a mile away.

Around this time Bill and I would enjoy the visits of my younger brother, Lawrence, when his Merchant Navy ship docked in the port. Always generous, he would arrive unexpectedly on the doorstep with a large chicken and presents for Mary. Bill and Lawrence would proceed to the pub for a pint, where they passionately discussed religion, politics and sport, while I cooked what seemed to us at the time a most wonderful feast. The animated and spirited discussions would continue, sometimes long into the night accompanied by glasses of home-made wine.[1]

It was in Stannington Grove that we made our first Catholic lay friends. Tom and Doris Stead lived almost opposite us and had two attractive daughters, Diane and Marion, who were about eight and four at the time. Tom taught in St Aidan's, the Catholic Grammar School for Boys, and he, in particular, impressed Bill and me. He told us he had gone to the seminary to train to be a priest, but that, after meeting Doris, he had left. There seemed a certain sad, wistful air about him, as if somehow he felt he had missed his true vocation in life, which made me wonder even then, as I have since, whether it would not be possible for the Church to allow priests to marry if they so wished. I am sure the Church has lost many good men and it might help to solve the desperate shortage of priests today.

Ruth's Birth

My second pregnancy was going well and, because there had been no complications with Mary's birth, I was told that the baby would be born at home, but that I would be assigned a midwife, who would be with me throughout the birth. A few weeks before Ruth was due, I was given a large cardboard box, which contained everything the midwife was likely to need. I had told Mary that she would soon have a little baby brother or sister, but she was only a year and a half old and only half understood. When we took the box home, she pointed to it and said, 'baby.' I think she thought the baby was in the box rather like a doll and that, when we opened the box, there the baby would be!

Bill's mother came several days before Ruth was due to give Mary time to get used to her and also in case Ruth came early, as Bill had never been practical and wouldn't have been able to cope on his own. In addition, the autumn term was just about to start and there was no paternity leave in those days. At this time, it was still believed that a woman should stay in bed for at least week after giving birth and not lift anything heavy, so Bill's mother would have to be doing virtually all the shopping, cooking, washing by hand, house work in addition to looking after Mary, as well as me and the new baby. Doris offered to help with shopping and also the washing, as she had a washing machine, which Bill's mother gratefully accepted, and Tom offered also to help in any way he could at the weekends.

A few days later, while we were watching a film during Friday evening, I felt the first pains, but said nothing in case it was a false alarm and we went to bed as usual. However, by about one a.m., they really started in earnest, so I woke Bill. We crept downstairs, so as not to awake his mother and were just debating whether it was too soon to go for the midwife, when she came rushing downstairs, all anxious, saying not to delay, a second baby could come very quickly. We had no telephone at the time, so Bill pulled his clothes over his pyjamas and went for the midwife.

The midwife arrived soon after Bill returned and, although Ruth was not to be born until about twelve noon, she never left my side and was kind and encouraging throughout. At some time in the morning, she asked Bill's mother to stand outside the door in case she needed a bowl of hot water or help. Bill noticed that whenever there was a groan from inside the birth room his mother groaned in sympathy. She suggested Bill should take Mary to the park, which he promptly did and stayed there for quite a long time. I think he felt relieved to be doing something useful but well out of the way of the birth!

Ruth's birth was the least stressful of my four daughters, not necessarily because it was less painful, but because of the gentle, yet efficient and kindly support throughout from the midwife. There was no panic or fear. She kept telling me how well I was doing, that everything was progressing as it should, that it wouldn't be too long before the baby was born. When Ruth was safely delivered, she said, as she placed Ruth in my arms, 'You have another beautiful little girl,' and again, as with Mary, I felt a flood of relief and joy. It was 8 September, the Birthday of Our Lady.

I thought it would be nice for Mary to have a sister, close in age to herself, which has certainly proved to be the case.[2] I had, of course, four much loved siblings myself and had enjoyed their company during our youth.

A few months later, we read in the local paper that the midwife had been granted a divorce on the grounds of cruelty and we felt really sorry for her and thought how generously and kindly she had looked after me at what must have been a very difficult time for herself.

Bill's mother came in expectantly to see her little granddaughter soon after Ruth was born. Ruth's fair skin had been under so much stress during the birth that she was bright red and Bill's mother privately thought, 'What have we got here?' but judiciously kept the sentiment to herself. Bill timed his return, diplomatically, to the point that he thought the birth would be all over, which indeed it was. He carried Mary into the room to see her little sister in the cot, as Mary still could not walk. This is one of Mary's earliest memories.

Bill and his mother were both very pleased and relieved by the arrival of Ruth. Ruth was very fair, in fact, her hair and eyebrows were almost white. She weighed 6lbs 2 ounces, exactly the same as Mary's birth weight and I followed exactly the same feeding routine, which had been so successful with Mary and, as with Mary, it worked equally well. Ruth's carrycot was by my side of the bed and when she cried at night because she was hungry, I lifted her out, fed her, put her back and we all slept peacefully. Bill said he couldn't remember a disturbed night.

In the daytime the midwife would come to check everything was all right. She would bath Ruth, while Mary sat on Bill's mother's lap and watched. She would say before she left, 'These are the two most beautiful babies on my rounds', which left me feeling proud and happy. Nana, as Mary and later Ruth called her, thought Ruth was growing more beautiful with each day and she used to say to me, 'Her little cheeks are filling out.' Gradually Ruth's downy wisps of white hair changed and grew into soft golden curls.[3]

However, I think Mary might have been having some doubts about 'this little intruder', who had usurped her place! She was very good with Bill's mother in the day but liked to spend time in the bedroom with me, where she became quite possessive. Bill would jokingly put his face against my cheek and say, 'Ah, Mummy' and Mary would say emphatically, 'No, my Mummy.' She didn't like it when Bill's mother put her to bed in her cot and used to cry, which she had never done before. I had always been the one, who did this and she probably couldn't understand the reason for the change and possibly was upset that Ruth remained with me, while she was taken away. I have since thought we stuck too rigidly to the advice given at the time about staying in bed.

For a while, Bill and I were undecided whether to name our new, little daughter Clare or Ruth. We had both been recently touched by reading the life of St Clare, but had always been deeply moved by the story of Ruth in the Old Testament and her loyalty to her mother-in-law, who had lost all her sons. After much discussion, we opted for Ruth as the first name and Clare as the second name.

There was now no problem over godparents. Tom and Doris were delighted to accept and had been good friends to us. Ruth was baptised when she was just two weeks old, which was customary at the time and we invited Tom, Doris, Diane and Marion afterwards for a buffet meal, which Bill's mother had stayed behind to prepare. We also toasted Ruth with glasses of the homemade wine, probably the sweet rose-hip for the women and the strong maize for Bill and Tom. Ruth, like Mary, slept throughout her baptism. I noticed that Tom looked at her with an expression of love in his eyes and, when Ruth started to smile at him a few weeks later, he seemed really moved and said what a beautiful smile she had.

Bill's Reception

It was round this time that Bill phoned Father Caden to say he felt ready to be received into the Catholic Church and Father Caden was delighted. I think Bill had come to feel he might, indeed, be in danger of resisting grace if he delayed any longer. He took his preparation for his First Confession extremely seriously and said it would take him ages to get through it all and would be a real ordeal. I must admit, I did wonder if Bill was being over-scrupulous.

It was also around this time that Bill's mother unexpectedly said she would have to return home. I was somewhat taken aback, because she had stayed much longer when Mary was born and, with two young children, I could have done with the help even more now. I still felt rather washed out and Bill's mother and I got on very well and she was generally very supportive of my needs. Also, she enjoyed being with her grandchildren and had developed a loving relationship with Mary. However, I said nothing. She later told me that she had left so suddenly, because she didn't want to be there when Bill committed himself to the Catholic faith. At the time she did not hint at her true motive, nor did Bill and I guess at it. Strong emotions were aroused by conversion to Catholicism and Bill's mother did not want her feelings on the subject to affect her close bond with her son and his family. However, as time went on, she modified her attitude and was keen to see Mary in her First Communion dress. The dress was in good condition, though second hand, and Lilian washed, dried it in the sun and carefully ironed it.

A week after Ruth's baptism, Tom drove Bill through to Dipton. I wasn't able to go, because with two young children and Ruth having frequent feeds, it didn't seem practical, but I felt pleased and relieved Bill had made this final step and felt sure it would bring him peace of mind.

Bill said it had been a tremendous relief to get through his confession, that after it he felt as if he was just a few days old. Because of Bill's scrupulosity and great respect for the sacrament, he went into his first confession with a wad of file paper covering his entire life. After receiving Holy Communion he was full of joy. He also said later, when looking back on his life, that the period following his reception was the happiest time. He felt fulfilled in love, his young family were thriving, he was successful in teaching and now he had been received into his beloved Church. Bill also said that he had never since doubted or regretted his decision for a moment, even in times of difficulty or ill health.

Sister Peter visited us and was also delighted that Bill had been received into the Catholic Church. She said there were now 'two more small scraps of the Body of Christ.' Because Ruth came four days late, Sister Peter said she had waited for the birthday of Our Lady.[4] She looked lovingly at Mary and Ruth and said, 'There will be a special blessing on these two children,' and, indeed, we did feel blessed.

Notes

[1]   Later, after Lawrence was married to his American wife Martha in 1962, our four daughters would spend exciting, action-packed weekends with them at their home in Reading. Martha would play her guitar and beautifully sing folk songs. They would go to folk concerts, row on the River Thames and have Chinese take-aways. Although Lawrence and Martha's religious position was agnostic, they always respected our faith and conscientiously made sure the girls attended Mass on Sunday morning.

[2]   After Bill and Win moved to Barrow-in-Furness in August 1964, they had two more daughters: Sarah on 29 January 1965 and Cathy on 15 January 1970. The four sisters have grown up greatly enriching each other's lives.

[3]   It went on to be one of the coldest winters on record and so we were grateful and relieved to be settled in our own home.

[4]   In the summer of 1987, I wrote to Sister Peter to tell her Ruth was in a few weeks going to enter the Poor Clare Convent at Woodchester and sent her some photos, which I'd taken during a family walk in the Lakes. I received a lovely warm letter in reply, expressing her delight.

Part II

Bill's Search

11 THE INTELLECTUAL GROUNDS

Bill

T O SAY THAT it is not merely cognitive is not to deny that there are serious rational grounds for belief. It was these which preoccupied Win and me for most of our inquiry and it is these which I would like to consider first. I think it is important to re-emphasise that what I write here will not be an entirely accurate account of what I thought at the time. As I said in my introduction, this book is really about conversion and confirmation, so what I offer here, on this and other matters, is an account of ideas developed early and expanded and consolidated over many years.[1]

Faith then is, in part, an act of the intellect, a rational assent to the testimony of credible witnesses. The earliest apologists, the Apostles and the authors of the New Testament, insist on this, maintaining that their claims are rooted in the word of eyewitnesses, testifying to true events. Hence St Luke begins his Gospel with:

> Seeing that many others have undertaken to draw up accounts of the events that have reached their fulfilment among us, as these were handed down to us by those who from the outset were eyewitnesses and ministers of the word, I in my turn, after carefully going over the whole story from the beginning, have decided to write an ordered account for you, Theophilus, so that your Excellency may learn how well founded the teaching is that you have received (Lk 1:1–4).

It is interesting to reflect on this passage at a time when the infancy narratives of Matthew and Luke have been subjected to much sceptical scrutiny, even by Christian biblical scholars. Can we believe that the author of Luke's Gospel, having insisted on his scrupulous deference to historical objectivity, should immediately proceed to fantasise in his account of the Annunciation, the Nativity and the early infancy of Christ?

Moreover, another interesting question arises here, one posed by the French Catholic writer, Francois Mauriac. If it is indeed fantasy that we are dealing with in Luke's and Matthew's accounts of Christ's conception, birth and early childhood, why did the fantasising stop there? Why, between these narratives and the beginning of Jesus' public ministry, should we have only one recorded incident: the finding of the twelve year old Jesus in the temple? (Lk 2:41–51) In Mauriac's words:

> [W]hy was the web of imaginings interrupted, after the first moments of childhood? Why didn't it apply to Christ as a little boy, as an adolescent or as a young man?[2]

According to Mauriac, Luke himself had learned nothing notable about these thirty years. He therefore recorded nothing—he who told us about the mystery of Christmas. His silence concerning the hidden life of Nazareth authenticates the Gospel of the Annunciation and the Holy Night, and all those things which he could have learned only from Mary. On this matter, we must remember the scrupulosity which Luke manifested at the beginning of his narrative.

These questions regarding the historical credibility of Luke's testimony might also be asked about the author of St John's Gospel, who insists in his Prologue, that his testimony is that of a reliable witness 'sent by God'.

> A man came, sent by God.
> His name was John.
> He came as a witness,
> to bear witness to the light,
> so that everyone might believe through him.
> He was not the light,

He was to bear witness to the light (Jn 1:6–8).

Later, in the same Prologue, he insists on the carnality and visibility of 'the only Son of the Father':

> The Word became flesh,
> he lived among us,
> and we saw his glory,
> the glory that he has from the Father as only son of the Father,
> full of grace and truth (Jn 1:14).

Again, the first letter of John speaks of the Incarnate Word as something 'heard', 'seen', 'watched' and 'touched' (1 Jn 1:1).

> Something which has existed since the beginning,
> which we have heard,
> which we have seen with our own eyes,
> which we have watched
> and touched with our own hands:
> the Word of life-
> this is our theme.
> That life was made visible;
> we saw it and are giving our testimony ... (1 Jn 1:1–2).

Again, the first preaching of Peter at Pentecost, after Christ's Resurrection and Ascension, appeals to the witnessed fact that 'God raised this man Jesus to life, and of that we are all witnesses' (Ac 2:32), a claim frequently echoed by Paul throughout his ministry, which he insists would amount to perjury were it not true fact (1 Co 15:15–6). This admission would, of course, apply to the whole of the New Testament. If it is not reliable testimony, it is vulnerable to the charge of being a sustained perjury, a continuous narrative of blasphemous mendacity. This is difficult to believe given that the Bible (both Testaments) is rooted in the experience and testimony of Israel and given the deference which the Jews, bound to the Mosaic Decalogue, had for their God. To repeatedly lie about Him, or to make claims about Him on insubstantial ground, would have been unthinkable. Even to speak or write His name could not be undertaken lightly.[3]

This claim to veracity is confirmed by the Gospels themselves; they are self-authenticating. They have the hallmarks of credibility all over them, not least in the abundance of convincing detail which characterises so many of the narratives, in particular, the miracle narratives. These details are often not necessary to the account; they do not enhance its apologetic force. The only reason for their inclusion would seem to be that they are part of what actually happened to specific persons at a specific time and place. Moreover, this anchoring of the narratives in named place and person is highly significant. It means that the alleged events could be checked. Many of the persons named, or their relatives, would still be alive when the Gospels were written, so the claims made would be open to verification or falsification.

Furthermore, the account of the ministry of Jesus, given in the Gospels, is profoundly convincing and coherent in both the consistency of character and behaviour of all He encounters, in particular, of His disciples and the Pharisees, and the penetrating moral light which He sheds on all mankind. His ministry is a continuous acted parable on God's relationship to a sinful, faithless, weak and vulnerable people. He constantly rebukes the disciples for their blindness, cowardice, self-seeking and weak faith (Mt 16:8; 17:20). He upbraids the Pharisees for their impeccable but sterile rectitude and the self-righteous pride and heartlessness which derive from it (Mt 23). On the other hand, when confronted by the sick, the weak, sinners who are repentant and open to grace, He is inexhaustible, even scandalous, in His compassion and mercy (Lk 7:36–50). He is a bit like Hamlet in some ways, only better, for while Hamlet is the acute luminary on all that 'is rotten in the state of Denmark,'[4] including himself, Christ is even more penetrating and illuminating, because, unlike Hamlet, He is the perfect light in which, not just Israel, but all humankind are exposed and challenged.

In fact, it is in this unmistakably real and unique Person that the truth of the Gospels is established. He is a Person of sublime moral and spiritual stature, who always speaks with characteristic authority and whose Person, words and actions illuminate, challenge and confirm our own deepest moral and spiritual intuitions, the light which Scripture maintains 'gives light to everyone' (Jn 1:9).

According to Francois Mauriac:

> With Christ, authority is always the striking characteristic; even as a child, he always speaks as one having authority. He questions the doctors; but he dazzles them with his own answers.[5]

Throughout His ministry there is an unerring moral accuracy about everything He says and does, which both addresses and transcends the immediate situation. To the crowd wanting to stone the woman taken in adultery He says: 'Let the one among you who is guiltless be the first to throw a stone at her' (Jn 8:7). This is a typical utterance, addressed not just to those present but to every lynch mob that has ever existed. To all of us, preoccupied as most of us are, with the things of this world, He says: 'Wherever your treasure is, there will your heart be too'(Mt 6:21) and: 'What gain, then, is it for anyone to win the whole world and forfeit his life?'(Mk 8:36) In two brief, pregnant utterances we are all radically challenged to re-evaluate our lives.

Many writers, both Christian and non-Christian, speak of the clear identity of Christ's personality and words. To quote Mauriac again:

> 'Though heaven and earth should pass away, my words will stand,' And indeed they have not passed away; they still fire us; they have created a new humanity; for generations of believers they have changed hearts of stone into hearts of flesh and blood. And for many, even after they have lost the faith, those hearts remain.[6]

And again, in the same book, speaking of the unmistakable identity of Christ's character and voice, Mauriac writes:

> The man whose name is Jesus and around whom the Gospels centre is not a disincarnate creature; he possesses

a definite, clear-cut character and he said nothing that did
not have a particular tonality—so much so that the 'words
of the Lord' (which were first transmitted orally) retain a
kind of tremor in which their tone and accent remain
perceptible.[7]

Not only are the words of Jesus always characteristic and enlightening, they have extraordinary power to comfort and console.
How many of the dispirited have found new hope and reassurance
in His all-embracing invitation:

> Come to me, all you who labour and are overburdened,
> and I will give you rest. Shoulder my yoke and learn from
> me, for I am gentle and humble in heart, and you will find
> rest for your souls. Yes, my yoke is easy and my burden
> light (Mt 11:28–30).

Mauriac quotes St Teresa of Avila, in Chapter Three of her *Sixth
Mansion*, where she speaks of the words which God speaks to the
soul, writes of the enlightening and healing power of the simplest
of Christ's utterances:

> A soul finds itself in pain, in trouble, and these few words:
> *do not be troubled*, calm it, fill it with light and dissipate
> all its troubles—troubles from which, a few moments
> before, it would not have believed the wisest men in the
> world could have delivered it. Another person is in afflic-
> tion and fear; he hears only these words: *It is I, fear not*,
> and suddenly all his apprehensions disappear. Another is
> worried about the success of some important business, and
> hears these words: *peace be to you* ...'[8]

To which Mauriac adds the following reflection:

> 'Be not troubled: It is I, fear not, peace be to you' —this is
> the human language God uses when He speaks to suffering
> man, as to the sea troubled in its depths. Immediately there
> is a great calm; in this calm the Master is recognized...'[9]

According to the New Testament, Christ's words have an authority immediately recognised by all who hear Him with open minds,

an authority which surpasses that of all the religious leaders of the time: 'Jesus had now finished what he wanted to say, and his teaching made a deep impression on the people because he taught them with authority, unlike their own scribes' (Mt 7:28–9). This authority is, of course, challenging to those who believe they are in authority, as Luke points out:

> He taught in the Temple every day. The chief priests and the scribes, in company with the leading citizens, tried to do away with him, but they could not find a way to carry this out because the whole people hung on his words (Lk 19:47–8).

Aidan Nichols in his recent book, *The Realm* quotes from the writings of Samuel Taylor Coleridge which defend this unique, unerring authority:

> [T]he Coleridge scholar Jeffrey Barbeau maintains that:

> [R]ather than arguing for subjectivism in biblical interpretation, Coleridge... emphasises the objective sources of revelation expressed in Scripture and the church traditions handed over from the apostles.

> Coleridge did not deny that Scripture is a unique vehicle of moral and religious truth, explicitly declaring indeed, that '[E]very sentence found in a canonical Book, rightly interpreted, contains the *dictum* of an infallible Mind'.[10]

This recognition of Christ's clear identity and luminous authority is not confined to Christian writers. The great Jewish scientist, Albert Einstein, when asked to what extent Christianity had influenced his life, answered:

> As a child I received religious instruction both in the Bible and the Talmud. I am a Jew but I am enthralled by the luminous figure of the Nazarene ... No one can read the Gospels without feeling the presence of Jesus. His personality pulsates in every word. No myth is filled with such life.[11]

Even the political revolutionary, Jean Jacques Rousseau, senses something superhuman in the character and thought of Christ.

Echoing Chesterton, who sees Christ as 'Tower[ing] ... above all the thinkers who ever thought themselves tall,'[12] Rousseau writes:

> I will confess to you further, that the majesty of the Scriptures strikes me with admiration, as the purity of the Gospel has its influence on my heart. Peruse the works of our philosophers, enriched with all their pomp of diction: how mean, how contemptible are they, compared with the Scriptures! Is it possible that a book at once so simple and sublime should be merely the work of man? Is it possible that the sacred personage, whose history it contains, should be Himself a mere man? Do we find that He assumed the tone of an enthusiast or ambitious sectary? What purity, what sweetness in His manners! What an affecting gracefulness in His delivery! What sublimity in His maxims! What profound wisdom in His discourses! What presence of mind, what subtlety, what truth in His replies! How great the command over His passions! Where is the man, where the philosopher who could so live and so die, without weakness and without ostentation?...The death ... of Jesus, expiring in the midst of agonizing pains, abused, insulted ... is the most horrible that could be feared ... but in the midst of excruciating tortures, [He] prayed for His merciless tormentors. Yes, if the life and death of Socrates are those of a sage, the life and death of Jesus are those of a God.[13]

Notes

1   Win and Ruth are now taking up Bill's consideration of the unfolding of his search for faith from where we left it half way through Chapter Seven.

2   F. Mauriac, *The Son of Man* (London: The World Publishing Company, 1960), p. 27.

3   See Ex 20:7.

4   W. Shakespeare, *Hamlet*, Act 1, Scene 4, l. 90.

5   Mauriac, *The Son Of Man*, pp. 28–29.

6   *Ibid.*, p. 40.

7   *Ibid.*, p. 63.

8   *Ibid.*, p. 65.

9   *Ibid.*

10   A. Nichols, *The Realm: An Unfashionable Essay on the Conversion of England* (Oxford: Family Publications, 2008), pp. 84–85.

11   G. S. Viereck, 'What Life Means to Einstein: An Interview by George Sylvester Viereck', *The Saturday Evening Post*, 26 October 1929, p. 17.

12   Chesterton, *Orthodoxy*, p. 277.

13   J. J. Rousseau, *Profession of Faith of a Savoyard Vicar* (Read Books Ltd, 2011), pp. 101–103.

12 THE DIVINE NATURE OF CHRIST

Bill

Miracles

BUT, CONTRARY TO what some modern theologians appear to think, even if we are prepared to concede all that has been said about the moral and spiritual stature of Christ, it would not be sufficient to establish the credibility of His Divinity. Supreme wisdom and virtue alone would not substantiate John's claim that 'Through him all things came into being, not one thing came into being except through him' (Jn 1:3). Or Paul's claim that 'in him were created all things in heaven and on earth: everything visible and everything invisible' (Col 1:16). This is abundantly recognised throughout the New Testament, where the evangelists always present the challenge of Christ in terms of word and sign. So Mark ends his Gospel with the picture of the Apostles going out preaching, with 'the Lord working with them and confirming the word by the signs that accompany it' (Mk 16:20). And the signs that the New Testament appeals to, both in the account of Jesus' ministry and that of the early Church's evangelisation, are of two kinds: miracles performed and prophecies fulfilled. The twofold nature of the signs is illustrated by Peter's sermon on the day of Pentecost, when, having explained the miraculous outpouring of the Holy Spirit as the fulfilment of the words of the prophet, Joel (Ac 2:16), he proceeds to proclaim Jesus to the crowd as the 'man commended to you by God by the miracles and portents and signs that God worked through him' (Ac 2:22). The culmination of these signs, according to Peter, is Jesus' Resurrection, a miracle foretold by David, confirming Jesus as 'both Lord and Christ' (Ac 2:36).

First let us consider the miracles attributed to Jesus. The Gospels are so full of them that it is difficult to see how anyone can doubt their credibility without questioning the credibility of the Gospels as a whole. I suggested earlier that Jesus sustains His credibility because He always speaks and acts characteristically and this applies to the miracle narratives as to everything else. They are an expression of His inexhaustible compassion, and, linked as they are to the Person of Jesus, they seem as natural and characteristic as everyday events in the lives of ordinary people.

Moreover, they are integral to the whole narrative and cannot be extracted from it without doing violence to all intellectual and imaginative integrity. Miracles are often the occasion of doctrine, and doctrine illuminates the miracles as in John's Gospel when Jesus uses the miracles of the feeding of Israel in the wilderness and His own feeding of the five thousand to illustrate and authenticate His teaching on the Eucharist (Jn 6:33; 6:49). Similarly, the miracle of the raising of Lazarus from the dead offers the perfect occasion for Jesus to proclaim that He Himself is the Resurrection and that whoever believes in Him will never die (Jn 11:26). It is a foretaste of the definitive Resurrection which is to come.

As I have suggested here, there is a necessary reciprocity between the miracles reported and the extraordinary claims made by Jesus and the Church as to His own identity. The miracles are not only signs of God's compassionate love but of His immanence and power. Words alone, however wise and profound, could not have established a sufficient ground for the doctrine of the Incarnation. Only a Christ, who in His sovereignty over nature, sickness and death could have been perceived and proclaimed by Jewish witnesses as One echoing the name and power of Jehovah given to Moses (Ex 3:14) when He says of Himself: 'I tell you most solemnly, before Abraham ever was, I Am' (Jn 8:58).[1]

Interestingly, when, in Matthew's Gospel, Jesus rebukes the citizens of the three towns by the lake for their refusal to believe and repent, it is to His miracles rather than to His moral authority that He appeals:

Then He began to reproach the towns in which most of His miracles had been worked, because they refused to repent.

Alas for you, Chorazin! Alas for you, Bethsaida! For if the miracles done in you had been done in Tyre and Sidon, they would have repented long ago in sackcloth and ashes. Still, I tell that it will be more bearable for Tyre and Sidon on Judgement Day than for you. And as for you, Capernaum, did you want to be raised as high as heaven? You shall be flung down to hell. For if the miracles done in you had been done in Sodom, it would have been standing yet. Still, I tell you that it will be more bearable for Sodom on Judgement Day than for you (Mt 11:21–4).

The same appeal to the miraculous is made by the Apostles after Christ's Ascension. The account given in the Acts of the Apostles is as full of miracles as the Gospels themselves. Together with the Resurrection of Jesus and the claim that He is the fulfilment of the prophecies of the Old Testament, the miracles are one of the primary motives of credibility for faith and repentance. We are told that

Many signs and wonders were worked among the people at the hands of the apostles so that the sick were even taken out into the streets and laid on beds and sleeping-mats in the hope that at least the shadow of Peter might fall across some of them as he went past. People even came crowding in from the towns round about Jerusalem, bringing with them their sick and those tormented by unclean spirits and all of them were cured (Ac 5:14–6).

It is because of these miracles that 'the numbers of men and women who came to believe in the Lord increased steadily' (Ac 5:14).

We are told that the first Deacon, Stephen, prior to his arrest and execution 'was filled with grace and power and began to work miracles and great signs among the people' (Ac 6:8). Similarly the preaching of Philip in Samaria is confirmed by the miracles he works: 'The people unanimously welcomed the message Philip preached, because they had heard of the miracles he worked and because they saw them for themselves' (Ac 8:5). After his conversion and baptism, Simon, the magician, who 'went round constantly with Philip... was astonished when he saw the wonders and great miracles that took place' (Ac 8:13).

Significantly, it is through the power and example of Christ living in them that the Apostles were able to work these miracles. This is illustrated by the cure of Aeneas, 'a paralytic who had been bedridden for eight years.' Peter says to him: 'Aeneas, Jesus Christ cures you: get up and make your bed,' and Aeneas gets up 'immediately' and 'everybody who lived in Lydda and Sharon saw him, and they were converted to the Lord' (Ac 9:34–5). Similarly, with the miracle that follows, Peter's raising of Tabitha to life. Following the example of Christ, witnessed by Peter at the raising of Jairus' daughter, (Ac 9:40) Peter sends everyone out of the room before he works the miracle which is instrumental in the conversion of many: 'The whole of Jaffa heard about it and many believed in the Lord' (Ac 9:42).

It is interesting and noteworthy that, according to the New Testament, Christ and the Apostles should appeal to the miracles so frequently, regarding them as one of, if not the decisive motive, for the credibility of Jesus' claim that He has been sent by God, and for His call to humankind to faith and repentance. Why, one is tempted to ask, when confronted by this flood of testimony, have some Christians become so miracle-shy in recent decades? Why has it become fashionable in some academic circles to play down the miracles, regarding them as bait only for the simple and the credulous? Why was Bishop Jenkins, the former Anglican Bishop of Durham, taken seriously when he dismissed the popular conception of the Resurrection as 'a conjuring trick with bones'[2]? I personally have never met any Christian who thinks of it in those terms.

The Protestant theologian, R. Bultmann, regarded miracles as impossible to believe in our scientific age which has seen the discovery of electricity:

> The wonders of the New Testament are ... finished as
> wonders ...We cannot use electric lights and radios and,
> in the event of illness, avail ourselves of modern medical
> and clinical means and at the same time believe in the
> spirit and wonder world of the New Testament ...[3]

What the scientific discovery of electricity and modern medicine
has to say about the repeated biblical and historical claims that
miracles can and do happen is beyond me. Even the widely
respected biblical scholar, Raymond Brown, when considering
the veracity of the New Testament, appears to admit only
grudgingly that he wouldn't rule out the supernatural.[4] Wouldn't
rule it out! I should think not. If you took the supernatural away
from the New Testament, there would be very little left.

This scepticism with regard to miracles was certainly not the
view of Christ and the Apostles according to the authors of the
New Testament, and it is certainly not the view of many Catholic
intellectuals in the modern age. Of philosophers like Jacques
Maritain, Edith Stein and John Haldane and of theologians like
Scheeben, Newman, von Balthasar and Karl Rahner. For example,
according to Rahner, Christ's miracles are indisputable.[5] According-
ing to Professor Haldane, it was the miracles of Jesus and the
Apostles which formed the primary apologetic for Christianity
in its infancy. Hence:

> This ... was one of the main points of traditional episcopal
> responsibility: to preach and teach the miracles testified
> by the writers of the Gospels and Epistles. It was and
> largely still is the case that Christians believe in the divinity
> of Christ because of the miraculous signs recorded in
> Scripture: Now Jesus did many signs in the presence of the
> disciples, which are not written in this book; but these are
> written that you may believe that Jesus is the Christ
> (Messiah), the Son of the Living God' (Jn 20:30).[6]

'[A]nd that believing this you may have life through his name' (Jn
20: 31). If the first Christians had taken the view of Church leaders

such as Spong, Jenkins, Holloway and Carnley, it is hard to believe
that Christianity could have survived the lifetime of the Apostles.
What is the theological significance of miracles? Surely it lies in
the blatant and universal force of their appeal. Wisdom can be
resisted, even contradicted, but the impact of the miracles, such
as those recorded in the New Testament has irresistible power
to blow away the doubts of all but the most obdurate sceptic.
Miracles indicate in an instant what words can never do: the
actuality, immanence, power and benevolence of God.

How should the enquirer or the committed Christian respond
to the New Testament witness to the miracles? What strikes me
as significant is that the Gospels repeatedly use the word 'signs'
when referring to the miracles. They are certainly not presented
as 'conjuring tricks', the term used by the former Bishop of
Durham when he spoke of the Resurrection of Jesus. Nor are they
something the believer should be constantly demanding by way
of confirmation in faith. Jesus Himself says it is a 'perverse
generation' which is always demanding them (Mt 17:17). What
they represent is not magic, aimed at coercing belief or reassuring
the sceptic, but invitations to faith in the God who is immanent
and who invites us to believe and reshape our lives in response
to His call. This is illustrated by the story of Peter and the
miraculous catch of fish. The disciples in the boat have, for a long
time, caught nothing. Directed by Jesus, they suddenly land an
enormous catch. Peter might have responded by a request for
more. Instead his response is: 'Leave me, Lord; I am a sinful man'
(Lk 5:8). This should be the response of any believer or anyone
open to belief, when confronted by a sign of God's favour. Not
what else can you do, but, Lord, I believe. This was illustrated for
me by an acquaintance of mine who believed he was instantane-
ously cured of a crippling condition at Lourdes. His first thought
was: 'I have no enemies.' He felt overwhelmed by a sense of
gratitude and forgiveness towards all who had ever hurt him; and
confirmed in his faith.

Scissors and Paste[7]

Coming back to the question of the credibility of the miracle narratives, a book which influenced me at an early stage of my spiritual journey was *Now I See* by Arnold Lunn. Lunn was himself a Catholic convert who, prior to writing this book, had engaged in written controversy with the philosopher C. E. M. Joad on the truth of Christianity, and with the Catholic priest, Ronald Knox, on the truth of Catholicism. Interestingly, Joad, partly as a result of the controversy, ended up a committed Christian, just as Lunn, after his correspondence with Knox, ended up a committed Catholic.

In an important chapter of *Now I See* entitled 'Scissors and Paste', Lunn addresses the question of the miracles and the problem many people have with them, even though they admire the moral teaching of Jesus and quote verbatim from the Gospels in support of their arguments. About his controversy with Joad, Lunn wrote:

> But Mr Joad does not regard the Gospels as spurious, for he expresses the greatest admiration for Christ, and his admiration is based on the records of Christ's teaching in the Gospels, records which Mr Joad is constantly quoting to establish his own view of Christ's character as against the traditional view.[8]

He goes on to develop the point:

> 'I do not think,' I wrote to Joad, 'that you can logically quote *any* text against me until you have explained on what principle you accept certain texts and reject others. Your cheerful theory that any text which suits your preconceived theories must be, and any text which does not suit them cannot possibly be, authentic, does more credit to your heart than to your head.' To this Mr Joad made no reply.[9]

Lunn goes on to demonstrate how characteristic of Christ the miracles are, issuing as they do 'from a pity that knew that it had the power to heal men's sickness and to supply their physical needs.'[10] Moreover, they provide occasions to authenticate Jesus' teaching:

> Note how often these miracles give occasion, as Bishop Gore points out, for sayings and gestures of Christ which bear the unmistakable touch of authenticity. 'Is it lawful on the Sabbath day to do good or to do harm, to save life or to kill?' Surely you hear the authentic voice of Jesus in these words, and if you do, how can you refuse credence to the setting of these words, the man with a withered hand which was healed?[11]

Lunn concludes his chapter with a commentary on the story of the healing of the blind man in the ninth chapter of John's Gospel. It is challenging and illuminating to read his commentary to see if it supports Lunn's contention that the

> [S]tory is full of natural touches, incidents and remarks which develop naturally out of what proceeds. Every character is true to type. The blind man and his parents, Jews, act and talk just as we might expect them to act and talk.[12]

Notes

[1]   We have retained this passage in its older translation from the Jerusalem Bible.

[2]   The controversial remark by Bishop David Jenkins was made in a pre-recorded interview for BBC Radio in October 1984.

[3]   R. Bultmann, *New Testament and Mythology* (Philadelphia: Fortress Press, 1984), p. 4.

[4]   R. E. Brown, *Responses to 101 Questions on the Bible* (New York: Mahwah, Paulist Press, 1990), pp. 66–67.

[5]   K. Rahner, *The Teaching of the Catholic Church* (Cork: The Mercier Press, 1964), p. 42.

[6]   J. Haldane, *An Intelligent Person's Guide to Religion* (London: Duckworth, 2003), p. 28.

[7]   Bill intended to develop this chapter even more in order to explore the further implications of 'Scissors and Paste.'

8   A. Lunn, *Now I See* (London: Sheed and Ward, 1955), p. 174.

9   *Ibid.*

10   *Ibid.*, p. 175.

11   *Ibid.*

12   *Ibid.*, pp. 175–176.

13 MAD, BAD OR GOD

Bill

AN INTERESTING APOLOGETIC argument for Christianity emerges from all I have said so far about the credibility of Christianity. It is the well-known 'Mad, Bad or God' argument. *Bad, Mad or God*[1] is the title of the excellent book by John Redford in which he addresses this question among others. I first came across the argument as a student at Durham University, and it has stayed with me ever since. It is an extension, in some ways, of Arnold Lunn's 'Scissors and Paste' argument. I wouldn't claim that the argument is irresistible but it is a powerful persuasion. It has a long history, which goes back at least to Coleridge, and it has been brilliantly developed in the last century by C. S. Lewis, G. K. Chesterton and others.

It runs something like this: If the claim to divinity made by Jesus in the New Testament (or at least by the Church for Him) is a false one, what does it tell us about His character? Does the image of supreme goodness and moral authority, recognised by believers and unbelievers alike, survive? Coleridge thought not. If Jesus was not God, He was not a good man he maintained. We can easily see how this could be developed. A man, who demanded from His followers a renunciation of the world, including the ties of family (Lk 14:26), who called them to the discipleship of the cross (Mt 16:24), even to the point of martyrdom (Mt 16:25), all for a lie, or delusion, could hardly be a good man. He was certainly not a sane one, as Lewis and Chesterton point out. 'A great man knows that he is not God and the greater he is the better he knows it,' argues Chesterton.[2] Those who make such claims are not usually numbered among the great, but rather among the patients of psychiatric units, as both Lewis and Chesterton maintain.[3] And yet, in the light of all that has been said by both believers and sceptics, who can question the eminent goodness and sanity of Jesus?

There is another problem here for the sceptic to ponder. How does he reconcile the moral integrity of Jesus, the unerring wisdom of His utterances with the relentless mendacity of the New Testament as a whole: miracles which did not happen, prophecies which were either not made or, if made, were not fulfilled, claims to divinity which bore no relationship to a purely human, historical Jesus. According to John's Gospel, the Jesus who says, 'Let the one among you who is guiltless be the first to throw a stone at her' (Jn 8:7), also says, 'Now, Father, glorify me with that glory I had with you before ever the world existed' (Jn 17:5). How can we reconcile the sanity and compassion of the first with the megalomaniac delusion of the second? Scissors and Paste?

The problem is neatly crystallised by C. S. Lewis in his book *Miracles*:

> The historical difficulty of giving for the life, sayings and influence of Jesus any explanation that is not harder than the Christian explanation is very great. The discrepancy between the depth and sanity and (let me add) *shrewdness* of His moral teaching, and the rampant megalomania which must be behind His theological teaching, unless He is indeed God, has never been satisfactorily got over. Hence the non-Christian hypotheses succeed one another with the restless fertility of bewilderment. Today we are asked to regard all the theological elements as later accretions to the story of a 'historical' and merely human Jesus.[4]

Lewis is particularly scathing towards those who are great admirers of Christ's ethical teaching but sceptical about His theological credentials. Politicians of both right and left (Church-ill and Atlee for example) figure prominently among them, as do excellent writers such as Clive James. Lewis will have none of it, maintaining that the distinction made is devoid of all integrity:

> I am trying here to prevent anyone saying the really foolish thing that people often say about Him: 'I am ready to

accept Jesus as a great moral teacher, but I don't accept His claim to be God.' That is the one thing we must not say. A man who was merely a man and said the sort of things Jesus said would not be a great moral teacher. He would either be a lunatic ... or else he would be the Devil of Hell. You must make your choice. Either this man was, and is, the Son of God: or else a madman or something worse. You can shut Him up for a fool, you can spit at Him and kill Him as a demon; or you can fall at His feet and call Him Lord and God. But let us not come with any patronising nonsense about His being a great human teacher. He has not left that open to us. He did not intend to.[5]

G. K. Chesterton develops Lewis' argument, emphasising the towering solitariness of Christ with regard to His claims, claims which distinguish Him from all other great luminaries, both religious and non-religious:

There is a sort of notion in the air everywhere that all the religions are equal because all the religious founders were rivals; that they are all fighting for the same starry crown. It is quite false. The claim to that crown, or anything like that crown, is really so rare as to be unique. Mahomet did not make it any more than Micah or Malachi. Confucius did not make it any more than Plato or Marcus Aurelius ... Normally speaking, the greater a man is, the less likely he is to make the very greatest claim. Outside the unique case we are considering, the only kind of man who ever does make that kind of claim is a very small man; a secretive or self-centred monomaniac. Nobody can imagine Aristotle claiming to be the father of gods and men, come down from the sky; though we might imagine some insane Roman Emperor like Caligula claiming it for him, or more probably for himself ... Nobody can imagine Shakespeare talking as if he were literally divine ...[6]

Just imagine a Bertrand Russell or a Richard Dawkins breaking off from an eloquent philosophical or scientific argument and suddenly asking God to 'glorify me with that glory I had with you before ever the world existed' (Jn 17:5), or claiming that 'Anyone who has seen me has seen the Father' (Jn 14:9). Their credibility and reputation would vanish overnight, beyond recovery. But this is not the case with Jesus. Not only did His contemporaries appear to take such claims seriously, they have been taken seriously by His many followers across the world for twenty centuries.

Moreover, even if the Church from the beginning and down the centuries had misrepresented Him and made claims for Him which He Himself would have disowned, the uniqueness of the phenomenon would not be undermined, as Chesterton again maintains:

> Even if the Church had mistaken his meaning, it would still be true that no other historical tradition except the Church had ever even made the same mistake. Mahomedans did not misunderstand Mahomet and suppose he was Allah. Jews did not misinterpret Moses and identify him with Jehovah. [According to St John's Gospel it was precisely because Jesus did make this claim that the Pharisees regarded Him as a blasphemer who had to be destroyed.] Why was this claim alone exaggerated unless this alone was made? Even if Christianity was one vast universal blunder, it is still a blunder as solitary as the Incarnation.[7]

To sum up, orthodox, Catholic Christology sees the consciousness of Jesus as perfectly integrated. It refuses to take seriously the contradictions implicit in the reflections of sceptics and half-believers: a great moral and spiritual teacher but grossly superstitious in His belief in the angelic and the demoniac; shrewd and firmly grounded in human reality, but wholly misrepresented in His alleged possession of miraculous powers and His claim to be the fulfilment of the prophets of Israel. The consciousness of Christ is indivisible. His moral and spiritual teaching are often inextricably rooted in the miraculous and the prophetic as I have tried to show.

Notes

1   J. Redford, *Bad, Mad or God? Proving the Divinity of Christ from St John's Gospel* (London: St Paul's Publishing, 2005).

2   G. K. Chesterton, *The Everlasting Man* (London: Hodder and Stoughton, 1953), p. 237.

3   *Ibid.*, p. 235.

4   C. S. Lewis, *Miracles* (London and Glasgow: Fontana Books, 1960), p. 113.

5   C. S. Lewis, *Mere Christianity* (London and Glasgow: Collins, 1958), pp. 52–53.

6   Chesterton, *The Everlasting Man*, p. 235.

7   *Ibid.*, p. 234.

14 REASONS OF THE HEART

Bill

B
UT, IN MATTERS of faith, arguments such as I have tried
to develop are not always the deepest motives of credibility. Newman, I think, speaks for many converts and cradle
believers when he insists that the real grounds for faith and for
love lie beyond argument, and are too deep for words.[1] Like Pascal
in his *Pensées* he knew that the heart has reasons which reason
itself knows nothing about:[2]

> Do not be surprised to find simple people believing
> without reasoning ... God inclines their hearts to belief.
> We shall never believe with a helpful and real faith unless
> God inclines our hearts; and once He inclines them we
> shall believe. This was well known to David: 'Incline my
> heart unto thy testimonies'.[3]

Hence, echoing Pascal's words, Newman writes:

> Can it, indeed, be doubted that the great majority of those
> who have sincerely and deliberately given themselves to
> religion, who take it for their portion, and stake their
> happiness upon it, have done so, not on an examination
> of evidence, but from a spontaneous movement of the
> heart towards it? They go out of themselves to meet Him
> who is unseen, and they discern Him in such symbols of
> Him as they find ready provided for them.[4]

A reflection of Pope John Paul II, offers a development of
Newman's contention that Christ offers the perfect complement
to all the aspirations of the enlightened heart, to all our latent
idealism, heroism and generosity; and to our dissatisfaction with
mediocrity and compromise:

It is Jesus that you seek
when you dream of happiness;
He is waiting for you
when nothing else you find satisfies you;
He is the beauty to which
you are so attracted;
it is He who provoked you
with that thirst for fullness
that will not let you settle
for compromise;
it is He who urges you
to shed the masks of a false life;
it is He who reads in your heart
your most genuine choices,
the choices that others try to stifle.
It is Jesus who stirs in you
the desire to do something
great with your lives,
the will to follow an ideal,
the refusal to allow yourselves
to be ground down by mediocrity,
the courage to commit yourselves
humbly and patiently to
improving yourselves and society,
making the world more
human and fraternal.[5]

This would seem to confirm what St Augustine writes after his conversion to Catholicism:

[Y]ou made us for yourself and our hearts find no peace until they rest in you.[6]

Similarly, Carl Ullmann in *The Sinlessness of Jesus: An Evidence for Christianity* writes not only of the extraordinary appeal to the human heart that Jesus makes,[7] but of His power to transform hearts, an appeal and a power which could not have been invented and which establishes the reality of the historical Jesus.[8]

Ullmann argues from the New Testament portrait of Jesus and from Jesus' testimony concerning Himself to the conclusion that Jesus was, in fact, sinless, as befits the Redeemer of humankind.[9] To the objection that the Gospel portrait might be fiction Ullmann replies with Rousseau:

> The inventor of such an image would be greater and more astonishing than his subject.[10]

Then he adds that the effects of the manifestation of Jesus in the religious regeneration of the world would not have a proportionate cause except in a real person. He especially who has felt in his own heart the peculiar power experienced by the Gospel delineation of the Lord Jesus will entertain no kind of doubt as to its reality and origin.[11]

Ullmann's appeal to the experience of radical regeneration effected through Christ is reiterated by August Tholuck in *Guido and Julius, or Sin and the Propitiator: Exhibited in the True Consecration of the Sceptic*[12] in which he praises the joyful experience of rebirth in Jesus and maintains that the newness of life granted to our hearts by the Holy Spirit is its own assurance. The Catholic Theologian, Karl Rahner, confirms and develops these ideas, maintaining that Christ alone satisfies fully the longing deeply implanted in the human heart for the 'absolute bringer of salvation.'[13]

Avery Dulles describes Rahner's theology of salvation like this. '[Rahner] sees the religions of the world as flowing together into a single stream ... The other religions ... are intrinsically ordered toward Christ as their unacknowledged fulfilment':[14] Dulles continues:

> All human beings, [Rahner] maintains, are in search of salvation, the definitive success of our existence as a whole. Experience teaches them that such salvation is unavailable within the relativities of history, but at the same time that salvation must be sought within history in association with our fellow human beings. Spontaneously, therefore, we

look for a human person in whom God's saving power would be wholly and manifestly successful. By considerations of this kind, Rahner believes, we can project the idea of 'the absolute bringer of salvation' to whom God definitively communicates Himself in absolute fullness and whose definitive success is manifested by a death for others and a victory over death. Whoever is on the lookout for such a figure in history is practicing what Rahner calls a 'searching Christology'... On the other hand, a priori arguments do not take the place of reasoning from facts. Actual history alone can tell us that the absolute Saviour has appeared and has done so in Jesus of Nazareth.[15]

Notes

[1]   St J. H. Newman, *Oxford University Sermons* (London: Longmans, Green, and Co, 1909), p. 225.

[2]   B. Pascal, *Pensées* (Middlesex, Penguin Books Ltd, 1961) p. 286.

[3]   *Ibid.*, p. 286.

[4]   Newman, *Oxford University Sermons*, p. 225.

[5]   John Paul II, St, 'Address at World Youth Day', Rome, 19 August 2000.

[6]   St Augustine of Hippo, *The Confessions* (London: Penguin Books, 1961), p. 21.

[7]   C. Ullmann, *The Sinlessness of Jesus: An Evidence for Christianity* (London, Dalton House Ltd, 2018, reproduction of Edinburgh, T. and T. Clark, 1863), p. 60.

[8]   *Ibid.*, p. 64.

[9]   *Ibid.*, pp. 70–71.

[10] *Ibid.*, p. 64.

[11] *Ibid.*, pp. 81–90.

[12] F. A. D. Tholuck, *Guido and Julius, or Sin and the propitiator: exhibited in the true consecration of the sceptic* (Boston: Gould and Lincoln, 1854).

[13] In 'Jesus Christ in the Non-Christian Religions,' *Theological Investigations*, Vol. 17, trans. M. Kohl (New York: Herder & Herder, 1981), pp. 39–50, Rahner describes this longing as a 'seeking *memoria.*' His theology of Christ as the 'Absolute bringer of salvation who alone fulfils this inner seeking' is elaborated in 'What Does it Mean Today to Believe in Jesus

Christ?' *Theological Investigations*, Vol. 18, trans. E. Quinn (New York: Herder & Herder, 1983), pp. 143–156.

[14] A. Dulles, *A History of Apologetics* (San Francisco: Ignatius Press, 2005), p. 333. See K. Rahner, 'On the Importance of the Non-Christian Religions for Salvation,' *Theological Investigations*, Vol. 18, trans. E. Quinn (New York: Herder & Herder, 1983), pp. 288–295.

[15] Dulles, *A History of Apologetics*, pp. 333–334. Dulles cites two of the key sources: K. Rahner, 'Christology Today.' in *A New Christology* (New York: Seabury Press, 1980), pp. 3–17 and more fully in chapter 6 of Rahner's *Foundations of Christian Faith: An Introduction to the Idea of Christianity (New York: Seabury Press, 1978)*, pp. 193–212. Dulles, *A History of Apologetics*, p. 333, footnote 21.

15 THE PARADOXES IN CHRIST'S TEACHING

Bill

T RUTH IS OFTEN paradoxical: it comprehends and reconciles what at first sight might appear to be contradictions; and, as a corollary to that, one of the hallmarks of true wisdom and virtue is an appreciation of that truth. Hence Socrates, one of the wisest of men, believed he knew nothing.

According to C. S. Lewis, Christ's teaching is like that; it exhibits all the paradoxes of a message that has come from the centre of reality.[1] For example, He challenges the wisdom of the worldly wise and insists that His truth is accessible only to those who are open to it with childlike simplicity:

> I bless you, Father, Lord of heaven and earth, for hiding these things from the learned and the clever and revealing them to little children. Yes, Father, for that is what it pleased you to do. Everything has been entrusted to me by my Father; and no one knows the Son except the Father, just as no one knows the Father except the Son and those to whom the Son chooses to reveal him (Mt 11:25–7).

Indeed, in Mark's Gospel, He says that unless we become like children we cannot enter the kingdom of heaven:

> In truth I tell you, anyone who does not welcome the kingdom of God like a little child will never enter it (Mk 10:15).

These are significant statements, very pertinent to our own time, when there are many in the Christian community who question the authority of Scripture and the Church and who appear to think that it is only the 'professors' (biblical scholars and radical theologians) who have access to the truth.

Again, paradoxically, His teaching both challenges and confirms us at the same time. It scrutinises us without mercy, renders us transparent to ourselves, yet it is the very embodiment of compassion and mercy, the mercy of the One who comes not to condemn the world but to redeem it (Jn 3:17), to call, 'not the upright but sinners to repentance' (Lk 5:32). As the saying goes, it is perfectly calculated to 'afflict the comfortable and comfort the afflicted.' It challenges the virtuous to accept the discipleship of the cross (Lk 9:23), and yet it welcomes the weak and struggling to the comforting yoke of God's compassionate embrace (Mt 11:28–30).

Christ's treatment of the Mosaic Law is typically paradoxical. He demands that we accept it in its entirety: 'In truth I tell you, till heaven and earth disappear, not one dot, not one little stroke, is to disappear from the Law until all its purpose is achieved' (Mt 5:18). But He reduces its negative imperatives to the two positives of love of God and love of neighbour (Mt 22:37–40). And there is a further paradox, which illustrates His insights into the complexity, the ironies, in moral reality. In the parable of the Pharisee and the tax collector (Lk 18:9–14) He sees the irony that those who are impeccably faithful to the letter of the law can, through self-righteous pride, alienate themselves from God's mercy, while the humble penitent, who acknowledges his sinfulness, has access to it, and goes home at rights with God. Similarly, in the lovely story of the Pharisee and the woman with 'a bad name in the town', which I have already mentioned, it is the woman who shows 'such great love', covering Christ's feet with kisses, whose many sins are forgiven, while the scandalised Pharisee is rebuked (Lk 7:36–50).

In fact, Christ's whole relationship to the Pharisees is very illuminating; it offers a further illustration of the paradoxes in His understanding. Throughout the Gospels He castigates them for their pride, hypocrisy and heartlessness, threatening them with damnation: 'You serpents, brood of vipers, how can you escape being condemned to hell?' (Mt 23:33) and yet, paradoxically, He upholds the teaching authority of the very same Pharisees:

> Then, addressing the crowds and his disciples, Jesus said, 'The scribes and the Pharisees occupy the chair of Moses. You must therefore do and observe what they tell you; but do not be guided by what they do, since they do not practise what they preach' (Mt 23:2–3).

Similarly paradoxical is Jesus' relationship with His disciples. Throughout His ministry they are shown to be inadequate and wrong most of the time: cowardly and weak in faith when tested (Mk 14:50), blind and uncomprehending in their response to His teaching (Mk 8:17). Yet these are the men chosen to judge the twelve tribes of Israel (Mt 19:28) and commissioned to evangelise the nations (Mt 28:19).

These paradoxes are highly significant. God's chosen and covenanted representatives have not merited their vocation. Like the kings and prophets of the Old Testament, they are called and sent, not because of their virtues, but in spite of their weaknesses. Their teaching authority derives ultimately from God, not from themselves, because it is God's truth they are called to proclaim, not their own.

G. K. Chesterton confirms this perception of paradox in the life and teaching of Jesus when he writes that Christ 'turns our values upside down until we realise that they have been turned right side up'.[2] So, He is supremely a king, but His kingdom 'is not a kingdom of this world' (Jn 18:36) for, unlike many worldly kings, such as Marlowe's Tamburlaine, who dreams of 'rid[ing] in triumph through Persepolis',[3] Christ chooses to ride into Jerusalem on a donkey, and allows Himself to be crowned with thorns and executed like a criminal. He comes as Israel's liberator, but the liberation He offers is a moral and spiritual liberation, a liberation from sin, not a political liberation from Roman oppression which many had hoped for.

In fact, the values He affirms throughout His ministry, in particular, in the Sermon on the Mount, are the absolute antithesis of the values of this world. It is the 'poor in spirit', 'the gentle', 'those who mourn', 'those who hunger and thirst for uprightness', 'the merciful', 'the pure in heart', 'the peacemakers', those who patiently endure 'persecution' and 'calumny' who are truly 'blessed' and whose 'reward will be great in heaven' (Mt 5:1–12).

And the downside of all this, according to Luke, is:

> But alas for you who are rich: you are having your consolation now. Alas for you who have plenty to eat now: you shall go hungry. Alas for you who are laughing now: you shall mourn and weep. Alas for you when everyone speaks well of you! This was the way their ancestors treated the false prophets (Lk 6:24–6).

Apart from the paradoxes in His utterances, Christ, Himself, is the supreme paradox, embodying perfectly all the apparent contradictions, the ironies and balances we associate with personal integrity: strength and chosen vulnerability, heroic courage and sympathy for those who lack it, perfect sanctity and compassion for sinners. Born in a stable, living in humble obscurity for thirty years, homeless for the three years of His ministry, executed with criminals, yet He claims to be wiser than Solomon and the fulfilment of Israel's law and her prophets (Mt 5:17; 12:42). According to Matthew's Gospel, He is the fulfilment of the prophecy of Isaiah, which speaks of the one who will speak softly, who will be gentle to the weak and faint-hearted, but who will be the leader whose voice will proclaim the true faith to the nations, who will lead the truth to victory and fill the world with hope:

> Here is my servant whom I uphold,
> my chosen one in whom my soul delights.
> I have endowed him with my spirit
> that he may bring true justice to the nations.
> He does not cry out or shout aloud,
> or make his voice heard in the streets.
> He does not break the crushed reed,

nor quench the wavering flame.
Faithfully he brings true justice;
he will neither waver, nor be crushed
until true justice is established on earth,
and the islands are awaiting his law (Is 42:1–4).[4]

So He comes as the perfect embodiment of that image and of so many others in the New Testament. He is the spotless lamb of God who is led like a lamb to the slaughter, the gentle consoler of the afflicted, who has come 'to call not the upright but sinners to repentance' (Lk 5:32), the prophet of peace who blesses the peace-makers (Mt 5:9).

But again, paradoxically, this same Christ is no soft touch. He can be fiercely critical towards the Pharisees, as we have seen, hostile to the point of physical chastisement towards those who desecrate His Father's house (Mt 21:12–7), frightening in His condemnation of anyone who damages the faith of children (Mt 18:6) and challenging to us all. In these encounters and others, He is no lamb, but, in the words of T. S. Elliot, 'Christ the tiger'[5], one who comes not to bring peace 'but a sword' (Mt 10:34), to divide families (Lk 12:51–2), who calls His followers to the discipleship of the cross (Lk 9:23), who asks the rich man who has kept all the commandments to go one step further and give all he has to the poor (Mt 19:21). Scandalous and inexhaustible in His mercy to penitent sinners, He, nevertheless, insists that 'not one dot, not one little stroke, is to disappear from the Law until all its purpose is achieved' (Mt 5:18), and that 'anyone who infringes even one of the least of these commandments and teaches others to do the same will be considered the least in the kingdom of Heaven' (Mt 5:19).

Notes

[1]   Lewis, *Mere Christianity*, p. 70.

[2]   G. K. Chesterton, *The Hibbert Journal* (April 1910). The article was reprinted in *Christian Faith and Life*, Vol 12 (January to June 1910) under the title '"Jesus" or "Christ"?... The Latest Bubble Punctured'.

[3]   C. Marlowe, *Marlowe: Tamburlaine the Great*, Part 1, Act 2, Scene 5.

[4]   We have retained this passage in its older translation from the Jerusalem Bible.

[5]   T. S. Eliot, 'Gerontion' *Collected Poems: 1909–1935* (London: Faber and Faber Ltd, 1959), p. 37.

16 READING AND ASKING QUESTIONS

Bill

ALL THIS TIME, while Win was moving towards the Church, I was reading everything I could put my hands on. I read the works of Catholic converts of the twentieth century: G. K. Chesterton, Ronald Knox, Arnold Lunn, C. C. Martindale, B. C. Butler, Father Maturin, William Orchard, Jacques Maritain, Thomas Merton. I spent a fortune on Catholic Truth Society pamphlets. I read the lives of some of the saints.

I was particularly interested in the Fathers of the Church for the picture they gave of the historical Church in its infancy. Here I was helped by an Anglican view of the Fathers, lent by a colleague at school, and by a massive book, *Thou Art Peter*,[1] by a man called A. D. Howell Smith, which looked at the Fathers and the whole of Christian tradition from the impartial standpoint of an agnostic. I was particularly helped by Newman's great book, *The Development of Christian Doctrine*,[2] in which he defends the thesis that the Christianity of Scripture is seminal Catholicism, that the Christianity of the early centuries is, increasingly, explicit Catholicism, and that in Catholic tradition we have, gradually unfolding, the full, integrated development of the Faith, which lies deeply dormant in the Bible.

I read anti-Catholic books as well, to check that I wasn't missing anything, notably the celebrated book by George Salmon, *Infallibility of the Church*,[3] which Anglicans regarded as the final answer to the Catholic claims. This book helped me a lot. It was clearly the work of an important scholar and polemicist, but I felt he was blowing up trifles and ignoring the main issues. What he seemed to be attacking was 'creeping infallibility', a widely used term for the assumption that the Church believes she would never be mistaken about anything, which is not in fact what the Church claims. He kept insisting that he had no serious case to answer, and yet he was spending nearly five hundred pages answering it. Above all, he failed to do justice to the thesis he was opposing, always a bad sign in a work of this kind. Even I, by this time, knew that the Church's belief that she could ultimately determine what is and what is not her own faith was an eminently reasonable one, with a solid biblical foundation to it. In this respect the book compared unfavourably with the works of Catholic Apologetic I was reading. B. C. Butler, for instance, in *Church and Infallibility*,[4] his reply to Salmon's book, stated clearly every significant point Salmon had made and answered it. Likewise Newman in *The Development of Christian Doctrine* began by frankly admitting the difficulties his theory involved.[5] As did Bellarmine in his great response to the Reformation, *The Controversies*.[6] The first two volumes of that work stated the case against the Church so powerfully that they became handbooks of Protestant Apologetics all over Europe. It was only when the later volumes, defending the Church, were published that Protestants were made to realise that they had a case to answer. I finished Salmon's book with a sense of relief, feeling there was nothing manifestly untenable in the Church's claims.

Most important of all, I reread the whole of the New Testament, underlining passages which pointed to Rome or elsewhere.

While I was reading my mind teemed with ideas: questions, arguments, counter-arguments: 'I wish to set forth my faith',[7] as Chesterton described this state of mind. The experience of moving towards the Church is not so much one of seizing ideas as being seized by them. They will not leave you alone. It is an absorbing state that keeps invading your time. Newman describes this state in his novel, *Loss and Gain* written while he was studying for the priesthood in Rome after his reception into the Catholic Church:

[H]is lectures and other duties of the place, his friends and recreations, were the staple of the day; but there was this undercurrent ever in motion, and sounding in his mental ear as soon as other sounds were hushed. As he dressed in the morning, as he sat under the beeches of his college-garden, when he strolled into the meadow ... when he threw himself on his sofa ... at night, [these] thoughts ... were busy within him.[8]

Of course, I asked many questions because Catholicism is a big subject, which, in a sense, raises all the questions. But basically the questions, which tormented me boiled down to three:

1. Is Christianity true?
2. If it is, through what agencies does its truth come to us?
3. And what is the nature of the truth it proclaims?

Now, the first question I had already answered. I had accepted Jesus as the Divine Messenger. It was the other two questions, which were to preoccupy me and form the basis of my enquiry. These were the questions fundamental to the Catholic and Protestant view of Christianity: How is Christ's saving truth given to us, and what is that truth?

With these questions in mind, I decided to look closely at the character of first biblical Christianity and then historical Christianity, on the assumption that, if it is from God and true, it would not be misinterpreted in its infancy and throughout the ages. Christ had promised to be with His Church in its teaching mission all days until the end of time (Mt 28:20). Scripture speaks of 'the faith ... once and for all entrusted to God's holy people' (Jude 3) and of 'Jesus Christ [who] is the same today as he was yesterday and as he will be for ever' (Heb 13:8). So, I studied the New Testament and the early centuries, looking for the evidence for the Catholic and Protestant positions.

Notes

[1]   A. D. H. Smith, *Thou Art Peter, A History of Roman Catholic Doctrine and Practice* (London: Watts and Co, 1930).

[2]   St J. H. Newman, *An Essay On The Development Of Christian Doctrine* (London and New York: Sheed and Ward, 1960).

[3]   G. D. Salmon, *The Infallibility of the Church: A Course of Lectures Delivered in the Divinity School of the University of Dublin* (London: John Murray, 1914).

[4]   B. C. Butler, *The Church and Infallibility* (New York: Sheed and Ward, 1954).

[5]   Newman, *An Essay On The Development Of Christian Doctrine*, pp. 3–23.

[6]   *The Controversies* emerged out of lectures St Robert Bellarmine delivered at the Roman College and were published in three volumes at Ingolstadt from 1586 to 1593.

[7]   Chesterton, *Orthodoxy*, p. 3.

[8]   St J. H. Newman, *Loss and Gain* (Oxford: Oxford University Press, 1986), p. 49.

17 THE MYSTERIOUS NATURE OF THE GOSPEL

Bill

A PERCEPTION, which was to develop early and strengthen, was of the mysterious nature of the Gospel. It is both deeply mysterious, with a language and concepts which are uniquely and strangely its own, and yet given and guaranteed. Christianity is a revealed religion, a gift from God to His people. It is not the fruit of human speculation like the philosophies of the world. St Paul makes this very clear in his Epistle to the Galatians:

> Now I want to make it quite clear to you, brothers, about the gospel that was preached by me, that it was no human message. It was not from any human being that I received it, and I was not taught it, but it came to me through a revelation of Jesus Christ (Ga 1:11–12).

And again, in the First Epistle to the Thessalonians we are invited to accept God's message 'for what it really is, not the word of any human being, but God's word' (1 Th 2:13). This message is, says G. K. Chesterton, dependent upon 'transcendental doctrine,'[1] that is, doctrines which are beyond human speculation, coming purely from above on the initiative and authority of the revealing God. Again, Scripture speaks of revelation as the mystery hidden from the ages, and, at last in the fullness of time, revealed to the little ones of Christ, to those who can receive it like children in the 'obedience of faith' (Rm 1:5).

At the heart of this mystery is the Cross, the supreme mystery, which, above all others, in the words of St Paul, 'destroy[s] the wisdom of the wise and bring[s] to nothing the understanding of any who understand' (1 Co 1:19), a mystery transcending all powers of human cognition, which can only be grasped obscurely in faith:

> Since in the wisdom of God the world was unable to recognize God through wisdom, it was God's own pleasure to save believers through the folly of the gospel ... we are preaching a crucified Christ; to the Jews an obstacle they cannot get over, to the gentiles foolishness, but to those who have been called, whether they are Jews or Greeks, a Christ who is both the power of God and the wisdom of God. God's folly is wiser than human wisdom, and God's weakness is stronger than human strength (1 Co 1:21–5).

Notes

[1]   Chesterton, *The Everlasting Man*, p. 279.

18 THE INADEQUACY OF SCRIPTURE ALONE

Bill

S O, FROM THE outset, I found myself looking for a theory of Revelation, which could sustain this idea of God-givenness, and bring light to the mysteries in the gift. Moreover, it had to be a theory, which would make Revelation accessible to everyone, in particular to the little ones of Christ, to whom, according to St Matthew's Gospel, the mysteries of faith would be revealed when they were hidden from 'the learned and the clever' (Mt 11:25).

What soon became clear to me was that Scripture alone neither sustains the givenness nor resolves the mystery. Though the Bible is a wonderfully thematic and echoic book, with a profound coherence in the testimonies of both Testaments, nevertheless, on its own, it remains deeply mysterious on many matters. The fragmented Christendom of the Post-Reformation centuries offers a sad testimony to that. According to the Internet, current estimates as to the number of Protestant sects can vary from 20,000 to 30,000, or even more. The truth is that Scripture alone does not answer many of the questions it poses. It offers no clear creed or catechesis, no fully coherent, clearly resolved corpus of doctrine. The Bible is a collection of writings, different in kind, written by different people over a long period of time, usually for certain immediate purposes. These writings are often fragmentary, sometimes apparently contradictory, always calling for interpretation. Scripture, itself, admits as much:

> 'How could I,' [understand] asks the Ethiopian of the Apostle, Philip, as he puzzles over a passage from Isaiah, 'unless I have someone to guide me?' (Ac 8:31)

Again, while Paul, in his Second Letter to Timothy, maintains that 'all Scripture is inspired by God' (2 Tm 3:16), Peter, on the other hand, insists that no interpretation of Scripture is valid unless it is prompted by the Holy Spirit (2 P 1:21).

So, from early on in my enquiry, I realised that the Protestant doctrine of *sola scriptura*, the contention that Scripture alone is the sole guide in matters of revealed truth, bristled with difficulties. These difficulties were highlighted for me by the French writer, Antonin Eymieu, in his book, *Two Arguments for Catholicism*:

> The founders of Protestantism wanted this insensate role to be played by a book that dealt with the most difficult subjects which the human mind can approach, and those most liable to be influenced by passions and prejudices; by a book composed by the most dissimilar authors, who adopted in turn every kind of literary style, from description and anecdote to the most pronounced lyrical poetry; a book filled with allusions to facts, to proverbs, to the mentality and civilisation of a different race and another age; a book written in an unknown tongue;...a book which, to be properly studied, would require a man's whole lifetime, and, moreover, a man accustomed to the severest intellectual training, possessing a knowledge of Greek, Hebrew, Aramaic...ancient history and pre-history: Yet it is claimed that it is right to say to every Christian—to the ignorant, the working-man, the house-wife, the child— 'Take this book, it will tell you everything. It is the sole teacher of truth. Listen to it alone!'

> Everyone will find it perfectly clear, for Scripture, according to Calvin, 'has the power to make itself understood, and this by a perception as manifest and infallible as that possessed by black and white objects in exhibiting their colours or by sweet and bitter things in imparting their flavour.' 'It is the most certain, the easiest and the clearest thing in the world,' said Luther of the Bible. 'Scripture is its own interpreter. It is clearness itself.' 'We must hold

this as undeniable, that it is a light ... much clearer than the sun.'

Of certain passages of Scripture this is true; but not everywhere and always ... Even the clearest passages, when passion becomes involved in them, are rendered perplexing ... Luther and Calvin saw with their own eyes their disciples wrangling blindly and furiously for and against the clearest texts of the Gospel.

Hoc est corpus meum [This is my body], for example, is a clear expression. But, before the end of the sixteenth century, (1577), the Protestants had already produced two hundred different interpretations of it! The first two words, *Hoc est*, alone gave rise to three sacramental theologies (those of Luther, Calvin, and Zwingli) mutually irreconcilable, subdivided indefinitely in their turn ... and incomprehensible to the uninitiated ...

And Luther, who had extolled the clearness of the Scriptures, and had boasted of not finding, for his part, a single difficult word in the Bible, subsequently exclaimed—passing from one extreme to the other— 'We cannot claim to fathom completely the meaning of a single verse of Scripture; we succeed in apprehending only the ABC of it, and even that imperfectly.'

And he ended by exclaiming: 'If the world is to last, there will be, in view of so many different interpretations, only one means of preserving the unity of the faith, and that will be to take refuge in the decrees of the councils.'[1]

Eventually, I came to realise that all 'private' interpretation of Scripture and all 'private' theology is speculative and without authority. Our only final ground for believing a particular doctrinal understanding (of the Sacraments, for example) to be authoritative is our faith in the prophetic discernment and judgement of the interpreting and teaching Church, operating on the given of her own prophetic word, because clearly, as the words of the Ethiopian and St Peter, quoted above, have indicated, Scripture requires the help of a power equivalent to the power which inspired it, if it is to be made intelligible and credible to all men and women.

Notes

[1]   A. Eymieu, *Two Arguments for Catholicism* (London: Burns, Oates and Washbourne Ltd, Publishers to the Holy See, 1928), pp. 70–72.

19 THE CATHOLIC CHARACTER OF THE BIBLE

Bill

NEVERTHELESS, WORKING ON the widely shared assumption that the New Testament offers the best account we have of Christianity in its infancy, and aware of the doctrinal issues, which divide Catholics from non-Catholics, for me the evidence of Scripture told emphatically for Catholicism. I saw Catholic doctrine on the Papacy, the Mass and the Sacraments jump out at me from Scripture. What had first challenged me in the manual from the Catholic Enquiry Centre expanded into an ever-clearer light. The more I read, the more Scripture seemed to teem with the doctrines of the Catholic Church, given sometimes seminally but nonetheless clearly given.

The French poet, Paul Claudel, had a similar experience. After his dramatic conversion from atheism to faith in Notre Dame Cathedral on Christmas Day, 1886; his immediate problem was, which church? So he went straight to his sister's Protestant Bible and, in no time, the question was settled for him forever.[1]

I agree with the theologians who argue that Catholicism is the true legacy of Jesus and that the Apostles guided the Church as Jesus intended. I believe that the emerging Catholic Church is already present in the age of the Apostles, without delay, directly after the death of Jesus.

What Friedrich Heiler conceded was apparent to me, not just on the most central issues such as the nature of the Church and the Sacraments, but on other matters as well.[2] For example, I became aware of the texts relating to Mary, few in number perhaps, but loaded with theological implications, as the recently canonized philosopher and convert, Edith Stein, has pointed out:

> Only a few words from the Virgin Mary have come down to us in the Gospels. But these few words are like heavy grains of pure gold. When they melt in the ardour of loving meditation, they more than suffice to bathe our entire lives in a luminous golden glow.[3]

Her point was reinforced for me by the radical, liberal theologian, Hans Kung, in his book, *The Council, Reform and Reunion*:

> What do we make of the numerous Marian passages in Scripture? Something positive and creative in theology and piety, or only something critical and defensive? Where do we stand in regard to Luther's undeniable Marian piety? ... Are Protestant Christians included or not in 'All generations shall call me blessed?' Is calling her blessed to be done only silently, only shamefacedly, only peripherally, only privately? Is it only to be taught (and often not even that) or to be lived as well? Can we raise our voices in praise of Christ without also raising them in praise of her who spoke the decisive *fiat* to Christ? Can we work at Christian theology without—though in a different way— working at Marian theology too? Considering how often it took centuries to plumb the depths of scriptural meaning, is it not possible that here too there were precious treasures lying hidden for quiet meditation and prayer to discover? ... Do we not here again need the undiminished Gospel, given its undiminished value and brought out into the full light of day?[4]

Protestants might be interested to read Luther's own eloquent defence of the Immaculate Conception.[5]

I like the phrase 'the undiminished Gospel'; it goes to the heart of my Catholic convictions, because Catholicism (and by that I mean orthodox Catholicism) is just that: the Gospel undiminished, affirmed in all its fullness, depth and integrity. It is 'the complete truth' which Christ promised would be the Holy Spirit's gift to His disciples (Jn 16:13).

In fact, what has become increasingly clear to me in the years following my conversion is that Catholic doctrine, far from being un-biblical, as many have maintained, comprehends the Bible more completely and affirmatively than any other interpreting tradition. In her understanding of the Church, the Papacy, the Sacraments (especially the Eucharist), Mary, the prescriptions of morality and spirituality, everything, in fact, in the Bible, relevant to our salvation and sanctification is gathered up, explicated and integrated into a profound and coherent whole. It is a whole which exemplifies a massive fidelity both to Scripture and to a continuous tradition spread over twenty centuries, a tradition which always seeks in Scripture an ever more, rather than a merely means which characterises certain recent fashions in biblical exegesis today.

Moreover, it is a tradition which sees in Scripture gifts, which were not just given once for Jesus' contemporaries, but which are still effectively present for us today, so that, for a Catholic, the promises Christ made to Peter are still operative in the Papacy, the Sacrifice of Calvary is made present for us in the Mass, Mary is still present as our Mother in the order of grace. Above all, Christ is still present for us in His mercy, as He absolves us through His priests in the Confessional and forgives us in the Mass and the Sacrament of the Sick. Among many Christian traditions, Catholicism is the one in which all the saving mysteries are made palpably available in the here and now of our lives.

Notes

1   J. Saward, 'Regaining Paradise: Paul Claudel And The Renewal Of Exegesis', *Downside Review* 114 (1996), p. 79.

2   Friedrich Heiler (1892–1967) was a German theologian. Born into a devout Catholic family in Munich he became a Lutheran without losing his attachment to his childhood faith.

3   Edited by L. Gelber and M. Linssen, *The Collected Works of Edith Stein: The Hidden Life: Volume Four* (Washington: ICS Publications Institute of Carmelite Studies, 1992), p. 106.

4   H. Kung, *The Council, Reform and Reunion* (London and New York: Sheed and Ward Ltd, 1961), pp. 186–187.

5   See W. Ullathorne, *The Immaculate Conception of the Mother of God* (London: Richardson and Son, 1855), pp. 137–140.

20 THE CENTRAL QUESTIONS

Bill

S O, IT WAS with this general sense of the essentially Catholic character of biblical Christianity that I began to consider the basic questions I referred to earlier: through what agencies does the revealing God give us His truth, and what is the nature of that truth?

Through What Agencies Is The Truth Given?

First, the question of agencies. This raises the fundamental question of the nature of the Church and her relationship to the Bible. All Christians agreed that there was a Church from the beginning and that it was still with us. But Catholics and non-Catholics disagreed as to its nature. What did Scripture have to say about this? Catholics and non-Catholics also disagreed about the relationship between the Church and Scripture as to which was the primary guide on matters of doctrine. Did Christ intend that we receive His truth primarily from the Bible or primarily from the Church? How did the one relate to the other?

On this most critical of questions, I soon came to the conclusion that all the evidence we have in the New Testament and early history points to the Catholic position: that it is the Petrine and Apostolic Church, the Church founded on Peter and the Apostles, which Our Lord intends to be the primary vehicle of His Gospel. If Scripture is not clear about this, then, for me, it is not clear about anything.

First, let us consider the nature of the Bible. God did not drop it from the sky. It was written over many centuries by a considerable number of men. And its authority, like that of all books, can only be as reliable as the authority of its authors. Equally true, as we have established, is that a reliable understanding of it can only be achieved through an authority we can trust to interpret it.

In fact, the Bible itself makes it clear that God never begins His revelation with the gift of a book. He begins always by calling individuals to His service. The Judaeo Christian Revelation begins with the calling of Abraham. He is our father in faith, as the Church constantly reminds us at Mass. God calls Abraham to leave his own country and go to a land that God will show him. He is told that God will make from his offspring a great nation (Israel) through which all the nations of the earth will be blessed (Gn 22:18). So, too, with Moses, who is called to be the one, who will lead Israel out of slavery in Egypt and to be her prophet, priest and law-giver. So, too, with the other prophets and kings in the Old Testament. They are all chosen, called and sent by God to be leaders of the great community, which is Israel. It is within this community that the Scriptures of the Old Testament are written, and it is within this community that they are preserved, developed and interpreted by recognised authorities.

The same principle applies to the fulfilment of revelation in Christ. It does not begin with a book. It begins with the calling of individuals: with Mary, called by God, through an angel, to be the mother of His Son; with John the Baptist, called and sent by God to prepare the way for Christ; with the disciples, in particular, Peter, called by Christ to be the leaders of the community, which will continue His work after His Ascension; with Paul, called by the risen Christ to be the light to the Gentiles (Ac 26:23).

According to the Gospels, Christ Himself wrote nothing, nor does He commission others to write. It is His disciples He commissions to go out and preach the whole message to all nations, promising to be Himself with them always until the end of time (Mt 28:20). To equip them for this mission, He promises to send them the Holy Spirit, the Spirit of truth, who will be with them forever (Jn 14:16), and who will lead them 'to the complete truth' (Jn 16:13). It is because of this assistance that He can assure them that 'Anyone who listens to you listens to me; anyone who rejects you rejects me, and those who reject me reject the one who sent me' (Lk 10:16). Through the same assistance they are assured that 'whatever you bind on earth will be bound in heaven; whatever you loose on earth will be loosed in heaven' (Mt 16:19). According to St Matthew's Gospel, this charism was conferred first on Peter and subsequently on all the disciples. Interpreted narrowly, it meant, according to rabbinical tradition, the power to exclude from (binding) or readmit (loosing) to the community. A wider interpretation sees in it the gift of legislative authority over everything necessary to the well-being of the kingdom. (This would include decisions on matters of faith and morality.)

Among the disciples, Peter is to have a position of central and vital prominence, as the Church's rock foundation, the bulwark against the powers of darkness, the holder of the keys of the kingdom, possessing singly the powers to bind and loose, which would later be conferred on them all (Mt 16:19). He is to be the centre of unity that, when converted, and, assisted by the prayer of Christ, will strengthen his brethren in crises of faith, when Satan threatens 'to sift you all like wheat' (Lk 22:31). He is to be the chief shepherd of the whole flock, who is to feed Christ's lambs and look after His sheep (Jn 21:15–7). As I have already indicated, from the time when my attention was first drawn to these texts, I have never been able to see in them anything less than a permanent and foundational gift to the Church.

The picture of the Church given in the Acts of the Apostles and the Epistles confirms that of the Gospels. It is an Apostolic Church, founded on the Apostles, the one Body of Christ (Ac 2:1–5). Indwelt and guided by the Holy Spirit from Pentecost onwards, it teaches with divine authority the Word of God' (Ac 6:4). Though indeed a pilgrim Church, which sees 'only reflections in a mirror' (1 Co 13:12), it is nonetheless, in the words of St Paul, the 'pillar and support of the truth' (1 Tm 3:15). It is led by Peter and, when it meets in council to decide a matter of importance to its own mission to the Gentiles, it is confident of the assistance of the Holy Spirit. The decision is, in fact, made 'by the Holy Spirit and by ourselves' (Ac 15:28).

The Church does, indeed, refer with reverence to the Scriptures of the Old Testament, as did Christ Himself. Time and again the Apostles, in particular Peter and Paul, use the Old Testament to show to their Jewish audience that the Scriptures have been fulfilled in Christ (Ac 13:26–33). But nowhere does the Church refer to the composition of a New Testament, which has now become the primary guide in matters of faith. After all, the oral witness to our faith, guided by the teaching Church in the Apostles, existed before its written content was recorded.

From first to last, through the Acts of the Apostles and the Epistles, it is made clear that it is the Church, founded by Christ on the Apostles, which is the prophet and custodian of revealed truth. In the Epistle to Timothy, Paul speaks of it as 'the Church of the living God, which upholds the truth and keeps it safe.'[1] (1 Tm 3:15). In the Epistle to the Corinthians, he writes of the God who in Christ was 'reconciling the world to himself' and who has 'entrust[ed] to us [the Apostles] the message of reconciliation' (2 Co 5:19). The theme is developed in the Epistle to the Ephesians, where Paul speaks of the God 'who has put all things under his [Christ's] feet and made him, as he is above all things, the head of the Church; which is his Body, the fullness of him who is filled, all in all' (Ep 1:23). Again, in the same Epistle, Paul writes, 'You are built upon the foundations of the Apostles and Prophets, and Christ Jesus himself is the corner-stone' (Ep 2:20). And of the revelation he has been entrusted with by God, he says it is a:

> Mystery... now revealed in the Spirit to his holy apostles and Prophets ... unknown to humanity in previous generations ... the mystery kept hidden through all the ages in God ...The purpose of this was, that now, through the Church, the principalities and ruling forces should learn how many-sided God's wisdom is, according to the plan which he had from all eternity in Christ Jesus, Our Lord (Ep 3:5–12).

Of this Church Paul says:

> There is one Body, one Spirit, just as one hope is the goal of your calling by God. There is one Lord, one faith, one baptism, and one God and Father of all, over all, through all and within all (Ep 4:4–6).

It is through this Church that:

> we all reach unity in faith and knowledge of the Son of God ...Then we shall no longer be children, or tossed one way and another, and carried hither and thither by every new gust of teaching, at the mercy of all the tricks people play and their unscrupulousness in deliberate deception (Ep 4:14–5).

The Church in History

Leaving Scripture and moving on to history, as I studied the early centuries in the writings of the Church Fathers, I saw the picture of the Church I had seen in the Bible developing before my eyes with its essential identity preserved intact. The ministerial nature of the Church, which was to continue down the centuries and was very soon to call itself 'the Catholic Church', became increasingly clear. It was an apostolic Church, founded on the Apostles and deriving its authority from them through a principle of succession. A moment's reflection would suffice to show that this self-perpetuation was necessary, if the Gospel was to reach the nations as God had promised (Mt 28:19) and if its truth was to be faithfully kept (Mt 28:20). It is this which assures the Catholic that he has a life-giving contact with the original Apostles through the current of succession, which goes back to the beginning. It is through it that he knows that Jesus is 'the same today as he was yesterday and as he will be for ever' (Heb 13:8), that there is 'the faith which has been once and for all entrusted to God's holy people' (Jude 1:3), and that Christ is effectively with His Church in her teaching mission 'always; yes, to the end of time' (Mt 28:20).

This principle of Apostolic Succession is there embryonically in the New Testament. When the disciple, Judas, dies, another,

Matthias, is elected to make up the twelve. After Pentecost, we see the Apostles, guided by the Holy Spirit, extending their ministry. Through the 'laying on of the Apostles' hands', they hand on the gift of the Spirit to others (Ac 8:18), and this gift has been passed on to our own day by Episcopal consecration.

In the post-apostolic Church, the principle is clearly reinforced by St Clement of Rome. Writing to the Corinthians around the year 96 AD, he says that the Apostles themselves knowing 'through our Lord Jesus Christ that there would be strife for the office of bishop,' first appointed successors 'and afterwards added the further provision that, if they should die, other approved men should succeed to their ministry.'[2]

These were the bishops, and by the second century bishops were everywhere regarded as the rightful successors of the Apostles, inheriting their authority to govern and to teach. In them, the authority, which Christ had conferred on the Apostles, a participation in His own divine authority, was seen to be still operative. Hence, St Ignatius of Antioch, addressing the Ephesians around 110 AD, writes:

> For Jesus Christ, our inseparable life is the will of the Father, just as the bishops, who have been appointed throughout the world, are the will of Jesus Christ. It is fitting, therefore, that you should live in harmony with the will of the bishop—as, indeed, you do. Let us be careful, then, if we would be submissive to God, not to oppose the bishop...For anyone whom the master of the house sends to manage his business ought to be received by us as we would receive him by whom he was sent. It is clear, then, that we must look upon the bishop as the Lord Himself.[3]

Apostolic and Petrine

Apostolic in foundation and succession, the Church was also Petrine. That is to say she regarded the Bishop of Rome, the successor of St Peter, as the centre of unity and the ultimate judge as to whether a tradition of doctrine was truly from the Apostles.

Again, a brief reflection indicates the necessity for such a principle. Any college without a head will always contain the seeds of
division within it, and the Episcopate was no exception as history
has demonstrated on a number of occasions. When such divisions
occur, how are the ordinary faithful to discern the party to trust?
For Roman Catholics over the centuries, the answer has always
been the one in communion with the Bishop of Rome, the
successor of Peter, on whom singly Our Lord conferred the
fullness of Episcopal authority (Mt 16:18–9). Hence, it is the
councils whose decisions have been ratified by the Pope, which
have come to be regarded as authoritative in the development of
Catholic Doctrine. Historically, it took the Church some time
before the full implications of the Petrine texts were appreciated.
But the notion of Petrine or Papal authority was there in germ
from very early, acknowledged by Protestant scholars, such as
Lightfoot and Harnack. It was developed in the early centuries
and abundantly recognised in the fourth and fifth centuries, the
time of the great councils.

It was already implicit in the letter of St Clement, the Bishop
of Rome, written towards the end of the first century AD.
Addressing certain dissidents among the congregation at Corinth,
he writes:

> If anyone disobey the things which have been said by Him
> [Christ] through us, let them know that they will involve
> themselves in transgression and in no small danger ... You
> will afford us joy and gladness if, being obedient to the things
> which we have written through the Holy Spirit, you will root
> out the wicked passion of jealousy, in accord with the plea
> for peace and concord which we have made in this letter.[4]

A recognition of the same special authority is also implicit in
St Ignatius of Antioch's letter to the Romans written around 110
AD: 'You have envied no one; but others you have taught.'[5]

What was implicit in the letters of St Clement and St Ignatius
was made explicit in the testimony of St Irenaeus, Bishop of Lyons
(AD 140–202). In his apologetic work, *Against Heresies*, written

in approximately 189 AD, he affirms the principle of apostolic succession as the sure guide to authentic faith, insisting that 'everyone in every Church, who may wish to know the truth' has access to it through 'those who were instituted bishops by the Apostles, and their successors to our own times.'[6]

'But,' he goes on to say:

> [S]ince it would be too long to enumerate ... the successions of all the Churches, we shall confound all those who... assemble other than where it is proper, by pointing out here the successions of the bishops of the greatest and most ancient Church known to all, founded and organised at Rome by the two most glorious Apostles, Peter and Paul, that Church which has the tradition and the faith which comes down to us after having been announced to men by the Apostles. For with this Church, because of its superior origin, all Churches must agree, that is, all the faithful in the whole world; and it is in her that the faithful everywhere have maintained the Apostolic tradition.[7]

Apostolic in Organisation: Priests and Deacons

Founded on Peter and the Apostles, the Church was, from the beginning, apostolic in organisation. Serving under the Bishops and sharing in their ministry and authority, were the priests and deacons. This three-fold hierarchical structure we find embryonically present in the New Testament and developed with increasing clarity in the post-apostolic age. It is a structure, which has been preserved throughout the Church's long history, illustrating her continuity with and fidelity to her apostolic roots. The same continuity and fidelity applies to her doctrinal traditions, ministerial and doctrinal continuity being inextricably linked. The office of deacon, together with the name, goes back to the Acts of the Apostles (Ac 6). In the New Testament and early Church, the term priest, denoting a special priestly office, (as distinct from the priesthood of all the faithful) is rarely used, the term commonly used being 'elder' in the New Testament (Ac 22:5; Ac 15:6) and 'presbyter' among the early Church Fathers. But, the notion of a special office delegated by apostolic authority and subordinate to it is clearly there.

We also find it in Paul's letter to Titus:

> The reason I left you behind in Crete was for you to organise everything that still had to be done and appoint elders in every town, in the way that I told you (Tt 1:5).

We see it again when the Church meets for its first Council in Jerusalem; its decisions are made by the Apostles and elders working together:

> Then the apostles and elders, with the whole church, decided to choose delegates from among themselves to send to Antioch with Paul and Barnabus (Ac 15:22).

Historically, this hierarchical structure can be traced back to St Clement's letter to the Corinthians, which I have already mentioned. Referring to the Apostles, he writes:

> Through countryside and city they preached; and they appointed their earliest converts ... to be the bishops and deacons of future believers.[8]

And, rebuking the dissidents in Corinth, he writes:

> Shameful ... and unworthy of your training in Christ, is the report that on account of one or two persons the well-established and ancient Church of the Corinthians is in revolt against the presbyters.[9]

In the letter of St Ignatius of Antioch to the Magnesians (AD. 110), this three-fold hierarchy is even clearer:

> Now, therefore, it has been my privilege to see you in the person of your God-inspired bishop, Damas; and in the persons of your worthy presbyters, Bassus and Apollonius, and my fellow-servant, the deacon, Zotion. What a delight is his company! For he is subject to the bishop as to the grace of God, and to the presbytery as to the law of Jesus Christ.[10]

Notes

1   We have retained this passage in its older translation from the Jerusalem Bible.

2   Clement, St, Letter to the Corinthians, *XXXXIV.* See W. A. Jurgens, *The Faith of the Early Fathers,*Vol.1 (Collegeville: The Liturgical Press, 1970), p. 10.

3   Ignatius of Antioch, St, *Letter to the Ephesians,* III, 2; V, 3 and VI, 1. *Ibid.,* pp. 17–18.

4   Clement, Letter to the Corinthians, 1, LIX–LXIII. Ibid., p. 12.

5   Ignatius of Antioch, St, *Letter to the Romans,* III, 1. *Ibid.,* p. 21.

6   Irenaeus, St, *Against Heresies,* 3, III, *Ibid.,* p. 89.

7   *Ibid.,* p. 90.

8   Clement, Letter to the Corinthians, *XXXXII, 1. Ibid.,* p. 10.

9   *Ibid.,* XXXXVII, 6 *Ibid.,* p. 11.

10 Ignatius of Antioch, St, *Letter to the Magnesians,* II. *Ibid.,* p. 19.

21 CATHOLIC AND PROTESTANT VISIONS OF THE CHURCH

Bill

T HIS CHURCH SINGLE, visible, Petrine, apostolic, self-perpetuating and hierarchically organised is very different from the conception of the Church, which developed among Protestants after the Reformation. In understandable revolt against the appalling scandals and abuses prevalent in the pre-Reformation Church, the reformers rejected the whole notion of the Catholic Church as Christ's true representative on earth, the sole covenanted prophet and custodian of His saving truth and gifts. From henceforth it was to be 'sola scriptura', 'Scripture alone'[1], which was to be the only reliable guide in matters of faith. The first article of the Calvinist Geneva Confession represents the view of all the Churches of the Reformation on this question:

> First we affirm that we desire to follow Scripture alone as rule of faith and religion, without mixing with it any other thing which might be devised by the opinion of men apart from the Word of God, and without wishing to accept for our spiritual government any other doctrine than what is conveyed to us by the same Word without addition or diminution, according to the command of our Lord.[2]

This principle is echoed in the Thirty-Nine Articles of the Church of England, which in Article Six insists that:

> Holy Scripture contain[s] all things necessary to salvation: so that whatsoever is not read therein, nor may be proved thereby, is not to be required of any man, that it should be

believed as an article of the Faith or be thought requisite
or necessary to salvation.[3]

Following this principle of 'Scripture alone', the Reformers rejected
the whole notion of apostolic authority perpetuated in the Papacy
and the Episcopate, expressed in tradition and articulated definitively in ecumenical councils. Here there was some inconsistency
in that the reformers did not reject the creeds, which had been
defined by the Catholic Church in the councils of the fourth and
fifth centuries.

Moreover, in the case of the Anglican Church and the Eastern
Orthodox Churches, the first seven councils of the Catholic
Church continued to be regarded as authoritative, though the
Thirty-Nine Articles did insist that councils 'forasmuch as they
are an assembly of men, whereof all are not governed by the Spirit
and Word of God ... may err and sometimes have erred, even in
things pertaining to God.'[4] Not only was the authority of the Pope
and the Bishops repudiated, but the whole idea of a particular
priestly office with special powers to consecrate the Eucharist,
offer sacrifice (the Mass) and absolve sinners was rejected by the
Protestants. From now on, only 'the priesthood of all believers'[5]
was to be recognised. The Church itself was no longer to be
regarded as the hierarchically governed body I have depicted, but
as simply the community of believers held together by 'true faith'
in a faithful proclamation of God's Word (that is, Scripture) and
administration of the two Sacraments, Baptism and the Lord's
Supper, as instituted by Christ.

The Augsburg Confession (1530), the definitive confession of
faith for Lutherans, maintained:

> That one holy Christian church will be and remain forever.
> This is the assembly of all believers among whom the
> gospel is preached in its purity and the holy sacraments
> are administered according to the Gospel. For it is suffi-
> cient for the true unity of the Christian church that the
> Gospel be preached in conformity with a pure understand-

ing of it and that the sacraments be administered in accordance with the divine Word.[6]

Complementing that are the words of the Calvinist Geneva Confession (1536), aimed directly at the Catholic Church:

> But inasmuch as all companies do not assemble in the name of our Lord, but rather to blaspheme and pollute him by their sacrilegious deeds, we believe that the proper mark by which we rightly discern the Church of Jesus Christ is that his holy gospel be purely and faithfully preached, proclaimed, heard and kept, that his sacrament be properly administered ... On the other hand, where the Gospel is not declared, heard and received, there we do not acknowledge the form of the Church. Hence the churches governed by the ordinances of the pope are rather synagogues of the devil than Christian churches.[7]

In rejecting the old Church model and replacing it with the new, the Reformers were repudiating an understanding, which was clearly grounded in Scripture, had persisted for over fifteen centuries, and which, in spite of conflicts, scandals, occasions of stumbling (Lk 17:1), had held Christendom together in remarkable unity. What the Reformers replaced it with was a theology, which had the seeds of dissension and disintegration rooted in its first principles. Faith in the teaching and governing authority of Bishops and Popes, based on the apostolic succession, was a clear principle with the power to unify the Church, both locally and universally, as we have seen. The consequences of 'Scripture alone' and 'faith alone' (as defined by the Reformers) were soon apparent in the fragmented Protestantism we have witnessed since the Reformation. John O'Brien in his book, *The Faith of Millions*, describes Luther's own disappointment at:

> The religious anarchy to which his own principle of the private interpretation of Scriptures had given rise: 'There are as many sects and beliefs as there are heads. This fellow will have nothing to do with Baptism; another denies the Sacrament; a third believes that there is another world

between this and the Last Day. Some teach that Christ is not God; some say this, some say that. There is no rustic so rude but that, if he dreams or fancies anything, it must be the whisper of the Holy Ghost, and he himself a prophet.'[8]

What was also lost to the Reformers was the idea, deeply present in Catholic Christianity, of the Church as the full representation of Christ on earth after His Ascension. For Catholics, the Church is not just the minister of the Word, but the extension of the Incarnation: Christ Himself still present among us through 'the Church; which is his Body, the fullness of him who is filled, all in all' (Ep 1:23). Through His Church Jesus reaches us and communicates Himself to us in all His prophetic power to sanctify and redeem. In the words of Ludwig Ott:

> Christ delegated to the Apostles the mission which He, as man, received from the Father (Jn 20:21). Christ's mission embraces His three-fold office of Redeemer. He gave them the mandate to proclaim His Gospel through the whole world (Mt 28:19; Mk 16:15), endowed them with His authority (Lk 10:16; Mt 10:40), promised them a wide power of binding and loosing (Mt 18:18), and transferred to them the sacerdotal powers of baptism (Mt 28:19), of celebrating the Eucharist (Lk 22:19), of forgiving sins (Jn 20: 23).[9]

Notes

1   'Sola Scriptura' is the belief that Scripture alone, as it appears to the subjective and undirected mind, contains all that is necessary to interpret the meaning of the Word of God and the teaching of the Church in order to achieve salvation. The concept of 'Sola Scriptura' was the foundation of the 16th century Protestant Reformation which challenged the authority of the Catholic Church.

2   *The Library of Christian Classics; Volume XXII; Calvin Theological Treatises* : The Geneva Confession of Faith: 1536: Article 1: The Word of God

3   *The Thirty-nine Articles of Religion; Church of England,* 1571. Article VI Of the Sufficiency of the Holy Scriptures for Salvation (Eternal Sun Books, 2017), p. 8.

4   Ibid XXI: Of the Authority of General Councils.

5   In 1523 Martin Luther wrote a treatise to Christians in Bohemia which expounded this concept. See C. Methuen, *Luther and Calvin: Religious Revolutionaries* (Oxford: Lion Hudson plc, 2011), pp. 100–101.

6   The Augsburg Confession VII, 1530. C.T. Knippel, *The Augsburg Confession and Its Apology* (St Louis: Concordia Publishing House, 1999), p. 66.

7   *The Library of Christian Classics; Volume XXII; Calvin Theological Treatises*: The Geneva Confession of Faith: 1536: Article XVIII: The Church.

8   Luther writing in 1525. See J. A. O'Brien, *The Faith Of Millions: The Credentials Of The Catholic Religion* (London: W. H. Allen and Co. Ltd, 1962), p. 185.

9   L. Ott, *Fundamentals of Catholic Dogma* (Cork: The Mercier Press, 1960), p. 277.

22 CHURCH AND SCRIPTURE

Bill

O N THE CENTRAL question as to whether it is the Church or Scripture, which we take as our guide in matters of faith, what I eventually came to realise was that God does not give us His truth either through the Church or Scripture in isolation from one another, but through both in a profound and indissoluble relationship. For Catholics, the key principle for theological understanding is not Scripture alone, but Scripture as read by the Church. (As a matter of fact, there is, strictly speaking, no such thing as 'Scripture alone.' What all Christian bodies, both Catholic and non-Catholic, offer is Scripture interpreted. So, the question of the legitimacy of the interpreting agent, whether it be Lutheran, Calvinist, Anglican, Eastern Orthodox or Roman Catholic, is always of fundamental importance.)

I have already indicated that the revealing God always begins His self-disclosure, not with a book, but with individuals and communities called into discipleship. It is within these communities that the Bible is written, and, for Catholics as for Jews, this relationship between book and community is never broken. It is only within the community that the book can be fully understood. It is helpful here to begin with Jesus, the Word Incarnate, the Founder of the Church. Throughout His ministry, He appeals to the divine authority of the Scriptures of the Old Testament. In St Matthew's Gospel, He tells Jewish religious leaders that God was speaking to them through the Scriptures: 'Have you never read in the scriptures' (Mt 21:42). Again, in St John's Gospel, He refers to the Old Testament as a certain confirmation of His divine mission: 'You pore over the Scriptures ... it is these scriptures that testify to me' (Jn 5:39). And in Luke's account of the walk to Emmaus, after His Resurrection, Jesus points to all that was written of Him through Moses and the Prophets (Lk 24:27). Significantly, in these statements and others, Our Lord is saying that Scripture can only be fully understood in relationship to Himself. So He is, in effect, establishing the principle that Scripture needs an interpreter, in this case Himself. Without that interpreter, Scripture does not shed its full light. The Old Covenant can only be understood in the light of the New.

This principle is acknowledged and developed in the apostolic Church. It is one of the key motives of credibility in her evangelisation. She, too, constantly appeals to the authority of the Old Testament. On the day of Pentecost, for instance, in his first sermon, Peter appeals to some words of David, which, he claims, foretell Christ's Resurrection (Ac 2:25), and also to the words of the prophet, Joel, which, he maintains, are now being fulfilled in the miraculous outpouring of the Holy Spirit (Ac 2:16–21). St Stephen, before he is stoned to death, appeals to the prophecy of Moses, which speaks of the supreme prophet who is to come: 'From among your own brothers God will raise up a prophet like me' (Ac 7:37). Time and again, St Paul, on his missionary journeys, argues with a Jewish audience that their Scriptures point unmistakably to Christ. In fact, throughout the Acts and the Epistles, the principle is clearly articulated that it is through the Scriptures read, appropriated and understood by the Church that God gives us His definitive light in Christ. This is made very clear in the story of the Ethiopian to which I have referred. He is reading Scripture, but is unable to make sense of it until he is enlightened by the Apostle, Philip, who shows him that the passage he is troubled by points to Christ.

> 'How could I, [understand] unless I have someone to guide me?' he says (Ac 8:31).

According to his second letter to Timothy, St Paul clearly believes that 'All Scripture is inspired by God' (2 Tm 3:16), but St Peter, in his second letter, insists 'that the interpretation of scriptural prophecy is never a matter for the individual.' Why? 'For no prophecy ever came from human initiative. When people spoke for God it was the Holy Spirit that moved them' (2 Pt 1:21). This is the Spirit, which Christ promised to His disciples, as an abiding presence which would lead them into 'the complete truth' (Jn 16:13), enabling them to regard the Church as 'God's family...the Church of the living God, which upholds the truth and keeps it safe'[1] (1 Tm 3:15).

This implied confidence, among the Apostles, in the relationship between the Holy Spirit, Scripture and the Church has remained in Catholic Christianity down the centuries from the beginning. It is the source of the Church's trust in tradition, which keeps the Christian people faithful to the apostolic truth, assured that Jesus Christ is 'the same today as he was yesterday and as he will be forever' (Heb 13:8), and also of her absolute confidence in the decisions of the Church in Council, which have resolved the great doctrinal disputes. The necessary bond between Scripture and Church was articulated very early by St Irenaeus in his treatise, *Against Heresies*, in which he takes it for granted that every Christian diligently reads the Scriptures in company with the priests in the Church with whom lies apostolic doctrine.[2] The relationship was powerfully confirmed by the Church in the Second Vatican Council document *Dei Verbum*:

> Sacred Tradition, then, and holy Scripture are closely joined and connected, each with the other. Both spring from the same divine fountain, and so in some manner merge into a unity, and tend towards the same end. For holy Scripture is the utterance of God, in so far as it was written down under the Holy Spirit's inspiration; while sacred Tradition hands on in its entirety the word of God, that was committed to the apostles, by Christ Our Lord and the Holy Spirit to their successors, in order that being enlightened by the light of the Spirit of Truth, they may in their preaching faithfully preserve, set forth and dissemi-

nate it. In this way it comes about that the Church does not derive from holy Scripture alone the certainty she possesses on all revealed truths. Therefore both Scripture and Tradition should be accepted with equal sentiments of devotion and reverence.[3]

This unifying bond between Scripture, Tradition and Church authority is neatly summarised in the recently published pocket edition of the *Catechism of the Catholic Church*:

Scripture, Tradition and the Magisterium are so closely united with each other that one of them cannot stand without the others. Working together, each in its own way under the action of the one Holy Spirit, they all contribute effectively to the salvation of souls.[4]

In this connection, the situation of the Church in Council is illuminating, whether we think of Church as the Roman Catholic Church or as one of the Churches of the Reformation. In either case, the principle of 'Scripture alone' is clearly inadequate, because all the important conciliar decisions, both Catholic and Protestant, represent an ecclesial discernment and judgement, which appeals not to 'Scripture alone' but to one interpretation of Scripture as distinct from another. For Catholics, this is no more true of the conciliar decisions, which gave us the creeds of Nicea, Constantinople and Chalcedon against the Arians, than the doctrinal decisions on Justification and the Sacraments made at Trent against the Reformers. The same is true of the councils of the Reformation, which articulated the doctrines of Protestantism; their appeal was not in effect to 'Scripture alone' but to Scripture as they interpreted it in opposition to the Catholic understanding. The difference between the decisions of Trent and those made by the councils of the Reformation was that Trent offered an ecclesial reading of Scripture with centuries of tradition behind it,[5] whereas the Reformers could only offer a late, new reading, what Edmund Campion called 'upstart'[6] sentiments, without any substantial, traditional support. Hence, the Catholic position would seem to confirm Christ's promise to be an abiding presence in the Church in her teaching mission; the position of the Reformers is fraught with difficulty in this respect.

Notes

1   We have retained this passage in its older translation from the Jerusalem Bible.
2   Irenaeus, *Against Heresies,* 4, XXXIII. Jurgens, *The Faith of the Early Fathers: Vol.1,* p. 97.
3   *Dogmatic Constitution On Divine Revelation, Dei Verbum* (Catholic Truth Society: Publishers to the Holy See), p. 15.
4   *Compendium of the Catechism of the Catholic Church* (London: Catholic Truth Society: Publishers to the Holy See, 2006), p. 26.
5   Fourth Session, Decree Concerning The Canonical Scriptures. See H. J. Schroeder, *The Canons and Decrees of the Council of Trent* (Charlotte: Tan Books, 2011), pp.17–20.
6   E. Campion, St, *Ten Reasons Proposed To His Adversaries For Disputation In The Name Of The Faith And Presented To The Illustrious Members Of Our University* (London: The Manresa Press, 1914), p. 97.

23 THE NATURE OF JUSTIFICATION

Bill

THE SECOND PROBLEM I felt I had to resolve was the nature of the Church's message. It was a problem inextricably linked to the first one about the relationship between the Church and Scripture, as I hope to show. Convinced that the Church was apostolic in foundation, in succession and in organisation, I had to be equally sure that she was apostolic in faith. Christ had commissioned His disciples to go out and preach the Gospel to every person (Mk 16:15). But what was that Gospel? All Christians agreed that it was a Gospel of salvation, of God's saving love for fallen humankind and radically alienated from Him; but they disagreed seriously about its content. Granted that Christ came into the world to save sinners, how is that salvation, won for us on Calvary, to be applied to each of us? In what does salvation or 'justification,' to use the more technical term, consist? This question was the principal bone of contention between Catholics and Protestants at the Reformation. 'If we had not this article [the doctrine of justification by faith alone] certain and clear,' said Luther, in his *Table Talk*, 'it were impossible we could criticise the pope's false doctrine ... and other abominable errors'.[1] And at the Council of Trent, a central preoccupation of the Bishops was to clarify the Catholic tradition on the matter, in opposition to the teaching of the Reformers.[2]

Now, the first thing that struck me in approaching this question was that 'Scripture alone' does not answer it clearly. The biblical teaching on justification is scattered, fragmentary and often apparently contradictory. There are texts, particularly in John's Gospel and the Epistles of St Paul, which might suggest that faith alone is sufficient to save us. Others suggest that faith must be accompanied by baptism (Mk 16:17). Again, others stress the necessity of repentance (Lk 13:1–9). According to Mark, Christ begins His proclamation of the kingdom with the exhortation to 'Repent, and believe the Good News' (Mk 1:15).[3] On the day of Pentecost, Peter affirms all three; those who have accepted his message of Christ crucified and risen are invited to repent and be baptised. Elsewhere, we are told it is not enough to believe, repent and be baptised; not all those who cry 'Lord, Lord' will enter the kingdom, only those who do the will of God (Mt 7:21). Indeed, the vision of the Last Judgement in Matthew might suggest that it will be our good works alone which will decide our fate before God. It is those who feed the hungry, clothe the naked, visit the sick and the imprisoned who will be welcomed into the kingdom (Mt 25:31–46), a passage which Luther would seem to have ignored in his insistence on faith alone.

Again, particularly in St John's Gospel, the vital importance of the Sacraments as foundational to our hope of salvation is emphasised. Our Lord tells Nicodemus that 'No one can enter the kingdom of God without being born through water and the Spirit' (Jn 3:5). This is complemented later in the Gospel by His teaching on the Eucharist when we are told that if we 'do not eat the flesh of the Son of man and drink His blood' we will 'have no life' in us (Jn 6: 53). Moreover, according to St John's Gospel, Christ's first gift to His disciples after His Resurrection was the transfer to them of His own authority to absolve sinners or refuse absolution. It is difficult for me to understand how many Christians cannot see the Sacrament of Reconciliation, at least in embryo, in this text (Jn 20:23).

Nevertheless, despite these texts, there are passages in St Paul's Epistles, which, taken out of context, might seem to imply that our salvation is grounded in faith alone. Read selectively, they might even suggest that we are not bound to keep the Mosaic Law:

> The promise to Abraham and his descendants that he should inherit the world was not through the Law, but through the uprightness of faith (Rm 4:13).

Again, later in the same Epistle, he insists that it is faith, which guarantees our salvation:

> So far then we have seen that, through Our Lord Jesus Christ, by faith we are judged righteous and at peace with God, since it is by faith and through Jesus that we have entered this state of grace in which we can boast about looking forward to God's glory (Rm 5:1–3).[4]

And yet in the Epistle of James we are told that faith without good deeds is useless; it is in fact 'if good deeds do not go with it...quite dead' (Jm 2:17). Hence, Luther, on his own initiative, dismissed the Epistle as 'a work of straw.'[5]

St John, on the other hand, places great emphasis on love of God and neighbour as the key to our salvation:

> Whoever fails to love does not know God, because God is love (1 Jn 4:8).

And:

> Anyone who says, 'I love God' and hates his brother is a liar, since no one who fails to love the brother whom he can see can love God whom he has not seen (1 Jn 4:20).

This seems to echo Our Lord's words about the two commandments of love, which are the fulfilment of the law (Mt 22:36–40). John is also supported here by St Paul in his Epistle to the Corinthians, where he says, in apparent contradiction to what he says elsewhere, that love is the greatest of the virtues, the one which endures when faith and hope have passed away. Without it, no amount of faith and good works will save us (1 Co 13:13).

Among these apparent confusions is the whole question of the part played by the Mosaic Law in our salvation. Christ Himself insists that He has not come to destroy the Law but to fulfil it:

> Do not imagine that I have come to abolish the Law or the
> Prophets. I have come not to abolish but to complete them
> (Mt 5:17).

But St Paul, on the other hand, in his Epistle to the Romans, seems
at one point to suggest that the Law no longer has a part to play
in our salvation. With the coming of Christ, he appears to say,
we are no longer under the law; we are saved through faith:

> [A]s we see it, a person is justified by faith and not by doing
> what the Law tells him to do (Rm 3:28).

But later, in the very same passage, he seems to contradict himself:

> Are we saying that the Law has been made pointless by
> faith? Out of the question; we are placing the Law on its
> true footing (Rm 3:31).

The comments of Jacques Maritain on these apparent contradictions are very illuminating:

> That man should thus always be held to the works of the
> Decalogue and that he is, nevertheless, saved by faith; that he
> should be freed by faith from the regimen of the Law whose
> moral prescriptions he is nevertheless required to fulfil-that
> is the central problem which Paul had here to solve, and
> which, in the course of centuries, has put great religious
> thinkers to the test. Many of them have stumbled over the
> problem because in this or that they have parted company
> with Paul. Here is not only a problem to be solved by a correct
> arrangement of concepts; it is also a mystery to be penetrated
> even more deeply by the intelligence of contemplation.[6]

Here, surely, Maritain puts his finger on the nature of all doctrinal
problems, which have bedevilled Christians down the centuries.
They are not solved ultimately through man's intellectual
resources, but through a contemplative docility to the Holy Spirit.

Central to everything the New Testament has to say about
justification is the question we have been considering, the
question of the Church. It is clear from the words of Jesus in the
Gospels and from those of the Apostles in Acts and the Epistles

that the Church has a central part to play in God's plan for our salvation. We are not saved as isolated individuals, but as members of the community Christ established during His ministry and confirmed at Pentecost with the outpouring of the Holy Spirit. It is within this community, which St Paul calls the Body of Christ, that the saving truth and gifts, the mysteries of faith, are made accessible to the faithful.

Moreover, Scripture makes it clear that we receive these gifts, not just through our membership of the Church, like the gifts we receive through our membership of a club, but through a mysterious incorporation in it. In fact, salvation is affected through a two-fold incorporation: incorporation through Christ made possible through incorporation in the Church.

Monsignor Gilbey, in his book *We Believe*, a reflection on the old Penny Catechism, develops this, recalling the descent of the Holy Spirit on the Apostles at Pentecost:

> When the Holy Spirit came, on the first Pentecost, it was with the twofold effect we have noticed: the personal indwelling of individuals (shown by the parted tongues of fire) and the corporate effect of uniting them in a single body of which the same Holy Spirit is the soul. And since He comes as the gift of the Word Incarnate from Whose fullness we have all received, we become one with Christ in the Holy Spirit. We form one mystical body with Him, He the head, we His members.[7]

In other words, we are saved, according to Monsignor Gilbey, through our solidarity with Christ, effected through our solidarity with the Church. This necessary incorporation is developed in the discourse at the Last Supper, where Our Lord compares His relationship with His disciples to the relationship between the vine and its branches. The true Christian is not simply one who believes in Christ, but one who is engrafted onto Him, who lives by His life:

> Remain in me, as I in you. As a branch cannot bear fruit all by itself, unless it remains part of the vine, neither can you

unless you remain in me. I am the vine, you are the branches. Whoever remains in me, with me in him, bears fruit in plenty; for cut off from me you can do nothing (Jn 15:4–5).

In brief, we become one living, growing, organic reality with Him.

According to Scripture, there are at least two other virtues, which have an important part to play in the state of justification. First of all, there is hope, which Paul mentions in his wonderful reflection on love. It is clearly, for Paul, a virtue, which he regards as foundational in the spiritual life, but subordinate to love, which will abide, when faith and hope have passed away (1 Co 13:13).

The second virtue is fear of the Lord, one of the gifts of the Holy Spirit, mentioned in both Testaments (Lk 1:50). I will deal with these virtues later when I try to resolve the problem of apparent contradictions in the biblical data.

Finally, a word, which is repeated in the New Testament in connection with justification, is the word 'grace'. It is made very clear that our hope of salvation lies ultimately, not in any merit of our own, but in the 'grace' of God, given to us in Christ. In the Prologue to his Gospel, St John speaks of the 'Word' that has been 'made flesh', whose glory we have seen, 'the glory that he has from the Father as only Son of the Father, full of grace and truth' (Jn 1:14). This grace, according to John, He has communicated to us:

> Indeed from his fullness we have, all of us, received—yes, grace in return for grace, since, though the Law was given through Moses, grace and truth have come through Jesus Christ (Jn 1:16).[8]

This is a principal theme of St Paul, who tells us in the Epistle to the Romans, that it is 'by faith and through Jesus that we have entered this state of grace in which we can boast about looking forward to God's glory' (Rm 5:1–2).[9] And, in the Second Epistle to Timothy, he speaks of 'the power of God who has saved us and called us to be holy—not because of anything we ourselves had done but for his own purpose and by his own grace' (2 Tm 1:9). As to what is meant precisely by the key word, 'grace', 'Scripture alone' does not appear to offer a clear explanation, though there are clues.

The fact of the matter is that 'Scripture alone' offers no clear answer to the most crucial question which lies at the heart of Scripture: what must a human being do to be saved? This fundamental problem makes it clear to me that Scripture can never be the sole vehicle of the Gospel. The proliferation of Protestant sects since the Reformation, many offering different solutions to the problem, is a confirmation of that truth. In fact, as we have said, there is no such thing as 'Scripture alone' in Christian history. From the early centuries, up to the Reformation and beyond, to our own time, all theology, Catholic and non-Catholic, is based on Scripture interpreted, so reliable agencies of discernment are always as important as Scripture itself.

A decisive factor for me in becoming a Catholic and remaining one was that the Catholic Church does really solve, in a profound and convincing manner, the problem indicated here, by offering a doctrine of justification, which comprehends and integrates all the fragmentary, apparently contradictory doctrines of Scripture into a meaningful whole. Without dealing with all the non-Catholic theologies, some of which have been modified over the centuries, I would suggest this about them: most of them are selective in what they regard as important, some putting the emphasis on faith, others on love, others on a moral life, active in good works. Some have a low doctrine of the Sacraments, not regarding them as crucial; others have a high one, believing them to be essential. None offers a fully comprehensive doctrine, which embraces all that Scripture has to say about the part played by Church, grace, preaching, faith, hope, love, fear of God, repentance, Sacraments, commandments and good works in the working out of our salvation.

Only the Catholic Church achieves this in, for example, The Council of Trent's tremendous response to the teaching of the Reformers.[10] 'The reason why Catholic tradition is a tradition is because there is only one living doctrine in Christianity...The life of the Church is the life of God Himself, poured out into the Church by His Spirit,'[11] wrote Thomas Merton in *The Seeds of Contemplation*, and here that truth is profoundly illustrated in Trent's wonderful synthesis of the whole biblical data, a synthesis which unified Catholic theology for centuries. In contrast to this, the Reformers' teaching on justification was, from the beginning, subjective, selective and deeply divisive.

Significantly, in their introduction to the question, the Bishops of Trent emphasise the solid ground on which the Church's position rests.[12] The credibility of doctrine is always inseparable from the credibility of its imponent. As Ian Ker points out, in *Newman and the Fullness of Christianity*, the primary question in approaching matters of doctrinal controversy is not which of the alternatives is true, but which of the disputants has been sent.[13] Or, as Scripture says: 'How will there be preachers if they are not sent?' (Rm 10:15) Of this more later.

So, in acknowledgement of this principle, Trent insists that its aim is to expound the true doctrine of justification which Jesus Christ, the author and finisher of our faith taught, which the Apostles transmitted and which the Catholic Church, under the inspiration of the Holy Ghost, has always retained.[14] In other words, her understanding in this, as in all matters, is grounded in the authority of Christ, transmitted to the Catholic and Apostolic Church, which is always guided in matters of faith by the Holy Spirit. For Catholics true faith is always ecclesial, never private.

Next, scrupulously faithful to the biblical data of both the Old and New Testaments, the Church affirms the impotency of fallen humanity, despite being given the law, to liberate himself from the sinful state in which through the victory of the devil he finds himself.[15] This liberation is always the work of God's grace, which the Church understands to be the action of the Holy Spirit on our minds and hearts and wills. This 'pre-disposing grace'[16] is offered to us unmerited, as a free gift, on God's initiative. It comes to us through 'hearing'[17] those who have been mandated by the Church to preach. And this hearing, assisted by the Holy Spirit, prompts us to make the first act of faith which means 'believing to be true what has been divinely revealed and promised, especially that the sinner is justified by God by his grace, through the redemption that is in Christ Jesus'.[18]

This first act of faith is accompanied by acts of fear, hope, love and repentance as the sinner realises the gravity of his situation and 'turns from the fear of divine justice' to hope in God's mercy, 'trusting that God will be propitious' to him 'for Christ's sake'; and to love of God 'as the fountain of all justice';[19] and finally to a repentance which involves a deep aversion to sin and the resolution to be baptised and begin a new life of fidelity to God's commandments.

After these preparatory acts, the state of justification is established in us, again through grace, this time sanctifying grace, which is an abiding presence of the Holy Spirit within us, providing that we don't extinguish it through serious sin. It is given to us initially through the Sacrament of Baptism,[20] and subsequently strengthened and nourished through the other Sacraments, in particular through Confirmation and the Eucharist. If we diminish it or lose it through sin, it can always be recovered through the Sacrament of Reconciliation.[21] It is a grace which, if we cooperate with it, will regenerate us, recreate us from within, making us into 'a new creation' (2 Co 5:17), giving us a share in the life of God Himself.[22] Through it we become God's adopted children, members of Christ in His Body the Church, capable of a deeper sustained life of faith, hope, repentance and of love, fruitful in good works. Deeper, because we no longer live out of the resources of our poor selves, but through Christ living and acting within us through His Spirit. The justified soul can echo the words of St Paul: 'I am alive; yet it is no longer I, but Christ living in me' (Ga 2:20). The Mosaic Decalogue is still valid, 'Not one dot, not one little stroke, is to disappear from the Law until all its purpose is achieved' (Mt 5:18), but the commandments are no longer a matter of cold rules written on stone, but a law of love, a joyful and generous fidelity to the charity which

God's Spirit has poured into our hearts,[23] providing us with an interior spring of living water which assures us that we will never thirst again (Jn 4:14).

My own experience of conversion followed exactly the doctrine proposed at Trent, both in the preparatory acts of faith, hope, aversion to sin, love, and in the extraordinary sense of liberation, renewal and new enabling which followed upon my Baptism, (conditional, as I had been baptised as a Protestant) first Confession and first Communion. The experience was extraordinary in its intensity and duration at the time, and is always to some extent repeated whenever I go to Confession and Communion. To read the Council of Trent on justification is like reading the most important chapter in my own life story. I recognise what Chesterton meant when he wrote that he always felt 'five minutes old'[24] after he had been to Confession.

It is interesting to me that Luther, before his break with Rome, felt no sense of liberation or consolation from the Sacraments; his sense of sin was so overpowering and crippling.[25] It was only the experience of fiducial faith, offered to him, he believed, in St Paul's Epistle to the Romans, an eruption of hope, which released him. With myself, it was the exact opposite. What faith I had as a Protestant never effected in me a serious sense of sin, of its gravity, its threat to the soul, of the need for radical repentance, of liberation from it. It was only when I encountered Catholic moral and sacramental doctrine that I perceived my own indigence and, through the Sacraments, experienced the release, reorientation and inner renewal, which they can affect.

In fact, the older I get and the more I reflect, the more the Church's teaching on Original Sin and justification corresponds to my own experience and my perception of the world. I experience my own sinfulness, not just as a perverse choosing, seeing the right path but taking the wrong one, but as something I intrinsically am: sin prone, governed by appetite and pride, 'a zoo of lusts, a bedlam of ambitions'[26] to use the phrase C. S. Lewis used to describe himself before his conversion. In St Paul's words:

> The Law, of course, as we all know, is spiritual; but I am unspiritual; I have been sold a slave to sin. I cannot understand my own behaviour; I fail to carry out the things I want to do, and I find myself doing the very things I hate (Rm 7:15–16).[27]

Similarly, the experience of conversion and the continuous experience offered by the Church in her teaching and sacramental life does hopefully effect a radical inner transformation and elevation, the new creation which St Paul describes (2 Co 5:17).

This succinct statement of Trent must be one of the most profoundly prophetic statements in the Church's history. It offers, not only a satisfying resolution to the biblical problem in its wonderful integration of the whole data, but an accurate diagnosis of the human condition which anyone with eyes to see ought to appreciate. It shows us men and women as we have revealed ourselves historically, and as we show ourselves today: as alienated from God or from any absolute values, at odds with ourselves and with the world, thrown, adrift, in need of radical reorientation, and the compasses moral and spiritual that can provide it; and, above all, the inner motivation, energy, nourishment which can effect and sustain it.

For me, Trent on justification[28] offers the perfect paradigm for all theological problems and their resolution. It is the supreme illustration of the prophetic discernment of the Church. It exemplifies the Church's fidelity to the whole biblical data, as it has been ecclesially read from the beginning, and this fidelity and comprehensiveness are characteristic of all Catholic doctrine on all questions. Catholicism, contrary to what many Christians believe, is the Bible fully comprehended, explicated, integrated and affirmed. This is true, not only of her understanding of justification, but of her theology of Christ, Our Lady, the moral and spiritual life. Nothing in the Bible on any of these matters eludes the scrutiny and embrace of the interpreting and teaching Church. Of this fidelity, Francois Mauriac writes in *The Stumbling Block*:

> At a time like this the only thing we Christians can do is
> to confront our appalling world with the Catholic Church,
> that ancient vessel of antique shape, still laden with the
> cargo of Truth, nothing of which, for nineteen centuries,
> it has allowed to escape into those waters of slime and
> darkness upon which it rides.[29]

And, again, in the same book, Mauriac writes of the fidelity of the
Catholic Church to the Church of the Fathers:

> When that day comes in which flock will the risen Fathers
> of the oldest Christian generation be ranged? In the one,
> I do not doubt, in which they will find intact that treasure
> of the faith which was received from the Apostles, and has
> been safeguarded to the end only by the Catholic Church.[30]

When Luther, in opposition to the Catholic tradition, claimed
that 'Scripture alone' and 'faith alone' were the keys to our
salvation, he was not, in effect, affirming the truth about either
Scripture or faith; what he was affirming was Luther alone, in
opposition to the whole Bible and fifteen centuries of faithful
reflection on it.

It is a sad irony that the Churches, which began with a rush to
the Bible, insisting on it as the sole reliable agent of Revelation,
have seen that Bible wither in their hands under the corrosive
effect of critical biblical scholarship and radical theology. It has
become for some of them a Bible that can only offer a low
Christology, a low Mariology, (sometimes none at all) a low
soteriology, and a vague and confused ecclesiology. By contrast,
orthodox Catholicism, operating within the Apostolic tradition,
has continued to advance in theological conviction, confirming,
clarifying and amplifying the doctrine of Trent and crowning
Tridentine faith with the two Mariological dogmas: The Immaculate Conception in1854 and The Assumption in 1950. And with
the dogmas of ecclesial and papal infallibility as defined by the
First Vatican Council.

There is a continuous advance in the development of Catholic
doctrine, while at the same time this doctrine is continuously faithful

to the original deposit of the faith, the faith entrusted to the saints. It is a development that derives from and recognizes a principle which Cardinal Newman describes as immutability in progress.[31]

The truths from which the Church derives her life emerge gradually into the light of day and clarify themselves. They need time to reach the fullness of their self-realization. They grow from their pregnancy into a self-authenticating maturity. This exemplifies the principle of doctrinal development. True to this gradual awakening of her inherited potential the Church has defined the nature of God in the Blessed Trinity and also the Blessed human nature of Jesus in its relationship with His own Godhead. From this perspective the Church has been able to describe the nature of humankind and our radical need for grace through the holy Sacraments, together with the Sacrifice of the Mass. True to this principle, the Church has defined the role of Mary the Mother of Jesus and the privileges which accompany her unique status. Mary shared her human nature with her son so that as a man He came from her, depended upon her and resembled her. The Church has also clarified her teaching on the Pope who uniquely shares the authority of Jesus as leader of the Church.

This is a thesis that Newman was to develop in *The Development of Christian Doctrine*. Of this more later.

Faith

At the heart of the problem of justification at the time of the Reformation and since was the question of faith itself. Both Catholics and the Reformers were in agreement that faith was foundational to our salvation. Both would have accepted St Paul's teaching that it is initially faith and not anything we have done for ourselves which gives us access to the state of grace which justifies us before God:

> Because it is by grace that you have been saved, through faith; not by anything of your own, but by a gift from God (Ep 2:8).

But there were serious disagreements about the nature and content of that faith, and the disagreements, though hopefully modified in recent years, are still with us. They are apparent, not only between Catholics and Protestants, but also between liberals and conservatives within the Catholic and non-Catholic Churches.

If I understand it correctly, the Protestant tradition has always understood faith as something deeply personal and subjective. It is essentially a trust in the Person of Christ as distinct from beliefs about Him. Central to this is a confident trust in His forgiveness and saving power, both offered to humankind on the Cross. To use the language of theology, it is fiducial faith, as distinct from confessional or dogmatic faith (belief in doctrines), which saves us. For the Reformers, the faith that justifies is not to be distinguished from the resolute confidence (fiducia) of the believing heart in the forgiveness of God that is given to us in Christ, notwithstanding the fact that we continue to be sinners. Or as *the Lutheran Augsburg Confession* of 1530 says:

> We receive forgiveness of sin and become righteous before God by grace, for Christ's sake, through faith, when we believe that Christ suffered for us and that for His sake our sin is forgiven and righteousness and eternal life are given to us. For God will regard and reckon this faith as righteousness, as Paul says in Romans 3:21–26 and 4:5.[32]

And later:

> The conscience cannot come to rest and peace through works but only through faith, that is when it is assured and knows for Christ's sake it has a gracious God as Paul says in Romans 5:1: Since we are justified by faith we have peace with God.[33]

These sentiments are echoed in the Calvinist Geneva Convention which defines faith as:

> [a] certain confidence and assurance of heart through which we believe in the promises of the Gospel and receive

> Jesus Christ as he is offered to us by the Father and
> described to us by the Word of God [that is Scripture].[34]

For a Catholic, true faith possesses these elements but it involves much more. It is a belief, prompted and sustained by the Holy Spirit, in the whole work of the revealing God, given through His Christ and through His Church. According to the Council of Trent, the justification of adults begins when 'Aroused and aided by divine grace, receiving 'faith ... from hearing' (Rm 10:17) [that is hearing those who have been sent by the Church], they are moved freely towards God, believing to be true what has been divinely revealed and promised, especially that the sinner is justified by God *'By the free gift of his grace, through being set free in Christ Jesus'* (Rm 3:24).[35] This understanding is confirmed by The First Vatican Council, which defined faith in the following words:

This faith which is

> [t]he beginning of human salvation the Catholic Church
> acknowledges to be a supernatural virtue whereby
> impelled and sustained by grace, we believe those things
> to be true, which God has revealed, not because we have
> perceived the intrinsic truth of these things by the light of
> our natural reason, but on the authority of God Himself
> who reveals them, who can neither deceive or be deceived.
> For faith, as the Apostle says, 'Is the substance of things
> hoped for, the evidence of things not seen' (Heb 11:1).[36]

Again, as in her understanding of justification as a whole, the Catholic conception of faith illustrates the integral comprehensiveness of Catholic doctrine, its fidelity to the whole biblical testimony. It embraces what the fiducial faith of Protestants affirms, in insisting on absolute confidence in the authority of the revealing God in His truth gift, as well as absolute trust in the mercy and forgiveness of God offered through the redemption that is in Jesus Christ (Rm 3:24). Faith in God's revealed truth is expressed every week by Catholics at Mass when they say the Creed; trust in the mercy and saving power of Christ every time they receive the Sacraments of Communion and Reconciliation with the appropriate dispositions.

A charge sometimes made by Protestants against the Catholic understanding of faith is that it is too impersonal. It involves beliefs *about* Christ rather than belief *in* Him as Person. Certain older catechisms in which the Faith is proposed in a dry and formulaic way might seem to support this view. But it has never been wholly true, not in the Fathers, the apostolic tradition, the theologians, the saints and the millions of ordinary believers. And it is certainly not the understanding given in the new *Catechism of the Catholic Church*, where faith is defined as 'a personal adherence of man to God. At the same time, and inseparably, *it is a free assent to the whole truth that God has revealed.'*[37] Again: '"to believe" has thus a twofold reference: to the person and to the truth: to the truth, by trust in the person who bears witness to it.'[38]

So, besides being personal and fiducial, faith for a Catholic means commitment, not just to the Person of Jesus and the saving power of His Cross, but to the Church's whole word in matters of doctrine, morality and spirituality. It is confessional as well as personal and fiducial. When converts are received into the Church, this is the act of faith, simple but comprehensive, they are asked to make: faith in all that the Catholic Church teaches. It is the act of faith believers make every Sunday, when they recite the Creed, which affirms the foundational truths of the Church's faith as Trinitarian, Christological, Ecclesial, sacramental and, by implication, doctrinal. This was the act of faith catechumens were asked to make in the early years of the Church before they were received into membership.

For Catholics, Jesus, as the object of faith, is not something privately extracted from Scripture. It is something received from the community, because they believe that Jesus is present and incarnate in His Church through His Spirit and gives the whole of His revelation through her. Hence, the orthodox Catholic cannot be accused of picking and choosing, of what has come to be called 'cafeteria theology.' The Jesus, who invites confident trust (fiducial faith), when He says: 'Come to me, all you who labour and are overburdened, and I will give you rest' (Mt 11:28) and 'And when I am lifted up from the earth, I shall draw all people to myself' (Jn 12:32), this same Jesus invites ecclesial faith, when He says: 'Thou art Peter and on this rock I will build my Church' (Mt 16:18); and confessional faith when He says: '[I]f you do not eat the flesh of the Son of Man and drink his blood, you have no life in you' (Jn 6:53). When we speak of faith in Jesus, we cannot separate Him from His teachings, or from the teachings of the apostolic Church to which He repeatedly commits Himself, or select from within them. If we do, the object of our faith becomes ultimately not the Word of God, but what Newman in *Loss and Gain* calls 'the measure of Scripture' and 'some view of things in [the] mind',[39] and perhaps, we might add, rooted in our own psychology, in our mutable and questionable subjective preferences. Such a notion of faith is utterly at odds with what we find in the New Testament, where faith always involves assent to all the utterances of the One, who is 'the way, the truth and the life' (Jn 14:6), and to those of the Church, which, in the words of the Apostle, is the Body of Christ (1 Co 12:12–4), the 'pillar and support of the truth' (1 Tm 3:15).

So true faith for a Catholic means unconditional, fully committed assent to the whole Word of God in Revelation, as proposed by the Church, which is Christ's representative on earth. It is not a selection from within it, chosen by the individual believer. As such, it is certainly personal and fiducial, but also and always Trinitarian, Christological, ecclesial and doctrinal.

The perfect model for this faith is Mary's faith. At the Annunciation, she believes all that God tells her through His angel, and commits herself to it in total self-surrender: 'I am the handmaid of the Lord. Let what you have said be done to me' (Lk 1:38).[40] And, having said yes to this Word, she will continue to ponder it fruitfully in her heart (Lk 2:19) and live it in charity from the Visitation to the foot of the Cross.

Indeed, Mary is not only a model for us in the virtue of faith; she is also an agent in the gift of faith to others, which all Christians are called to be. At Cana, through her intercession, she helps to inaugurate the ministry of miracles, which initiates Jesus' disciples into faith (Jn 2:1–11). On Calvary, she is given to us as a mother in the order of grace (Jn 19:25–7), which comes to us through faith. At Pentecost, her faith and prayers help to bestow the gift of the Holy Spirit, who is the source and sustainer of the Church's faith. In the words of *The New Catechism*:

> Throughout her life and until her last ordeal when Jesus her son died on the cross, Mary's faith never wavered. She never ceased to believe in the fulfilment of God's word. And so the Church venerates in Mary the purest realisation of faith.[41]

Finally, Mary's faith illustrates what I tried to say in my reflection on justification; namely that, though faith is foundational to our salvation, we are not saved, as Luther maintained, by faith alone. It must be accompanied by charity, fruitful in good works (Jm 2:16–7). Mary's whole life is the perfect example of this; it is a life wholly animated by self-offering love for God (Lk 1:26–38) and neighbour (Lk 1:39–56).

A quotation taken from *The Tablet* might help to illustrate the points I have tried to make: Marie Schwan wrote that Mary offers the perfect example of a faith deeply interiorised and fruitfully lived:

> Mary is the first disciple. She is the model of what it means to live totally centred in God, and what it means to go 'With haste' to our neighbour in need, what it means to ponder the mystery of life as it unfolds, what it means to stand firm in the midst of suffering in the conviction that for a follower of Jesus, it is death that leads to the fullness of life.[42]

Notes

1   T. S. Kepler, *The Table Talk of Martin Luther* (Mineola, New York: Dover Publications, 2005) p. 107.

2   Sixth Session, Decree Concerning Justification. See H. J. Schroeder, *The Canons and Decrees of the Council of Trent* (Charlotte: Tan Books, 2011), pp. 29–47.

3   We have retained this passage in its older translation from the Jerusalem Bible.

4   *Ibid.*

5   'St James' epistle is really an epistle of straw... for it has nothing of the nature of the Gospel about it.' M. Luther, *Prefaces to the New Testament* (Milton Keynes: Lightning Source), p. 10.

6   J. Maritain, *The Living Thoughts of St Paul* (London, Toronto, Melbourne and Sydney: Cassell and Company Ltd, 1945), p. 5.

7   A. N. Gibley, *We Believe* (Herefordshire: Gracewing, 2011), p. 77.

8   We have retained this passage in its older translation from the Jerusalem Bible.

9   *Ibid.*

10 Seventh Session, Decree Concerning The Sacraments. See H. J. Schroeder, *The Canons and Decrees of the Council of Trent* (Charlotte: Tan Books, 2011), pp. 51–55.

11 T. Merton, *Seeds of Contemplation* (London, Hollis and Carter, 1949), p. 84.

12 Sixth Session, Decree Concerning Justification. See H. J. Schroeder, *The Canons and Decrees of the Council of Trent* (Charlotte: Tan Books, 2011), p. 29.

13 I. T. Ker, *Newman and the Fullness of Christianity* (Edinburgh: T and T Clark, 1993), p. 26.

14 Sixth Session, Decree Concerning Justification. See H. J. Schroeder, *The Canons and Decrees of the Council of Trent* (Charlotte: Tan Books, 2011), p. 29.

15 *Ibid.,* pp. 29–30.

16 *Ibid.,* p. 31.

17 *Ibid.*

18 *Ibid.,* p. 32.

19 *Ibid.*

20 *Ibid.,* p. 33.

21 *Ibid.,* p. 39.

22 *Ibid.,* p. 41.

[23] *Ibid.,* p. 44.

[24] '[W]hen a Catholic comes from Confession, he does truly, by definition, step out again into that dawn of his own beginning and look with new eyes across the world...[I]n that brief ritual, God has really re-made him in His own image... The accumulations of time can no longer terrify. He may be grey and gouty; but he is only five minutes old.' G. K. Chesterton, *Autobiography* (London: Grey Arrow, 1959), pp. 303–304.

[25] J. Gonzalez, The Story of Christianity (New York: Harper Collins Publishers, 2010), p. 23. See also K. James, *Luther The Reformer* (Minneapolis: Augsburg Fortress Publishing House, 1986), p. 79.

[26] C. S. Lewis, *Surprised by Joy* (London and Glasgow: Fontana Books, 1959), p. 181.

[27] We have retained this passage in its older translation from the Jerusalem Bible.

[28] Sixth Session, Decree Concerning Justification. See H. J. Schroeder, *The Canons and Decrees of the Council of Trent* (Charlotte: Tan Books, 2011), pp. 29–47.

[29] F. Mauriac, *The Stumbling Block* (London: The Harvill Press, 1956), p. 84.

[30] *Ibid.,* p. 86.

[31] Newman, *An Essay on the Development of Christian Doctrine,* pp. 54–55.

[32] The Augsburg Confession IV, 1530. C. T. Knippel, *The Augsburg Confession and Its Apology* (St Louis: Concordia Publishing House, 1999), p. 41.

[33] *Ibid.,* p. 59.

[34] *The Library of Christian Classics; Volume XXII; Calvin Theological Treatises:* The Geneva Confession of Faith/ 1536 /Article XI/Faith.

[35] Sixth Session, Decree Concerning Justification. See H. J. Schroeder, *The Canons and Decrees of the Council of Trent* (Charlotte: Tan Books, 2011), p. 32.

[36] Vatican Council 1, *Dogmatic Constitution, Dei Filius,* Chapter 3, 1870.

[37] *Catechism Of The Catholic Church,* 3.150.

[38] *Ibid.,* p. 44.

[39] Newman, *Loss and Gain,* p. 261.

[40] We have retained this passage in its older translation from the Jerusalem Bible.

[41] *Catechism Of The Catholic Church,* 3.149.

[42] M. Schwan, *Come Home: A Prayer Journey to the Centre Within* (Notre Dame: Ave Maria Press, 2020), p. 17.

24 BY WHAT AUTHORITY?

Bill

THE INEVITABLE QUESTION we come back to in all these statements, Catholic and non-Catholic, about the nature of the Church, justification and of faith is not simply who is right, but, more fundamentally, on what authority do the answers come to us? Who is the reliable imponent of one particular understanding as distinct from another?

I hope I have already made it clear that the Council of Trent begins its statement on justification, not by expounding its teaching, but by grounding it in the authority which the Fathers of the Council believed they possessed: the authority of Christ, transmitted to the one holy, Catholic and apostolic Church, which for Catholics has always meant the Church, which could trace its ministerial and doctrinal continuity and identity back to the Church founded on the Apostles.[1] The Reformers were unable to do this. Rejecting the authority of the Catholic Church as historically understood, their appeal was to Scripture alone as interpreted by themselves. This was, as Edmund Campion pointed out, a position of 'upstart Doctors,'[2] without biblical or historical foundation.

The problem of legitimate authority was the one, which tormented a number of converts from Anglicanism in recent centuries. By what authority was the question which, 'like an aching tooth', would not go away for Ronald Knox in the years leading to his conversion in the early 1920s. In his contribution to *The Road to Damascus*, he wrote:

> As an Anglican, then, I stood outside of the one evidently continuous and self-reproducing fellowship which went

back to the Apostles. As an Anglican clergyman, I was
taking it upon myself to exercise a jurisdiction which
proceeded, in the last resort, from no more respectable a
source than a Tudor Queen. These were the considerations which were most formidably present to my mind
when I made my submission to the Catholic Church.[3]

The same question haunted another famous convert from
Anglicanism in the previous century, the Jesuit poet Gerald
Manley Hopkins. As a high Anglican, Hopkins held and cherished
the Catholic doctrine of the Real Presence of Christ in the
Eucharist. But he realised that, given the massive rejection of that
doctrine by the Reformers, including the majority of Anglicans,
the doctrine could only stand on reliable authority. When he
came to realise that the claim of Anglo-Catholics could not be
sustained that they, together with Rome, possessed that authority,
he was left with only one alternative, as he explained in a letter
to his father:

> I shall hold as a Catholic what I have long held as an
> Anglican, that literal truth of Our Lord's words by which
> I learn that the least fragment of the consecrated elements
> in the Blessed Sacrament of the Altar is the whole Body of
> Christ born of the Blessed Virgin, before which the whole
> host of saints and angels as it lies on the Altar trembles
> with adoration. This belief once got is the life of the soul
> and when I doubted it I should become an atheist the next
> day. But ... it is a gross superstition unless guaranteed by
> infallibility. I cannot hold this doctrine confessedly except
> as a Tractarian [High Anglican] or a Catholic; the Tractar-
> ian ground I have seen broken to pieces under my feet.[4]

An even more eminent and influential convert, Cardinal
Newman, (1801–1890) had similar problems to Knox and Hopkins. Like them, he remained an Anglican for many years in the
belief that the Anglican Church, at least the Anglo-Catholic wing
of it, could sustain the claim that it was a true part of the Catholic
Church. That belief was seriously challenged for him when,

studying the Fathers, he detected remarkable similarities between Anglicanism and the heresies of the early centuries. The belief was further damaged when his defence of the Anglo-Catholic position, given in the famous Tract 90, was rejected by the Anglican authorities. This prompted him to resign his living as Vicar of St Mary's in Oxford, retire to Littlemore, and write his great book, *The Development of Christian Doctrine*,[5] which clinched his conversion to Catholicism.

Newman's Anglican doubts were not only ecclesial, with regard to the external credentials of the Church, but doctrinal. In particular, he was troubled by the Thirty-Nine Articles, to which Anglicans were expected to subscribe. He came to regard them as unclear, open to different interpretations, contradictory and weak in their foundation. These doubts are powerfully articulated in *Loss and Gain*, the novel he wrote while studying for the Catholic priesthood in Rome after his conversion in 1845. The novel describes the faith journey of Charles Reding, an Oxford undergraduate, who is studying for the Anglican ministry. As his ordination approaches, he finds the Articles an insurmountable obstacle, which forces him to turn his attention to the only Church which, he believes, can sustain its credibility, as heir to the Church of the Apostles.

Charles sees the Articles as lacking coherence, clarity and foundational credibility, as he indicates in the following reflection:

> He saw that the profession of faith contained in the Articles was but a patchwork of bits of orthodoxy [Catholicism], Lutheranism, Calvinism and Zwinglism; and this too on no principle; that it was but the work of accident, ... that it had come down in the particular shape in which the English Church now receives it, when it might have come down in any other shape; that it was but a toss-up that Anglicans at this day were not Calvinists or Presbyterians or Lutherans, equally well as Episcopalians. The historical fact did but clench the difficulty, or rather impossibility, of saying what the faith of the English

Church was. On almost every point of dispute the authoritative standard of doctrine was vague or inconsistent, and
there was an imposing weight of external testimony in
favour of opposite interpretations.[6]

One difficulty, which Charles experiences, is whether, according
to the Articles, divine truth was directly given to us or whether
we had to seek for it in Scripture. He is told by his tutor that the
saving doctrine is neither given nor is it sought. It is proposed by
the Church and proved by the individual. To this Charles replies
that he cannot quite see the distinction between seeking and
proving, for how can we prove the doctrine except by seeking in
Scripture for reasons?

He presses the question by asking if the Christian religion
allows private judgement in matters of doctrine. This was a very
practical question with wide implications for all the Christian
Churches both Catholic and non-Catholic. Had Charles asked a
Methodist or any member of one of the unambiguously Protestant Churches, he would have had a clear answer in the affirma-
tive; had he asked a Catholic, he would have been told that we
use our private judgement to find the true Church, and then we
submit to its authority. But from this Oxford divine he could not
get a distinct answer.

To exemplify his dilemma, he focuses on a particular problem.
He has been told by his tutor that it is a sin to doubt the doctrine
of the Trinity; the first of the Thirty-Nine Articles implies that.
And yet on another occasion he is told that our highest state here
is one of doubt. What does this mean? Surely certainty is
necessary on some matters, such as the object of worship? How
can we worship God as Our Father unless He truly is Our Father?
Charles is told that this quest for certainty is dangerous.

These difficulties are amplified in a conversation Charles has
with Carlton, a friend he respects. Carlton insists that Rome has
as many difficulties as the Anglican Church, such as infallibility,
Transubstantiation, the veneration of the saints. He asks Charles
if he could subscribe to these, to which Charles replies:

It depends on this...on what authority they come to me. Of course I could if they came to me on the same authority as the doctrine of the Blessed Trinity comes. Now the Articles come on no authority; they are the views of persons in the sixteenth century; and again it is not clear how far they are, or are not, modified by the unauthoritative views of the nineteenth. I am obliged then to exercise my own judgement, and I tell you quite frankly that my judgement is unequal to so great a task.[7]

This brings us back to the question which Knox and Hopkins had to face, and indeed one which confronts any thoughtful Christian: not so much what do I believe but on what authority do I believe anything? The interesting and significant question is this: if Newman, widely regarded as one of the most profound and acute thinkers in Christian history, had this problem, what about the man or woman in the street? On what possible ground can he or she claim to know that God is from all eternity a Trinity of Persons, that the second Person of that Trinity, the Eternal Word, became man in the Person of Jesus Christ, that through His Cross Christ has reconciled sinful humanity to God and that reconciliation is received by us either through fiducial faith alone, as Luther believed, or through the Sacramental system of the Catholic Church, in particular through the Mass, which makes present to us Christ's self-offering on the Cross and offers to us His sacred Body and Blood for our spiritual nourishment. These doctrines are, as Hopkins said of the Real Presence in the Eucharist, either false or, if true, stand on one ground alone: the authority of the revealing God, speaking through His own chosen and guided agencies. For Newman and for anyone who thinks the matter through, the question was this: is Christianity a religion, the truth of which was revealed by God, or are we dependent on purely human judgement on matters which are beyond it?

In his conversation with Carlton, Charles proceeds to outline the contradictions in the doctrine of the Thirty-Nine Articles, and between the Articles and the prayer book:

Well, for example, they (the Articles) distinctly receive the
Lutheran doctrine of justification by faith only which the
prayer book virtually opposes in every one of its offices.
One Article on the Sacraments speaks of the doctrine of
Melanchthon, another that of Calvin. One Article speaks
of the Church's authority in controversies of faith, yet
another makes Scripture the ultimate appeal.[8]

He contrasts this confusion with the consistency of the Catholic
position, consistency being a necessary hallmark of truth:

On the other hand, it has struck me ... that the Church of
Rome is undeniably consistent in her formularies; this is
the very charge some of our writers make upon her, that
she is so systematic... When a [theological] system is
consistent, at least it does not condemn itself. Consistency
is not truth, but truth is consistency ... When an oracle
equivocates, it carries with it its own condemnation ... St
Paul gives this very account of a heretic, that he is 'condemned of himself.'[9]

This consistency of principle, clear, simple, firmly grounded in
Scripture and tradition, accessible to all the faithful, was articulated by the Catholic Church in the profession of faith which was
the fruit of the Council of Trent, (the profession of the Tridentine
faith). Its unifying principles are clearly propounded in the first
five Articles, in particular in Article one, which demands that the
Catholic Christian with a firm faith believes and professes all and
every one of the things contained in that Creed which the holy
Roman Church makes use of, (that is the Nicene Creed).[10] Article
one asserts that in the doctrine of the Creed are contained all the
things that are to be held in the mind and heart according to the
discipline of the Christian faith.[11] Subsequent Articles develop
this in affirming the validity of Apostolic and ecclesiastical
traditions', the truth of Scripture, as understood in the sense
which the Church has held and does hold, the divine origin of
the Seven Sacraments, as opposed to the two retained by the

Reformers, and all other doctrines defined and declared by the general councils of the Church.

In other words, according to Trent, for Catholics the truth is given to us by God and received by the faithful in their docility to the Church, which, after Christ, is its primary imponent. In effect, historically, it comes to us through Scripture as ecclesially read; that is to say as interpreted by the Church, which is guided by the same Holy Spirit who inspired the biblical authors in the first place. The fruit of this ecclesial reading is dogma, which is the Church's definitive resolution of crucial doctrinal questions, a resolution usually effected by the Episcopate in communion with the Pope, or, occasionally, by the Pope alone, speaking ex cathedra.

Is this notion of faith too complex for the average layperson? I don't think so. For years, before and after my reception in the early sixties, I mixed with Catholics from all walks of life: lawyers, teachers, bricklayers, priests and nuns who all simply and sincerely believed what they had been taught in their catechesis: that God gives us His truth through the Church which He founded and promised to guide through His Spirit. Children made this act of faith every Sunday before receiving Communion. All converts, as I have said, made it without difficulty before reception. It was reinforced regularly for all practising Catholics from the pulpit. If there are difficulties with it today, it may be that with the emphasis now being on 'Thought for the day' on the Scriptures for the day, Catholics are less clearly aware of the doctrinal ground and content of their faith. As I have indicated, this understanding of justifying faith held the Catholic faithful, from high powered theologians to the ordinary laity, in remarkable unity for centuries, in contrast to the disunity which has characterised Protestantism from the beginning, and which, sadly, has, in the last few decades, begun to affect the Catholic community since the Second Vatican Council. Of this more later.

This is where Bill's manuscript, typed up by Win in his lifetime, finishes. On the last day of his life he was rereading his notes and planning how to proceed. These pages remain and we have included the following crucial passage on his reception in the next chapter.

Notes

[1] Sixth Session, Decree Concerning Justification. See H. J. Schroeder, *The Canons and Decrees of the Council of Trent* (Charlotte: Tan Books, 2011), p. 29.

[2] Campion, *Ten Reasons Proposed To His Adversaries For Disputation In The Name Of The Faith And Presented To The Illustrious Members Of Our University*, p. 97.

[3] J. A. O'Brien, *The Road to Damascus* (London: Love and Malcomson Ltd, 1955), p. 47.

[4] G. Roberts, *G. M. Hopkins, Selected Prose; Letter to his Father, 16–17 October 1866* (Oxford: Oxford University Press, 1980), p. 30.

[5] Newman, *An Essay On The Development of Christian Doctrine*.

[6] Newman, *Loss and Gain*, p. 89.

[7] *Ibid.*, p. 155.

[8] *Ibid.*, p. 156.

[9] *Ibid.*, pp. 156–157. (Tt 3:11).

[10] *The Catechism of the Council of Trent* (London: Routledge and Co, 1852), pp. 14–30.

[11] *Ibid.*, p. 9.

25 THE MOVE[1]

A ND SUCH, IN ESSENCE, was the final ground of my own conviction. I became a Catholic and remain one because I believe that Catholicism is the Christian Religion in the fullness of its possibility. The invitation to be Catholic resides overwhelmingly in the evidence God has given us in the burden of the Bible, in the burden of the living tradition of the Church, to use the marvellous concept of the American Jesuit, Weigel. 'The Catholic stand is simply that the Bible is in the Church and the Church is in the Bible.'[2] (The invitation to be Catholic resides overwhelmingly in the evidence God has given us within the Bible and within the Church's living tradition.) I joined the Church, following Newman and others, convinced that biblical Christianity was seminal Catholicism, that pre-Nicene Christianity was, increasingly, explicit Catholicism, that post-Nicene Christianity was, increasingly, emphatic Catholicism and that the Christianity of the second Millennium, that of Aquinas, of Trent and Vatican I, of Newman and of the great doctors of theology and of the spiritual life in the twentieth century is Catholicism in the fullness of its bloom. Vatican II has confirmed the conviction for me. The Catholic Church is ever in ministry and doctrine continuous with the Apostolic church, faithful to her scriptures and, essentially, consistent with her past. There is no point at which you can logically say, I will have the Church up to this date and not afterwards, or I will have these doctrines but not these. Like another famous, seamless garment,[3] it is all of a piece.

I realized the point at which I felt 'to delay longer'[4] would be to be sinning against grace.

Newman describes the state movingly in *Loss and Gain*. His central character, Charles, on the brink of his own decision says:

> [A]ll reason comes from God; our grounds must at best be imperfect; [for here we see through a glass darkly] but if

they appear to be sufficient after prayer, diligent search, obedience, waiting, and, in short, doing our part, they are His voice calling us on. He it is, in that case, who makes them seem convincing to us...I cannot resist the conviction which is upon me. This last week it has possessed me in a different way than ever before. It is now so strong, that to wait longer is to resist God.[5]

So in something like that frame of mind I rang up Father Caden and said, 'This is Bill Evans speaking.' 'Ah, so you've decided to give yourself up,' was the reply.

So my reception was arranged and in September 1962, shortly after the birth of my second daughter Ruth, I was received into the Catholic Church at the same Church at which Win had been received. My first confession was a bit of an ordeal for me, it was nearly as long as this paper—but the priest was very gentle and sympathetic. After it, I felt like Chesterton said he always felt after confession— 'five minutes old'[6]—and my First Communion, specially arranged for me at evening Benediction, was a great joy.

Notes

[1]   This is an extract from a talk Bill gave to the Methodist Debating Society about his conversion to the Catholic Church, in the early to mid-1970s.
[2]   G. Weigel, *Where Do We Differ?* (London: Burns and Oates, 1962), p. 27.
[3]   Jn 19:23.
[4]   Newman, *Loss and Gain*, p. 289.
[5]   *Ibid.*, p. 237.
[6]   Chesterton, *Autobiography*, p. 304.

26 CORRESPONDENCE BETWEEN BILL AND EDWARD

Win 2016

EDWARD GOLDWYN IS my first cousin on my mother's side. He is roughly the same age as me and over the years we would meet from time to time at family gatherings. I admired Edward for his lively mind, his enterprise and ability to embrace life to the full.

He married Charmian fairly soon after Bill and I were married and over the years they visited us both in Sunderland and Barrow. These visits were always characterised by passionate discussions, usually about religion, often late into the night. Edward would argue from a scientific, humanist, agnostic position, whereas Bill would put the case for Christianity and, in particular, the Catholic Church. At times, I feared that these discussions were becoming too heated, having seen how similar discussions had damaged Bill's relationship with my mother, but, in fact, the evening always ended with good will and mutual respect and were hugely enjoyed by both Edward and Bill.

Every Christmas we would receive a newsletter with family photographs from Edward and Charmian and it was clear that they were devoted parents, always there for their family, both in the difficult as well as the good times. In addition, they have supported friends and Charmian, a retired doctor, has worked tirelessly for *Medical Justice*,[1] which seeks to help asylum seekers, while Edward continues to be involved with films to encourage young people to go into science. At the end of these newsletters Edward would add a note, for example in 2013, he wrote, 'What a wonderful pope. I am feeling very Catholic. He may change the world. P.S. This is serious. I am not being flippant.' A year later came the message, 'Time for another day and night to put the world to rights' and in 2015, 'Must see you soon. It's been too long.'

In September 2016, this longed for visit took place, as Edward informed us that he and Charmian were going to a Creative Writing course in Keswick and would like to break their journey in Barrow. Our meeting was warm and friendly as always, but it lacked its usual animated religious discussion. This was partly because we had all been saddened by the death of Edward's younger brother, Neville, and more recently of my younger brother, Lawrence. In addition, Bill was frail, having suffered from frequent throat infections and poor mobility. In fact, when they left, Bill apologised whole-heartedly for his unusually subdued response to their presence, but wanted them to realise that it was a tribute to how highly he valued their friendship that he hadn't cancelled the visit due to ill health. However, he hoped to be feeling better later in the month, when we would meet them at Lawrence's Memorial Service. Sadly, this meeting never took place, as Bill's health further deteriorated.

The following correspondence was the result of Edward and Charmian's visit, but was unfortunately cut short by Bill. His health worsened and he became so weak and tired he feared his book would remain unfinished unless he tried wholly to devote his failing energy into completing it. Sadly, Bill died before he was able to do this.

Email One: Win to Edward

On Wednesday 21 Sep 2016, at 20:10, I wrote:

1. We will look forward to seeing you both on the Thursday at about 6/7ish.

Thank you for your generous offer to take us out for dinner, but we think it will be cosier to have the meal at home and better for conversation, Bill says. These days I use Marks meals quite often, which are easy and we find very good. I seem to remember Charmian is vegetarian. Is that correct? Is there any food that disagrees with you and what do you like for breakfast?

We can't think of anything we need bringing up, but thank you for the offer.

Hope all goes well,

Love from Winnie

Email Two: Edward to Win and Bill

Thursday 13 October 2016

2. Dear Winnie and Bill,

It was a treat to stay with you and catch up. You made us so welcome.

I had some expectations we would further explore our beliefs, but the sadness and reality of Lawrence pushed that to one side.

But I did have something Bill, I wanted your opinion on. If it interests you, respond.

It looks as though our life on earth is a test for the supernatural power to see if we are 'good', worthy or not. Very crudely, whether we shall be rewarded in heaven or hell. But what is this sorting out for? Does this 'testing' have some purpose?

Which also makes me wonder why, if the story is true, why not let everyone into heaven? Once one is sure God is running the show, who would not be 'good'? I suspect that almost everyone if they experienced God as unambiguously as Moses and the prophets would opt to be 'good'.

And what negative effects would there be from letting the sinners in? So why the testing?

If this does not interest you, just forget it.

See you soon in Reading.

As ever

Edward

Email Three: Bill to Edward and Charmian

Tuesday 18 October 2016

3. Dear Edward and Charmian,

Thanks for your email. Glad you enjoyed your stay. We enjoyed it too—very much.

My only regret is that I wasn't at my best health wise. If I had been, perhaps we could have discussed some of your questions relating to belief.

I must say, Edward, you do ask the most challenging questions. Implicit in them, lie all the relevant questions. I'll do my best with them, but you must realise that all I say now will only scratch the surface. To see them explored in more depth, you will have to read my book when I have finished it. Anyway, here goes.

The first point I would like to make relates to the nature of the knowledge claims, which both Israel and Christianity make. They are radically different to the claims made by any other truth seekers on this planet: scientists, philosophers, historians and so on. The difference being that the latter, in particular science, can all claim that their 'truths' are grounded in verifiable empirical data and rational reflection on it. Neither Israel nor Christianity can claim that. They can claim that their 'truth' has some kind of historical base to it (words truly spoken and events which truly happened), but their fundamental contentions transcend history and any mode of human cognition, verification or falsification known to man. I'll confine myself to Christianity because I know more about it than I know about Judaism.

Take the two most fundamental contentions of Christianity: the divinity of Christ and the reconciliation of mankind with God, effected by His death on the cross. Christians can legitimately claim that there was a man called Jesus, and that He was crucified under Pontius Pilate. But that this same man was also God, the eternal Son of God, through whom all things were made and that through His death we were all forgiven and given access to eternal communion with God, neither history nor human reason can touch that, either by way of verification or falsification. And yet, these claims have been and still are believed by hundreds of thousands of millions of people, by virtually every major English poet from Chaucer to T. S. Eliot and by most European philosophers over twenty centuries right up to our own day. On what ground then do these contentions stand, contentions that were a stumbling block to Israel and a madness to the Greeks? That is the question that we need to explore.

The other introductory point I would like to make relates to the conflict, which any religion, Israel, Christianity, Islam and so on, will inevitably have with the mind-set of contemporary man, shaped as it is by the serious claims of science and philosophical positivism. Who wins when a truth seeker, such as yourself, is faced with that conflict? A sceptic, Bertrand Russell or A. J. Ayers, for example, will say that nothing a believer might affirm can undermine their confidence in the validity of their own mind-set. Believers will say that the signs, which verify their religious faith, are so powerful that the claims of rational positivism crumble in the imperative light, which their faith offers. Again the question is: who is right?

A simple historical example might clarify the problem. Two men, both unbelievers, go to Lourdes in the nineteenth century. One of them, Alexis Carrol, a distinguished scientist, sees a cure so remarkable that his atheism crumbles as a result of the experience and very soon he finds himself returning to the faith of his childhood, the Catholic faith. The other man, Émile Zola, the novelist, says: 'All I want to see is someone with a cut finger put it in the water and find the cut healed. Then I will believe.'[2] In fact, he witnesses a cure much more spectacular.[3] It shakes him (he turns pale) but it does not shake his unbelief. Which of the two men made the right response?

The believer will say that the signs which confirm his faith: the wisdom and sublime goodness of Jesus, the miracles He works, the prophecies He fulfils, miracles and prophecies which continue throughout the history of the Church He founds, are more than sufficient to overwhelm any doubts he has. The unbeliever will not be convinced because he distrusts the biblical and historical testimonies and his innate scepticism, rooted in his positivist mind-set, (only what can be proved can claim to be true) is not seriously challenged by the biblical and historical testimonies.

The thing you must realise is that both belief and unbelief are each acts of faith. 'Atheism is a cruel, long-term business,' wrote Jean Paul Sartre. 'I believe I have gone through it to the end.'[4] (Apparently later in his life he reneged on his scepticism and committed himself to the Catholic faith.) His lover, Simone de Beauvoir, whose devout Catholicism Sartre had destroyed, suppressed his turn about, so the change was never widely publicised.

For myself, the motives of credibility for belief are so powerful that I can never imagine myself having the faith required for atheism. I can never imagine myself having the confidence that my own judgement on this matter surpasses the forty centuries of witness and discipleship—arguably the greatest consensus of great minds and noble souls the world has ever known.

So, I think the question boils down to this. If you are seeking for faith, you must examine the testimonies on which it stands. As a Christian, this means a careful reading of the New Testament and its relationship to the Old Testament. Christian apologists will insist that much of the Old Testament reads like a rehearsal for the drama yet to come. Certainly, the resonances between the two Testaments are very remarkable—I would say miraculous. As far as the New Testament itself is concerned, I would say the questions to ask are: what are we dealing with here: lies, delusions, a mixture of both—or the truth? For myself, the testimony has the hallmarks of truth all over it. That has been the judgement of so many believers over twenty centuries.

A final point: you say that God revealed Himself both to Israel and Christianity to test us, welcoming those who pass the test into heaven and sending those who fail to hell. There is some truth in that: there are tests that challenge us all. But my own Church never speaks in that language today. (I have never heard a sermon on hell in all my 57 years of worshipping in the Catholic Church.) It speaks of Christ, not as one who comes to test us, but as one who comes, not to condemn the world, but to redeem it, who comes to call sinful mankind to repentance and to communion with His love in this life, and to eternal communion with Him in the next. That will be the ultimate 'test': have we enough love in our hearts to enable us to be in communion with a God who is, by nature, self-offering love? Hell, for many contemporary theologians, would be a failure in that respect: to have hearts so full of hatred, resentment, unforgiveness, cruelty, self-centredness that we are incapable of communion with the blinding reality of perfect love.

I'll leave it there. As I said at the beginning, I am only scratching the surface. I haven't dealt with all your questions. Hopefully when I have finished my book, you will find the arguments sufficiently expanded.

We may have an opportunity to discuss the matter at Lawrence's Memorial Service. I hope to make it there but can't be absolutely sure, as my back and balance are still not right and will make the journey difficult.

With very best wishes to you both,

Bill

Email Four: Edward to Bill

Tuesday 18 October 2016

4. Dear Bill,

Thank you very sincerely for the above. It shows your sincerity and the absolute clarity of your faith, which I have never doubted and reads and sounds exactly like being with you.

I agree that religious faith and wanting verifiable evidence for hypotheses are fundamentally different. I don't myself experience what it must be like to believe in revelation and absolute authority. Well maybe I do but I am proud and determined 'not to give in to it'. It is not that the message of Moses, Jesus and some other great people do not contain the essentials of civilisation. I think they do. And it is their own creative insight in the same way as the theories of Darwin, Einstein and Crick were created.

In the religions it is that the authorities that interpret them do so corruptly to suit their power and politics.

Agreeing with all that, I still want you to think about my question.

Whether hell exists, there is a strong connection in religion that we should lead lives as set down by Jehova, and Jesus. Not to do that is to be barred from heaven. Unless the forgiveness of Jesus in the end forgives everyone everything.

So behaviour in this life is a qualification for heaven. In fact, it seems to be the main purpose of this life. What else is it for if not to sort the good from the bad?

So the question still is why does God set it up this way?

What would it matter if we all went to heaven?

Would not even the most evil see what it really is all about if they were there?

I hope you feel better now.

Best wishes to you both.

ED

Who knows? This could build to something you could put as an extra in your book.

Email five: Bill to Edward

Monday 31 October 2016

5. Dear Edward,

Thank you for your email. Sorry about the delay in replying. I have not been well recently.

Sadly, we won't be coming to the Memorial Service for Lawrence. My arthritis and balance are no better, and I don't think I am up to the journey. I am very sad about that, as Win and I had been looking forward to seeing you and Charmian again.

Coming now to your email—I thought I had dealt with your questions in my long reply (albeit in a superficial way), but apparently you don't think I have. So I'll try again.

You make an interesting point when you say: 'I don't experience what it must be like to believe in Revelation and absolute authority. Well, maybe I do, but I am proud and determined not to give into it.' The whole point about conversion to faith is that it begins in ourselves with our total openness to receive it (faith), if the grounds of credibility for belief are sufficiently compelling. The gift of faith will never be given to a person who is fixed, determined, in a resolute positivism or reluctance. It will only be given to one who is open in mind and heart and imagination to the invitation on offer; in other words to one who is ready to believe if convinced. It has another dimension; there must be a readiness to embrace the imperatives and constraints that come with belief—to repent and change one's life in accord with the teaching of Christ. This can be the most difficult part for some. A prolific novelist once said that conversion to Christianity would be difficult for him, because it would mean changing his character and his life. Conversion involves a fundamental reorientation of mind and of one's moral values.

I am glad you mention Darwin and Einstein. The Catholic Church has accepted Darwin's theory of evolution unlike some fundamentalist Protestants. *The Origin of Species*[5] did upset many Christians, when it was published—but not all. Cardinal Newman, one of the Church's best minds in the nineteenth century, maintained that the theory did not undermine the argument from design at all.[6] It was just as remarkable that creatures should evolve from the primeval soup into what they are—remarkably organised to function: to walk, run, fly, swim, reproduce themselves, hear and see. (Darwin, himself, was overawed by the thought of the eye.)

As for Einstein, you might be interested to hear what he thought of Christ. When asked to what extent Christianity had influenced his life, he answered:

As a child I received religious instruction both in the Bible and the Talmud. I am a Jew but I am enthralled by the luminous figure of the Nazarene (Christ).... No one can read the Gospels without feeling the presence of Jesus. His personality pulsates in every word. No myth is filled with such life.[7]

Even the political revolutionary, Jean Jacque Rousseau, himself not a Christian, sensed something superhuman in the thought and character of Christ. Echoing Chesterton, who sees Christ as 'tower[ing]...above all the thinkers who ever thought themselves tall',[8] Rousseau writes:

I confess to you that the majesty of the Scriptures strikes me with admiration, as the purity of the Gospels has its influence on my heart. Peruse the works of our philosophers, with all their pomp of diction, how mean, how contemptible they are compared with the Scriptures. Is it possible that a book at once so simple and sublime should be merely the work of a man? Is it possible that the sacred personage whose history it contains should be Himself a mere man? Do we find that He assumed the tone of an enthusiast or ambitious sectary? What sweetness, what purity in His manners! What an affecting gracefulness in His delivery! What sublimity in His maxims! What profound wisdom in His discourses. What presence of mind in His replies! How great the command over His passions! Where is the man, where is the philosopher who could so live and so die without weakness, without ostentation? ...Yes, if the life and death of Socrates were those of a sage, the life and death of Jesus were those of a God.[9]

Strange that a man of such stature should have megalomaniac delusions about Himself. Normally a great man knows that he is not God, and the greater he is the better he knows it. Moses never for a moment believed himself to be the equal of Jehovah any more than Mohamed thought that he was the equal Allah. Yet, here is One, who claims that He and the Father are one, and that anyone who sees Him has seen the Father—and His claim has been accepted by millions over twenty centuries.

Coming to your next point: 'In the religions, it is that the authorities that interpret them do so corruptly to suit their own power and politics.' This is not true of Catholic Theology. It is true that certain authorities (popes, bishops, monarchs, governments) have, at times, been up to their necks in the corrupting influences of power and politics. This is true of other Christian Churches too. But, the understanding of the Gospels, in matters of Revealed Truth, has been achieved through the work of great minds, such as St Augustine and St Thomas Aquinas, and holy souls, such as St John of the Cross, in a tradition of understanding over twenty centuries. There has been no politics or corruption in that—only a humble, prayerful reflection in faith on the meaning of the Bible.

And now, your final point—the one which seems to niggle with you the most, the problem of hell. I thought I had dealt with that (albeit in a brief and superficial way) in my last long email, but clearly not to your satisfaction. I'll try again. Yes, there is a doctrine of judgement, of reward and punishment in the Bible—together with other concepts, which can be difficult for contemporary man to swallow. But these problems are not, in my view, where you would start if you want to consider Christianity seriously. Is Christianity true? Has God spoken to the world definitively through the prophets of Israel, through Jesus and through the Christian Church? If you can believe that, then the problem of strange and troubling concepts falls into place. If you cannot believe it, then the problem of hell or heaven is irrelevant.

What I have suggested to you is that you speak of heaven and hell in a language that the Church no longer uses. It tries to make sense of judgement, of reward and punishment in other terms. In fact, my own Church virtually never preaches on hell. It speaks only of God's mercy, of the salvation offered to the world through Christ's life and death. It doesn't speak about 'tests to see if we are good,' about 'sorting out,' about letting people in or refusing admission.

When Christianity hit the world on the day of Pentecost, Peter, the first pope, was addressing an audience of Israelites, and—the world at large—who had been given the moral laws, but, along with all men and women, had failed to keep them. Peter's message was not one of God's condemnation, but of His mercy and forgiveness. What they had to do, he maintained, was believe that Christ had died and risen for them and to repent of their sins, however serious, and God would forgive them and pour His Spirit, (the Spirit of His love) into their hearts. That has been the message throughout the ages. So, it is not a question of 'sorting out' or 'testing', it is about accepting a generous invitation to enter into communion with God's love in this life and, hopefully, throughout eternity. This is what salvation or condemnation means. It is we, ourselves, who decide where we go. After that first yes to God's invitation, it is our responsibility to keep what we have been given—the gift of His love dwelling in us. We can only lose that gift by an act of serious sin, which we know to be evil. Even then, the mercy of God is still there for us if we repent and accept His forgiveness in the confessional or the Mass or at home in private prayer. Hell may exist as a possibility, but, for a Catholic, it is always overshadowed by a thousand getaway cars.

Salvation, then, for a Catholic means dying in the love we have been given, which enables us to be in eternal communion with the God who is love. Condemnation means the opposite—to be incapable of such a communion, because we have no love in us—we are resolute and unrepentant in our commitment to evil.

Cardinal Newman describes this final spiritual failure in the following words:

Heaven would be hell to [a man incapable of love]. We know how unhappy we are apt to feel…when alone in the midst of strangers…And this is but a faint illustration of the loneliness of a man of earthly dispositions and tastes, thrust into the society of saints and angels. How forlorn would he wander through the courts of heaven! He would find no one like himself; he would see in every direction the marks of God's holiness and these would make him shudder.[10]

I'll have to leave it there, Edward. Again, I realise this is only scratching the surface. Hope it is of some help. I'm afraid I'll have to end it there for the time being, as I am trying to get on with my book.

Love to you both,

Bill

Email Six: Edward to Bill

Monday 7 November 2016

6. Hello Bill

It's great reading your stuff. I hear your voice coming loudly through the words.

I appreciate the effort you put in and thank you.

I'm doing this because I hope that in our exchanges you can find some pleasure in the argument. But if it is not fun we should gracefully stop.

My first reaction to what you write is to say this.

We are in very different mind-sets.

I don't think there is a supernatural. So I look very hard at the evidence for it to see if there is sufficient reason to believe something I have previously rejected. I would need the evidence to be very convincing for that.

I think you do believe in the supernatural. I believe you will look at the evidence against the supernatural very hard. You would need that evidence to be *very* convincing to stop believing.

So our reaction to ideas, arguments and observations are going to be different. Mine defensive, critical and abrasive to anything that might upset my view that is so no supernatural. Yours defensive, critical and abrasive to anything that might [make] doubtful the Catholic Church's story.

I am sure you do understand me, but let me reproduce here some bits from the course on Proof in case this gives more insight into where I'm coming from.

To see why we need the scientific method, let's take a look at what people base their knowledge on in day to day life. People can accept something as true, based on intuition, or belief.

Let's consider my own strong belief that my cat, Misha, loves me most of all people in his life. I just know he loves me, more than anyone else. I feel this in my heart of hearts. Now is such a belief, a good basis for knowledge?

Well, no. Simply believing something doesn't make it so. Things we believe in strongly can turn out to be false. Also, what if someone else holds an opposing belief. What if my fiancée believes, that Misha loves her more? There is no way to settle who is right, just by pitting our beliefs against each other.

We could count the number of supporters for each belief, and require a majority, or a consensus. But, this isn't a very solid basis for knowledge either. Just because most people accept something as true, doesn't mean it is true. For centuries, practically everybody thought the Earth was flat. Turns out, they were wrong; it is round.

Another source of knowledge is an authority's opinion, also not a very good source. The opinion of authority figures like political leaders, experts, scientists is just that, an opinion. Authorities may have access to more or better knowledge, but they also have an important personal stake in getting their views accepted, their careers and reputations depend on it.

Suppose my fiancée gets a so called cat whisperer, to declare that Misha loves her more. Of course, I'm going to be sceptical about this expert opinion, especially if my fiancée paid for it. I can find my own cat expert to oppose my fiancée's cat whisperer. But, then we would just have two opposing opinions again.

What we need is evidence. So, how do we use evidence, to settle the argument of whom Misha loves more? Well suppose I regularly observe that after getting home from work, Misha always comes to sit on my lap and not my fiancée's. I'm supporting my statement about the world, that Misha loves me more, with an observation of the world. Namely, on whose lap she sits, after work. This gathering of evidence through casual observation is a better foundation of knowledge than the previous ones. But, it's still not good enough. This is because people just aren't very good at observing. We tend to selectively observe, and remember things that agree with our beliefs. For example, I might have forgotten very conveniently, that Misha always sits on my fiancée's lap at breakfast. There are many biases besides selective perception, that make casual observation a tricky source of knowledge.

And if you think about this we have no meaning for what 'love' is in a cat's consciousness? So maybe the question as put is not scientifically dealable with!

In this sense I have real problems when you talk about God's Love. I do not know what the words mean. His mercy?

So what do I think this conversation is about? What am I interested in? I deeply respect you, Bill, as a very religious person and simultaneously an honest, intelligent, rational human. How can you, who are rational in everyday life, submerge that rationality to accept a very improbable explanation of how the world is and what it is for? And not question the absence of almost any objective evidence? But see that questioning as somehow a betrayal of the gift of Faith. But I don't see Faith as a gift: it is a decision not to put the religion's story to the question. Does this make sense? Can I think of a simpler explanation?

So I am really interested to know how you deal with the conflict at the boundary between rationality based on evidence and all the old chestnuts you have to supress. For example, can God be both all good and all powerful? How can the death of a man/god 2000 years ago have any relevance to a murder I might commit tomorrow? How do we know what Jesus said?

The language I have heard in the church's answer to these old chestnuts is avoiding meaning by bending words into music. You must know what I mean.

I was raising a more novel chestnut than I thought, by asking why this elaborate structure, this life, is a test of a person's worth, the consequence of which being to go to heaven or not. What would it matter if everyone went to heaven? What kind of answer might I hope for from a believer? To a believer (with faith) there must be some purpose behind God's life for us on Earth? The purpose of this sorting out. What is it? What is the whole enterprise for?

What might you push me about?

From my end, I do not think there is a designer. I see no evidence that any supernatural being is remotely involved in me personally, humans or the world as a whole. I am sure you have some very probing questions and thoughts that might make me rethink.

So if this conversation is going to be both stimulating and rewarding we need to deal with each other's beliefs and see how complete and sturdy they are.

If that is a distraction from the book you are doing I shall fully understand.

As ever ED

Email Seven: Bill to Edward

Tuesday 22 November 2016

7. Dear Edward,

Many apologies for the delay in responding to your last email. I have not been too well recently.

Anyway—to address your questions—you do ask the most challenging questions, Edward. They are not only challenging, but they all beg half a dozen other questions, if I am to attempt to deal with them. Any one of them would take me a day, if I was to try to do justice to it.

Now, I haven't time to do that at the moment, so I think we had better leave it for a while until I have finished my book, which I hope may be of some help to you.

I will leave you with one question, which, I think, goes to the heart of the difference between us: the question of solid evidence. There are many kinds of 'evidence'. There is the evidence that would stand up in a court of law, the empirical evidence a scientist would demand, the evidence that would satisfy a logical positivist, or a professional historian. Now, I have dozens of convictions about my wife, none of which would satisfy the criteria of the above. But, I would willingly stake my life on them, or everything I own. Now, what I mean by 'evidence' in the case of my wife is a question we might profitably explore. —So, until we resume our correspondence—

Love to you both,

Bill

P.S. The point about convictions regarding my wife is not the best example of the principle I have in mind—which is that the evidence the Bible offers is not 'proof' of the kind you define but credible testimony. This is an idea I try to develop in my book. Chesterton has an interesting observation on the matter—he maintains that the most important things cannot be proved—the nature of love or our moral values, for example—but they can be believed—and the world would be a sorry place without that belief.[11]

Email Eight: Edward to Bill

Wednesday 23 November 2016

8. Bill, let us leave it till your book is done. And I look forward to reading it.

I agree with what you say about evidence. Most important things about people cannot be proved because the question is not definable exactly, or even approximately. What is honesty, loyalty, love? How measure it? Any measurement does not capture the full quality I might set out to know about.

But evidence is very important in deciding how probable something is. If we look to decide, say does Chum feel as I do about young grandchild, Zoe, there is no final test.

But by looking at how caring she is, how she will take on responsibilities to look after Zoe, we can see that 'a caring Chum' is much more likely to be a reflection of her than 'a selfish grandmother'. And evidence is about assessing the probability that something is true or not.

Is racial prejudice inherited or learnt? There is evidence that babies are born knowing if they are boy or girl, who their mother is, to prefer their mother's language.... all at 10 seconds after being born. Some evidence that these things are 'known' in the womb. So now how do we define prejudice in a newborn? The situation seems to me that the 'evidence' (itself only probability statements, applies to some 12% of babies perhaps) implies the baby is born with a scaffolding onto which racism can be imported from racist family.

So evidence piles up probability on beliefs.

Now does it matter if something is true or not? Depends what is at stake. God? Very high stake and very interesting. And now we get into explanation. Explanations that need to be elaborated every time a new observation or 'fact' comes up are a fragile theory. For the new explanations are not emergent from the original concept but added to stop it falling apart.

A lot of religion is like that. Explain why Abraham was instructed to kill his son. Why not eat milk and meat? Why Moses ordered the slaughter of the Jericho inhabitants? Why kill the people of Sodom? What does the multitude of special explanations do but make the whole scheme improbable, like Freudian analysis.

We have an intuitive common sense about what is likely. What amazes me is how most of the different peoples around the world throughout history have invented very implausible stories and come to believe them. If you think of all the gods now on the scrapheap with no belief in them, Thor, Zeus, Baal, all the tribal gods of India and S. America, there is nothing sacred about them. Just human folly to have executed thousands and fought wars on the belief they were in charge, telling us what to do.

But religion, as a human invention, does have some really important value. It is a receptacle to hold fundamental human discoveries about a decent life: the Ten Commandments, the two Jesus added, some Buddhist discoveries about our relationship to other living things.....

So when the book is finished we can continue this. Go well.

As ever

Edward

Notes

1   *Medical Justice* is a charity offering essential medical help to the most powerless in society. About 30,000 people a year are held in indeterminate immigration detention in the UK. Many of these have suffered torture or ill treatment and have significant and chronic related health problems. Being detained indefinitely itself causes serious health problems, including mental health issues. Clinicians volunteering for *Medical Justice* record detainees' scars of torture to help with their asylum claims and challenge medical mistreatment of those held in detention. These cases provide the evidence for research, publications and campaigns to improve the conditions of detainees.

2   'I only want to see a cut finger dipped in water and come out healed.' G. S. Johnston, 'Émile Zola at Lourdes', *A Voice for the Faithful Catholic Laity: Crisis Magazine* (1 December 1989).

3   Marie Lemarchand had deep tuberculous ulcerated areas on her face which were resistant to all treatment. She was born in 1874, in Caen and cured in her 19th year at Lourdes. Her cure was declared official.

4   J. P. Sartre, *Words* (London: Penguin Books, 1977), p. 157.

5   C. Darwin, *The Origin of Species* (London: John Murray, 1859).

6   C. S. Dessain and T. Gornall, *The Letters and Diaries of John Henry Newman*, Vol. XXIV (Oxford: Clarendon Press, 1973), p. 77–78.

7   G. S. Viereck, 'What Life Means to Einstein: An Interview by George Sylvester Viereck', *The Saturday Evening Post*, 26 October 1929, p. 17.

8   Chesterton, *Orthodoxy*, p. 277.

9   Rousseau, *The Profession of Faith of a Savoyard Vicar*, pp. 101–103.

10 J. H. Newman, St, *Parochial and Plain Sermons: Holiness Necessary For Future Blessedness*, Vol I (London: Longmans, Green and Co, 1907), p. 7.

11 Chesterton, *Orthodoxy*, pp. 267–268.

WIN'S EPILOGUE

2016–1 March 2017

ILL WAS LOSING weight and becoming frailer throughout 2016, suffering from severe arthritis, which made walking and standing difficult, and repeated chest infections, from which he found it hard to recover, but somehow we managed to get to Eastbourne and Brighton, where we had established a tradition of watching the Eastbourne Tennis Tournament live and the Wimbledon Tennis Tournament on television with Cathy, our youngest daughter, who shared our love of tennis.

On the way home, we stopped off at Lancaster, where we stayed in a comfortable hotel booked for us by Sarah, our third daughter, in order to be present at the graduation of our grandson, Joshua, Mary and Dominic's son. The sun shone and Dominic pushed Bill round the site in a wheel chair. We had wondered whether Bill would feel sensitive about the wheelchair but, in fact, in Dom's capable hands he felt secure and safe. Sarah and her husband, Derek, were also there as well as our other grandsons, Sam, John and Jacob and Dom's mother, Linda. Afterwards, we all celebrated by going to an Italian Restaurant and, as we toasted everyone, there was a light-hearted atmosphere. Mary said it was one of the happiest days of her life. Towards the end of the day Bill was very tired and asked Dom to drive him back to the hotel.

The whole family visited in the New Year. This was a well-established family tradition and, despite my misgivings due to his failing health, Bill was adamant he wanted it to take place as usual and his spirits and energy temporarily improved.

He had always been the heart and soul of this family celebration, organising a pool competition and card games, in which our four grandsons enthusiastically joined. He had also always taken a pride in his bar, making sure everyone had their favourite drink and buying bottles of elderflower, elderberry and blackberry wine from the Furness Abbey shop, in fond remembrance of our home-made wine-making days in Sunderland. However, this year Bill delegated the serving of drinks to Sarah and her husband, Derek. At the grand buffet meal, which our oldest grandson, Sam, helped me prepare, Bill ate better than he had for a while, but shortly afterwards he was exhausted and retired to bed early.

A few days after the family left, Bill's health took a turn for the worst. He started to fall frequently, had another chest infection and a temperature. Following the advice of the paramedics, he was admitted to hospital, where I was told the next day he was suffering from pneumonia and then a few days later from flu as well.

Bill was well supported by the whole family with cards, phone calls and visits. The nurses would say to him that he must be a very popular man, as we put all his cards up on the window sill of the little room he had been given behind the nurses' tables. I think they were rather bemused by the books Bill had asked me to bring in with titles such as *The Glories of Divine Grace*,[1] *Mary at the Foot of the Cross*[2] and *Regina Caeli*.[3]

Mary and Dom came often at weekends, sometimes with some of their sons and together they moved furniture, so that we could make a downstairs bedroom for Bill. Ruth stayed to help me and often did the evening visit, shopping and made meals, as I wasn't too well myself at the time. Bill really appreciated her visits and he liked Ruth to read to him from the newspapers so that he kept in touch with the news. Unfortunately, Ruth caught a severe throat infection and so had to return home for fear of giving it to Bill, whom we were hoping would be allowed home in the next day or two, so Sarah generously came to take her place and together we shopped excitedly and optimistically for everything we could think of which would be helpful for his return, stocking up on all the nutritious food the dietician had recommended.

The nurses were extremely kind to Bill and he was well supported by the Church, receiving the Sacrament of the Sick and Holy Communion from Father Darren and Father Manny. Bill told Father Manny that the two best decisions of his life were becoming a Catholic and marrying me, which deeply moved me when Father Manny told me this, as we crossed paths in the hospital corridor. Bill also received Holy Communion regularly from José, a Eucharistic Minister.

However, Bill was getting weaker all the time and finding it increasingly difficult to eat. He told me that he felt he would die if he remained in hospital but recover his strength if only he could return home. I pleaded with the ward sister to let him come home, who reluctantly agreed if certain tests proved to be satisfactory. To strengthen his case, Bill would tell the nurses that he had four daughters who would help to look after him. Later, I heard that the nurses were surprised I was taking Bill home and expected him to be back in hospital within two days.

The day Bill came home, he was triumphant. He said he would now be able to sleep and eat and build up his strength. It was preying on his mind that the book he was writing on his conversion, his spiritual biography, as he called it, would never be finished. His hope was to get well enough to go to our caravan in a few weeks' time where he could work undisturbed on his book.

He was really pleased with the warm little bedroom we had set up for him downstairs and reassured by the alert bell, which Sarah had fitted, so that I would know when he needed help, whether it was during the day or night. I could hear the bell as I carried the receiver box with me at all times. Bill used it many times in the day but never at night and, thankfully, surrounded by reassurance, he slept well. Although the bell was useful in the day, its main purpose was to guarantee our peace of mind, so that I would know if Bill needed help in the night.

Cathy offered to get compassionate leave from work and very much wanted to come. But when Sarah had to leave, Bill did not fully realize the gravity of his situation and said there was no hurry. Later, he said, he would enjoy watching Wimbledon with Cathy, but his immediate concern was to rest, build up his strength to get ready for our caravan in the lakes where, surrounded by beauty and away from all distractions, he longed to finish his book. I was aware of how unrealistic this dream was and had nightmares of how, cut off from all the medical support we were receiving, we would ever cope on our own but neither did I have the heart to destroy his hope. With hindsight, I am grateful I never voiced these fears.

Bill was happier at home and slept much better, but sadly his health was continuing to deteriorate. Nevertheless, he remained positive, appreciative and staunch in his faith. He would say, 'Thank you ever so much' to the doctor, the occupational therapist, the district nurses and our friend José, who brought him Holy Communion. He wrote each day in his diary, 'Prayers said' for fear he might miss them and even on his last day, he asked me to give him the folders of his book and was rereading the last chapter he had written in the hope of being able to start writing again. Then, at about 7 o'clock on Ash Wednesday he said he was so tired he would have to go to bed, but added could I wait a moment, as he felt too tired even to move from his chair. Suddenly, he collapsed gently in his chair. I rushed to our next-door neighbours for help, thinking he had fainted, but, in fact, he had died, just like that, quietly, peacefully.

Notes

[1]   M. J. Scheeben, *The Glories of Divine Grace: A Fervent Exhortation to All to Persevere and to Grow in Sanctifying Grace* (Indiana: Grail Publications, 1946).

[2]   *Mary at the Foot of the Cross* (Downside Abbey, Franciscans of the Immaculate, 2003).

[3]   Benedict XVI, *Regina Caeli: Reflections on Our Lady* (Oxford: Family Publications, 2010).

RUTH'S KADDISH[1]

My Father and the Historical Authority of Jesus[2]

MY FATHER'S FAMILY was working class, from the north of England, and he imbibed a rich popular culture from his mother, aunts and uncle, his two sisters and his friends. This included the cinema, radio programmes, a repertory theatre and the flourishing local rugby team. As an adult, he took on the music and lyrics of Leonard Cohen and Bob Dylan. Songs like *All along the Watch Tower*[3] and *Senor*[4] were deeply in tune with his understanding of life. These songs poetically express the plight of the human being, who, exposed to many risks and sorrows, struggles through an uncharted track of time, not in defiance but in a bewildered state. They are great songs about the burden of existential experience. At the same time they are by no means hymns to futility. The overall effect of these penetrating lyrics, combined with their poignant music, is uplifting. They hint at a mystical purpose within the struggle.

My father knew what this struggle felt like. And my father, who died on Ash Wednesday 2017, also knew about the delight of experience. As a student at Durham University in the mid-1950s, he fell deeply in love with my mother. In the early years of their married life, anxious to secure their love, they resolved to search together for the Christian Church which represented the full intention of Christ when He said to Peter, 'So I now say to you: You are Peter, and on this rock I will build my Church' (Mt 16:18). My mother had a serious intention to discover a Christian life within a Christian fellowship. But it was my father's tireless intellect which led them into the Catholic Church. The inexhaustible joy of this discovery, together with its intellectual excitement, was with him until the last hours of his life when he continued to review his writing on the subject. He used to say of the good news of Jesus, 'It is too good not to be true'.

Love and the Search for Faith

And so my father's life was not ultimately a story about moral bewilderment. Nonetheless, he was scarred by the bewildering experiences of his childhood which were the result of his parents' unhappy marriage. Out of this, there came both his understanding of human vulnerability and his profound need for certainty and truth.

His vision of life was softened by tenderness and joy, above all, I think in his experience of falling in love with my mother. She came from a different background to his. He was working class and had discovered his passion for English Literature through the resources of an excellent local Grammar school, eager to further the potential of local lads and enrich their options. (His two sisters who were equally promising did not receive the same encouragement to go to university. It was widely assumed they would leave school and work locally which they did.)

Dad did not have the practical aptitude that would have suited him to acquire a trade. The excitement of discovering his intellectual gifts enlarged his horizons. As a result, fortunately both for my father and the local shipyard, he left the hometown he loved, and went to Durham to study English literature. My mother was from a cultured middle class family which had made the advantages of literature, the London theatre and opera available to her from childhood. No doubt the stimulus of understanding each other and their differing perspectives was part of the attraction. Despite the disparities in their background, they formed a union which would assist my father through his existential journey.

As a young, recently married man soon to have a child, my father experienced a deepening of his need to rediscover the resource of Christian faith. In fact, it was I think the experience of falling overwhelmingly in love which fuelled his search. His youth had exposed him to the fragility of every encounter underpinned, as he knew everything to be, by human frailty and potential loss. The more precious the relationship the more deeply he felt this fear and he wanted to secure his love with my mother on the rock of Christian faith.

The problem was they did not know which version of Christianity to choose. My father and his siblings had been sent to the local Methodist Sunday School, chiefly to give their mother some necessary space in their cramped terraced home. This planted the seed of Dad's love for the human Jesus but it did not satisfy him as an intellectual. My mother came from a background of mixed influences. Her mother was Jewish and an atheist and her father was an agnostic with a sympathy for the figure of Jesus. Mum's schooling inclined her to accept Christianity as presented by the Church of England, a solution which would have appeared to satisfy her religious nature without too unduly distressing her mother. Dad's suggestion that they make enquiries about the nature of Catholicism was initially so shocking for Mum that it was a while before she could accompany him. Dad's mother was, in her quiet way, not happy about it either.

Mum writes,

> I was prejudiced against the Catholic Church, partly due to my mother, who was Jewish feeling her race had been persecuted by the Church and partly because I had imbibed a biased attitude to Catholicism at the Anglican school I attended and particularly in the history lessons about Henry VIII and Elizabeth I, so when Bill suggested looking into the Catholic faith, I wept, thinking that what I had believed would further strengthen our marriage might in fact prove to be an obstacle. But Bill, who also had inherited prejudices from his Methodist background, said, 'I do think we have to look at the largest of the Christian Churches in intellectual honesty, even if it is to discover that there are valid grounds to reject it'.

A little later, Bill noticed that some Jesuit priests were giving a course of lectures on the Catholic faith at Corby Hall and we decided to attend with an open mind. I remember being surprised by how many attended the lectures and by the sincerity and enthusiasm of the priests giving the lectures. The lectures were followed by discussion when people felt free to question and dissent. The priests didn't seem intolerant or fanatical, as I had imagined they might be, but listened with respect to the views expressed but then often quoted from Jesus' words to support the Catholic position. I remember we read again the Gospels and felt that they overwhelmingly supported the Real Presence and the Catholic position on the founding of the one true Church with Peter at its head and on the forgiveness of sins. Gradually, over the course of the lectures I found my perception of the Catholic Church was changing and so was Bill's.[5]

Meanwhile the quest took on a life of its own, as Dad described:

Win was beginning to come with me and, shortly before Christmas, 1959, we decided we would go to Mass together. We chose to go to the evening Mass at St Mary's, the church in the centre of Sunderland, thinking that there would be very few people there. We were in for a shock. The church held about six hundred people and it was jam-packed. Not only was it jam-packed, but it was full of the sort of people I'd never seen in Protestant churches. It was like the crowd at Roker Park, the local football ground … I felt throughout, particularly at the consecration and immediately afterwards, that there was a reverence, a depth and intensity of inward prayer there which I had never experienced before. The faith and devotion near the altar were almost tangible; you could cut it with a knife. The booklet from the Catholic Enquiry Centre had already introduced me to the idea of the Mass as a sacrifice. Here I had my first experience of it as a reality.[6]

My parents both felt indebted to the excellent catechetical instruc-
tion they received at Corby Hall. Mum was received into the
Church not long before she had my sister Mary, on 9 February
1961. Dad continued to scrupulously read and study. He continued
his enquiry to an extent that astounded the young curate, Father
Caden, who gently hinted; at a certain point, why not just give in!
     The issue of the intention of Jesus when He established what
He described as 'my Church' (Mt 16:18) was central to this search.
Thus the question of ascertaining the truth about the Church
which most comprehensively represented the authority of Jesus
while He acted as a man upon this earth took precedence for Dad
above all issues. This did not mean that he rejected the insights
that came from his Methodist past and my mother's Anglican
lessons at school. Father Caden left it to Dad to decide when he
was 'ready to give himself up', as he put it humorously, but
suggested that a point might come when one should yield to
grace. Dad came to feel this just before my birth. His painstaking
initial enquiry into the Catholic faith ended then with a joyful
reception into the Church about a year and a half after Mary was
born. By now it was September 1962. It was the same fortnight
as my birth on September 8 and then my Baptism.
     It was the beginning of a passion for Catholicism which lasted
until the end of my father's life and in the course of which he
attached huge importance to the teaching resources of the
Church. As he grew older he was troubled that this teaching, for
which he was so personally grateful, had lost some of it clarity
and thoroughness. This was not in its essence, to which his loyalty
never wavered, but in the way it was being presented. One of the
sources of his anguish was the state of modern scripture scholarship. You can see from my mother's recollections that my parents
turned to scripture to see if it backed up the interpretation of the
Church they were discovering from the local Jesuit programme.
An assumption about the essential historicity of the Gospels—
that the Gospels are not fictionalised documents—was a prereq-

uisite for this kind of analysis. In fact without this assumption it is difficult to see how they could have used this method.

As an older man Dad became distressed by the trend in modern scholarship of scripture which questions the historicity of almost every incident in the Gospels. He thought this trend was corrosive and never doubted the authenticity of his own approach to the scriptures. You can see that if, as modern scripture scholarship frequently implies, many of the recorded sayings of Jesus were devised by His followers for their own purposes, rather than what He actually said, the problem of ascertaining the intentions of Jesus becomes ambiguous. The premise of Dad's original search for faith, however, was that the intentions of Jesus did and do exist and are discoverable. While recognizing that the Gospels come down to us through a collection of human recollections and resources, he did not see this as any ground for dismantling the authenticity of the narrative they present and he was distressed to see the straightforward faith of some of his fellow Catholics, many of whom did not have the advantage of his own painstaking enquiry into the grounds of belief, disturbed. Although my father had studied the faith in depth there was nothing sceptical about his own conclusions. This, together with his working-class background, gave him sympathy for the plight of the 'man in the street' who knows his or her Catholic faith without intellectual self-confidence and feels worried by the scepticism of the academics.

For example, my father liked the story of the three wise men and did not understand why this, along with many other details of the infancy narratives, had become the focus of so much scholarly attack. The attack illustrated for him an increasing and troubling divide between modern scholarship and the consolations of the believer. Rather poignantly, these disputed narratives are at the heart of many believers' traditional celebration of Christmas and Christmas was one of the few days in my father's childhood when he could be sure of family harmony and happiness. Once to support him, I said that I thought the Son of God becoming a human baby was a more astounding story to swallow than the story about the three wise men. Was it really so difficult to believe that a few men of integrity, dedicated to truth within their natural lights, should have been guided on a journey by God to the scene of His Son's Nativity?[7]

I think my father may have identified with the predicament of the Magi who, passionate for a truth they did not yet possess, had to rely upon a mysterious star, their natural acumen and the wisdom they had inherited as a guide across the desert. My father's enquiring mind and the inherited insights of his Methodism, together with an increasing awareness of Catholic practice and belief, were the tools that he used to guide him towards the Church. His motives were personal but his tools were rational and academic, he depended on his intellect to guide him. He assumed that if God had established His truth on this earth through His Son, then this truth must be objectively available to the enquiring and sincere intelligence. Consequently, he was not in sympathy with the kind of relativism encapsulated in views such as, 'I'll carry on with this as long as it helps me'. 'It feels the right thing for me'.

Family Discussions about Jesus

Dad often said that the greatness of the figure of Jesus outstrips the literary context that portrays him, for example in the Gospel of Mark. In other words, there is nothing to suggest that anyone involved in the process of recording the gospel stories had the genius necessary to create the character of Jesus. Now I know that the Gospels are more skilled and complex as teaching narratives than they appear. But my father's point was that they would not be great literary works without the central figure they portray. Where then, if Jesus did not in fact live and breathe as described, does the genius to describe Him come from? Not from the imagination of His disciples who underestimate and misunderstand Him at every turn (Mk 4:38; 5:31; 6:37; 8:16–21; 10:13–4; Lk 9:54–5).

My father would speak of the apparent contradictions in the character of Jesus. What writer of fiction would have dared to have Jesus collapse in Gethsemane, overwhelmed in the face of the very thing that He has said that He must do? After all the exalted encouragement He has showered on His disciples, Jesus can barely overcome His own weakness (Mk 14:33–4). What writer of fiction would have had the audacity to present this broken, trembling man as the Son of God? But the absence of ostensible godlikeness in episodes like this has the effect of bringing the personality of Jesus to life. He possesses the inconsistencies and vulnerabilities of actuality. The contradictions in His personality ring true, they make Him cohere, not as an idea but as a human being.

I always liked the story of the woman taken in adultery and once I asked Dad why Jesus, confronted by her accusers, had merely stooped and written in the sand (Jn 8:7). It seemed to me a strange thing to have done at this tense moment when the onus was on Jesus to resolve the crisis by His teaching stature, His courage and His intellectual and moral brilliance. My father simply said that he thought Jesus was embarrassed by her situation.

We can only guess, of course, at what Jesus felt as He stooped. But I have never forgotten the ease with which my father attributed to Jesus this capacity for an ordinary and natural human reaction. It moved me far more than if he had offered a lofty explanation for Jesus' behaviour. I realized that not everything Jesus did and felt had to be extraordinary. It is, of course, quite plausible that Jesus experienced stress and shame at the sight of a woman who was being humiliated and threatened in public and that He needed to pause. Anxious at her peril and His responsibility to avert it what could be more natural for Him than to bend, and stir the sand while He composed His thoughts?

It is also probable that Jesus needed a strategy to relieve the ugly excitement and was repelled by the onlookers' voyeuristic enjoyment of the woman's plight. I understood then that Jesus was a sensitive man and the sight of a helpless and threatened woman could distress Him. We may tend to attribute to Jesus the exalted reactions which seem to us consistent with the grandeur of His Godhead and there is a danger that in doing this we forget that His experience included the range of simple human reactions which are familiar to us. I am sure I owe the fact that I had this insight about Jesus from a young age partly to my father.

Dad knew that in Jesus he was searching to understand an unfathomably great human being and that His humanity was united to the nature of God. But he also understood that Jesus really was a human being, capable of need. Both in Sunderland and then back in his hometown of Barrow-in-Furness, Dad worked as a gifted teacher but he found it stressful. He was not practical himself but he could imagine the solace and stability of the trade of the Son of Man who worked with His hands with wood. He spoke once of how he thought the manual trade of a carpenter would have been a sound basis for someone who needed to develop the resources necessary in order to carry out the demanding mission of Son of God. In other words, Jesus needed balance, security, agreeable work, and a manageable routine. He needed to prepare His strength and His capacities. It was better, Dad thought, that He was not over taxed in childhood.

Dad never took the sacraments for granted. He always saw them as a tremendous gift and aid through life, lovingly bestowed by a merciful God following his own arduous search for the truth. I have never met anyone more reverent of Jesus than my father. Often in my adult life I would feel moved in our sceptical age by the profound reverence with which I saw him approach the Eucharist. And again I understood from this that reverence for Jesus as Son of God did not exclude the effort to understand Jesus as a man.

Dad liked the story of the wedding feast of Cana. It struck a chord with him; he himself loved times of festivity, plentiful good food and wine. He would make the point that the first miracle of Jesus was about social joy and community, an act of pure generosity which affirmed our times of celebration. Dad had an extravagant streak, no doubt a response to the poverty of his childhood. He would buy in more food and wine for family gatherings than we could possibly need. When Mum challenged him on this he would say, 'Look at Jesus, a hundred and twenty gallons!' Although the story is funny I actually think it contains an interesting point. Jesus was abundantly generous, not only as the source of elevated spiritual gifts, but in the human encounters that He shared with us. There are stories which confirm His capacity for asceticism (Mt 4:1–2), but there are also incidents like this one which confirm His love of merrymaking (Mt 9:10–1). He needed the things that we do: celebration, laughter, interaction, festive community to lift His spirit.

Dad loved Mary the Mother of Jesus and he was aware of her human predicament. One of his favourite prayers was the Rosary. He once said that the phrase which struck him most forcibly from the Annunciation story when he mediated upon it was the words, 'And the angel left her' (Lk 1:38).[8] In other words, after the ecstasy of the angelic announcement, there was this experience of loneliness which for her must have felt close to abandonment. At this moment, the suffering of her unique destiny, notwithstanding its joy, could not entirely have escaped her thoughts.

Dad felt the sorrow of the Passion. He understood deeply that at the human level it was a story about betrayal and humiliation. He would always say that it all rang so true to the way human beings behave; the cruelty, the envy, the cowardice, the betrayal of greatness. I think the heartbreak of the story was with him, although we did not speak of it a great deal.

Conclusion

My father was a traditional and loyal Catholic but this did not mean his attitudes were exclusive and he certainly would not have had sympathy with any tendency to use the moral teaching of the Church as an excuse, say, for homophobia or a lack of respect for gay couples. He appreciated the social developments that he saw in his lifetime which gave people from minority groups a better access to the rights and opportunities of this society. He also appreciated the growth of an egalitarianism, coinciding at its height with his young adulthood and midlife years, that gave people from backgrounds like his own access to the good things of life through education and improved wages. He rejoiced in the welfare state, the great achievement of Clement Attlee's Labour government, which used to act as a badly needed security for vulnerable members of this society.[9]

On the whole, my father was not a fan of cinematic portrayals of Christ. He thought that no actor could adequately portray Jesus. With the exception of Pier Paolo Pasolini's wonderful *The Gospel According to St Matthew*,[10] he felt that the cinema had not been particularly illuminating in this regard. The popular *Jesus of Nazareth*[11] with Robert Powell did not escape this judgement. Later, I learned my father judged it less severely towards the end of his life when he was less driven by the thirst for new cinematic insights and was comforted by the film's simple portrayal of Christ in His compassion.

I do not know where Dad got the insight as a young man to define his search for the Church in such pure and objective terms and with such laudable deference to the intentions of Jesus. I guess that his intellectual integrity and longing for the truth were strong motivations. Also, he had an enquiring love for Jesus that he owed to his Methodist upbringing. It was a conviction about the historical truth of the revelation which comes to us in Jesus which marked Dad's Catholicism. And he believed that his discovery of Catholicism, together with embarking on his happy marriage, were the defining events of his own life.

Dad left behind an unfinished manuscript on his conversion and he worked on it a few hours before he died. Perhaps the grace of his conversion gave him the tranquillity necessary for this. Despite its intellectual stature, there was something childlike about the faith my father acquired. He had a tremendous confidence that through what Jesus did for us we have been saved. In the last year of his life, knowing how poor his prospects were, I saw him glance at a picture of the Annunciation. Our Lady encounters God's messenger and through the grace of the Holy Spirit is given the wisdom she needs to interpret her life in relation to the initiative of God and to respond completely to His gift of His Son. Dad looked at me and said, 'Something wonderful for us was accomplished there'.

When Dad died it was not just our family and friends who were saddened. It was also local taxi drivers, neighbours, the milkman and his companions in hospital. Former colleagues and pupils came to his packed funeral. They all appreciated my father for his kindness and generosity and for the way he shared with them a passion for sport, in particular football, rugby and cricket. I do not think they would have recognized my father as a deeply pious man. Although Dad did attend occasional retreats, on the whole he did not seek out specialized religious environments. Dad drew on the local resources of the Church: the parish Mass, the sacraments, discussions, days of recollection and a prayer group provided through the parish. This illustrated his confidence in the everyday provision of the Church and his affinity with the local community where he grew up. He did not need a rarefied atmosphere to believe he was on the road to salvation. He needed the parish Mass which filled his heart with awe as a young man and to which he entrusted himself and his family.

Notes

1   A 'Mourner's Kaddish' is a Jewish prayer in bereavement. The theme is the praise of the name of God from whom all blessings and all comfort come. The prayer does not mention death but praises God for the great gift of life. In contrast with the pain of loss, the prayer is hopeful and life-affirming.

2   This article is dedicated to the memory of my father William James Evans who died on Ash Wednesday, 1 March 2017. It is based on an article first published in *The Way*, Vol LVII, No 2, April 2018.

3   Bob Dylan, 'All along the Watchtower', *John Wesley Harding*, (1967), available at http://www.azlyrics.com/lyrics/bobdylan/allalongthewatchtower.html.

4   Bob Dylan, 'Senor', *Street-Legal*, (1978) available at http://lyrics.rockmagic.net/lyrics/bob_dylan/street_legal_1978.html.

5   From my mother's writings.

6   From my father's writings.

7   Incidentally, the integrity of the Magi is beautifully portrayed in *The Gospel According to St Matthew*, a 1964 Italian drama film directed by Pier Paolo Pasolini.

8   We have retained this line in its older translation from the Jerusalem Bible.

9   In July 1945, Clement Attlee succeeded Winston Churchill as Prime Minister of Britain. His reforming government enacted the welfare state.

10   *The Gospel According to St Matthew*, Pier Paolo Pasolini.

11   *Jesus of Nazareth* is a 1977 Anglo-Italian television mini-series directed by Franco Zeffirelli.

BILL'S EPILOGUE

Things Omitted[1]

I HAD HOPED TO deal with many more matters: other grounds of conviction such as the argument from holiness, just as powerful as any I have outlined. The Church is the Church of the Saints and is often generously acknowledged to be so by non-Catholic writers.

I had hoped to deal with the joys and consolations of Catholic living. 'She is full of divine gifts',[2] wrote Newman of the Church, a point echoed by Sister Peter in Sunderland in a letter she wrote to me in Sunderland. 'Such gifts' she wrote; 'we cannot cope with them'. And that has certainly been my own experience.

I had hoped to consider the mystery of Our Lady, a classical example of the development of doctrine, and a source of joy to those who believe in her.

I had hoped to reflect on life in the Church after Vatican II—the changes which have occurred and my reaction to them.

These and other matters which perhaps I will be able to discuss on some other occasion.

Notes

1 This was the end of Bill's talk on his conversion to the Methodist Men's Fellowship in the mid-1970s. As his book was unfinished and would have included these concerns, we think it makes a fitting Appendix.
2 J. H. Newman, St, *Sermons Preached on Various Occasions* (London: Longmans, Green, and Co, 1908), p. 202.

BIBLIOGRAPHY

Books

Bellarmine, St Robert, *The Controversies*. Ingolstadt, 1586 to 1593.

Belloc, H., *The Path to Rome*. London, Edinburgh and New York: Thomas Nelson and Sons Ltd, 1902.

Belloc, H., *Europe and the Faith*. London: Constable and Company Limited, 1920.

Bolt, R., *A Man for all Seasons*. London: Heinemann Educational Books Ltd, 1965.

Boylan, M. E., *This Tremendous Lover*. Cork: The Mercier Press Ltd, 1959.

Brown, R. E., *Responses to 101 Questions on the Bible*. New York: Mahwah, Paulist Press, 1990.

Butler, B. C., *The Church and Infallibility*. New York: Sheed and Ward, 1954.

Bultmann, R., *New Testament and Mythology*. Philadelphia: Fortress Press, 1984.

Caden, J., *Game, Set and Match*. Durham: The Pentland Press Ltd, 1997.

Campion, St Edmund, *Ten Reasons Proposed To His Adversaries For Disputation In The Name Of The Faith And Presented To The Illustrious Members Of Our University*. London: The Manresa Press, 1914, (1581).

Chapman, G., *Catechism Of The Catholic Church*. London: A Cassell imprint, 1994.

Chesterton, G. K., *The Everlasting Man*. London: Hodder and Stoughton, 1953.

Chesterton, G. K., *Orthodoxy*. London: Bradford and Dickens, 1957.

Chesterton, G. K., *Autobiography.* London: Grey Arrow, 1959.

Cristiani, L., and Rilliet, J., *Catholics and Protestants: Separated Brothers.* London: Sands and Co Ltd, 1960.

Darwin, C., *The Origin of Species.* London: John Murray, 1859.

Dessain, C. S., and Gornall, T., *The Letters and Diaries of John Henry Newman,* Vol. XXIV Oxford: Clarendon Press, 1973.

Dulles, A., *A History of Apologetics.* San Francisco: Ignatius Press, 2005.

Eliot, T. S., 'Gerontion' *Collected Poems:* 1909–1935. London: Faber and Faber Ltd, 1959.

Eymieu, A., *Two Arguments for Catholicism.* London: Burns, Oates and Washbourne Ltd, Publishers to the Holy See, 1928.

Franciscans of the Immaculate, *Mary at the Foot of the Cross.* Downside Abbey: Franciscans of the Immaculate, 2003.

Gelber, L., and Linssen, M., *The Collected Works of Edith Stein: The Hidden Life:* Vol. IV. Washington: ICS Publications Institute of Carmelite Studies, 1992.

Gibley, A, N., *We Believe.* Herefordshire: Gracewing, 2011.

Gonzalez, J., The Story of Christianity. New York: Harper Collins Publishers, 2010.

Hahn, S., *The Lamb's Supper: The Mass As Heaven On Earth.* New York: Doubleday, 1999.

Hardy, T., *The Woodlanders.* London and Basingstoke: Macmillan London Ltd, 1974.

Haldane, J., *An Intelligent Person's Guide to Religion.* London: Duckworth, 2003.

James, K., *Luther The Reformer,* Minneapolis: Augsburg Fortress Publishing House, 1986.

Kepler, T. S., *The Table Talk of Martin Luther,* Mineola, New York: Dover Publications, 2005.

Ker, I. T., *Newman and the Fullness of Christianity*. Edinburgh: T and T Clark, 1993.

Klein, J.W., *Pontius Pilate: Biblical Drama in Five Acts*. 29 Ludgate Hill: A. H. Stockwell, 1923.

Klein, J. W., *Charlotte Corday*. Great Britain: C. W. Daniel Company, 1927.

Knippel, C.T., *The Augsburg Confession and Its Apology*. St Louis: Concordia Publishing House, 1999.

Küng, H., *The Council and Reunion*. London and New York: Sheed and Ward Ltd, 1961.

Lewis, C. S., *Mere Christianity*. London and Glasgow: Collins, 1958.

Lewis, C. S. *Surprised by Joy*. London and Glasgow: Fontana Books, 1959.

Lewis, C.S., *Miracles*. London and Glasgow: Fontana Books, 1960.

Lunn, A., *Now I See*. London: Sheed and Ward, 1955.

Luther, M., *Prefaces to the New Testament*. Milton Keynes: Lightning Source.

Luther, M., *The Table Talk of Martin Luther*. Mineola: Dover Publications, 2005.

Marlowe, C., *Tamburlaine the Great*, 1587.

Maritain, J., *The Living Thoughts of St Paul*. London, Toronto, Melbourne and Sydney: Cassell and Company Ltd, 1945.

Franciscans of the Immaculate, *Mary at the Foot of the Cross*. Downside Abbey, Franciscans of the Immaculate, 2003.

Mauriac, F., *The Stumbling Block*. London: The Harvill Press, 1956.

Mauriac, F., *The Son of Man*. London: The World Publishing Company, 1960.

McCabe, H., *The Teaching of the Catholic Church: A New Catechism of Christian Doctrine*. London: Catholic Truth Society, Publishers to the Holy See, 1985.

Merton, T., *Seeds of Contemplation.* London, Hollis and Carter, 1949.

Merton, T., *The Seven Story Mountain.* New York: Harcourt, Brace and Company, 2009.

Methuen, C., *Luther and Calvin: Religious Revolutionaries.* Oxford: Lion Hudson plc, 2011.

Newman, John Henry St, *Apologia Pro Vita Sua.* London and Glasgow: Fontana Books, 1959.

Newman, John Henry St, *An Essay in Aid of a Grammar of Assent.* London: Longmans, Green, and Co, 1903.

Newman, John Henry St, *Parochial and Plain Sermons: Holiness Necessary For Future Blessedness*, Vol I. London: Longmans, Green and Co, 1907.

Newman, John Henry St, *Sermons Preached on Various Occasions.* London: Longmans, Green, and Co, 1908.

Newman, John Henry St, *Oxford University Sermons.* London: Longmans, Green, and Co, 1909.

Newman, John Henry St, *An Essay On The Development Of Christian Doctrine.* London and New York: Sheed and Ward, 1960.

Newman, John Henry St. *Loss and Gain.* Oxford and New York: Oxford University Press, 1986.

Nichols, A., *The Realm: An Unfashionable Essay on the Conversion of England.* Oxford: Family Publications, 2008.

O'Brien, J. A., *The Road to Damascus.* London: Love and Malcomson Ltd, 1955.

O'Brien, J. A., *The Faith Of Millions: The Credentials Of The Catholic Religion.* London: W. H. Allen and Co. Ltd, 1962.

Ott, L., *Fundamentals of Catholic Dogma.* Cork: The Mercier Press, 1960.

Pascal, B., *Pensées.* Middlesex: Penguin Books Ltd, 1961.

Prescott, H. F. M., *The Man on a Donkey*, London, Harper Collins, 1993.

Rahner, K., *The Teaching of the Catholic Church.* Cork: The Mercier Press, 1964.

Rahner, K., *Foundations of Christian Faith: An Introduction to the Idea of Christianity.* New York: Seabury Press, 1978.

Rahner, K., *A New Christology.* New York: Seabury Press, 1980.

Rahner, K., *Theological Investigations.* New York: Herder & Herder, 1992).

Redford, J., *Bad, Mad or God? Proving the Divinity of Christ from St John's Gospel.* London: St Paul's Publishing, 2005.

Roberts, G., *G. M. Hopkins, Selected Prose; Letter to his Father, 16–17 October 1866.* Oxford: Oxford University Press, 1980.

Rousseau, J. J., *Profession of Faith of a Savoyard Vicar.* Read Books, 2011. (1839).

Salmon, G. D., *The Infallibility of the Church: A Course of Lectures Delivered in the Divinity School of the University of Dublin.* London: John Murray, 1914.

Sartre, J. P., *Words.* London: Penguin Books, 1977.

Sayers, D. L., *The Man Born to Be King: A Play-Cycle on the Life of Our Lord and Saviour Jesus Christ.* San Francisco: Ignatius Press, 1943.

Scheeben, M. J., *The Glories of Divine Grace: A Fervent Exhortation to All to Persevere and to Grow in Sanctifying Grace.* Indiana: Grail Publications, 1946.

Schroeder, H. J., *The Canons and Decrees of the Council of Trent.* Charlotte: Tan Books, 2011.

Schwan, M., Come *Home: A Prayer Journey to the Centre Within.* Notre Dame, Ave Maria Press, 2020.

Shakespeare, W., *Hamlet.* 1599–1601.

Shakespeare, W., *Antony and Cleopatra.* 1607.

Slaughter, F. G., *The Crown and the Cross*. Norwich: Jarrolds, 1972.

Smith, A. D. H., *Thou Art Peter, A History of Roman Catholic Doctrine and Practice*. London: Watts and Co, 1930.

The Official Handbook of the Legion of Mary. Dublin 7: Concilium Legionis Mariae, 1993.

Tholuck, F. A. D., *Guido and Julius, or Sin and the propitiator: Exhibited in the True Consecration of the Sceptic*. Boston: Gould and Lincoln, 1854.

Ullathorne, W., *The Immaculate Conception of the Mother of God*. London: Richardson and Son, 1855.

Ullmann, C., *The Sinlessness of Jesus: An Evidence for Christianity*. London, Dalton House Ltd, 2018, reproduction of Edinburgh, T. and T. Clark, 1863.

Ward, M., *Gilbert Keith Chesterton*. London: Penguin Books, 1958.

Weigel, G., *Where Do We Differ?* London: Burns and Oates, 1962.

Articles

Anderson, L., 'Hundreds attend service for Father John Caden', *The Northern Echo* (4 March 2013).

Chesterton, G. K., '"Jesus" or "Christ"?...The Latest Bubble Punctured', *Christian Faith and Life*, Vol XII (January to June 1910).

Johnston, G. S., 'Émile Zola at Lourdes', *A Voice for the Faithful Catholic Laity: Crisis Magazine* (1 December 1989).

Leatherdale, D., 'Former Prime Minister Tony Blair leads tribute to popular Sedgefield priest', *The Northern Echo* (24 February 2013).

Saward, J., 'Regaining Paradise: Paul Claudel And The Renewal Of Exegesis', *Downside Review*, 114 (1996).

Viereck, G. S., 'What Life Means to Einstein: An Interview by George Sylvester Viereck', *The Saturday Evening Post* (26 October 1929).

Patristic Texts

Augustine of Hippo, St, *The Confessions*, London: Penguin Books, 1961.

Clement, St, Letter to the Corinthians.
Ignatius of Antioch, St, *Letter to the Ephesians.*
Ignatius of Antioch, St, *Letter to the Romans.*
Irenaeus, St, *Against Heresies.*

Papal Documents

Benedict XVI, *Regina Caeli: Reflections on Our Lady.* Oxford: Family Publications (2010).
John Paul II, St. *Address at World Youth Day*, (19 August 2000).

Vatican Documents

Vatican Council I, *Dogmatic Constitution, Dei Filius* (1870).
Vatican II, *Dogmatic Constitution On Divine Revelation, Dei Verbum* (1965).
The Catechism of the Council of Trent (1566).
Compendium of the Catechism of the Catholic Church (2006).

Lutheran, Calvinist and Anglican Documents

The Augsburg Confession (1530).
The Geneva Confession of Faith (1536).
The Thirty-nine Articles of Religion; Church of England (1533–71).